China's New Cultural Scene

Claire Huot

China's New Cultural Scene

A Handbook of Changes

Duke University Press Durham and London 2000

© 2000 Duke University Press
All rights reserved
Printed in the United States of America on acid-free paper ∞
Designed by C. H. Westmoreland
Typeset in Minion with Frutiger display by Tseng Information Systems
Library of Congress Cataloging-in-Publication Data
appear on the last printed page of this book.

Some of the material in this book appeared in
La petite révolution culturelle by Editions Philippe Picquier, 1994.

Frontispiece art: Recreation of a calligraphy for the series
"word": Introduction to English Calligraphy.
Ink on paper, by Xu Bing, 1998.

Contents

Acknowledgments

Some artists and critics who are mentioned in the body of the text and in the notes have been of crucial importance in the making of this book. There are also other individuals who cannot be acknowledged anywhere else but here. I would like to join these names now and thank them all, whether they have provided me with a valuable tip or a constant flow of information and support. They are: James Carl, hungry artist; Chen Xiaoming, critic of Chinese literature and culture; Rey Chow, critic of Chinese culture; Pascale Coulette, Ph.D. candidate (Chinese anthropology); Annie Curien, sinologist; Dai Jinhua, critic of Chinese culture; Joël Fronteau, *Yijing* exegete; Gao Minglu, art critic; France Guévin, acupuncturist; Hu Min, Ph.D. candidate (Chinese film); Hu Xiangwen, Ph.D. candidate (Chinese film); Guy Huot, my brother; Lin Qing, Ph.D. (comparative literature); Lü Tonglin, critic of Chinese literature; Catherine Mayor, M.A. (Chinese advertising); Frank Muyard, Ph.D. candidate (Chinese sociology); Danielle Noiseux, librarian at the Centre d'Études de l'Asie de l'Est, Université de Montréal; Elisabeth Papineau, Ph.D. candidate (Chinese anthropology); Reynolds Smith, Maura High, and Pam Morrison at Duke; Xu Bing, artist; Xu Xiaoyu, journalist; Wang Yichuan, professor; Wu Wenguang, videomaker; Zhang Yiwu, critic of Chinese culture; Henry Y. H. Zhao, editor.

My closing words sound like a will. I thank (without much money to offer) my two research assistants, for whom I was a "red guard": Sébastien Bage (especially for his thoroughness in the final technicalities, for the Chinese glossary, and for his serene composure); Sean Macdonald (for his linguistic revisions — especially his colloquial renderings of rock lyrics — and his irreverent humor).

And last a very, very, very gentle pat to my dumb dog.

China's New Cultural Scene

Introduction

But if the little fox,

After nearly completing the crossing,

Gets his tail in the water,

There is nothing that would further.

Hexagram 64, "Before completion," *Yijing*

In 1994, I published a book in French on new Chinese cultural phenomena entitled *A Small Cultural Revolution*.[1] I believed that a revolution in the cultural sphere had occurred and so attempted to present the radically manifest changes that I had tracked in the different cultural spheres (literature, music, theater, television, arts) and in the new words that were being used all over China—while ordering them into an organic whole. To my mind, the year 1993 marks the end of that cultural revolution, which lasted some ten years.

Since then, there have been further changes, sequential ones, smaller ones. That is, evolution and continuation. Nothing is ever absolutely at rest; nonchange is also a form of change, or so claims the *Book of Changes* or *Yijing*.[2] Now that more than ten years have gone by, it is possible to reassess the transformations, to reorder them into generations, successions that were not visible while they were in process.

This present work attempts to be a handbook of the changes that Chinese culture has undergone in the past decade. The index will allow the reader to locate (discussions of) specific events and their agents, and the glossary of main Chinese terms will contribute to its usefulness as a reference book. At the same time, this book aims to interpret (or "reveal," to use a *Yijing* term) the meaning of events. These last few years have allowed me a certain perspective on the process, and I now detect more connections among the various phenomena and between them and the real world, in China and outside of China. Nothing is self-contained. I have read between the lines and brought to the fore some configurations discernable in China's cultural scene. There are many more to be explored by anyone who is willing to look otherwise.

Unlike the *Book of Changes*, this present work, needless to say, is not a book of wisdom nor a fortune telling handbook. The outcome of these various changes cannot yet be assessed. Upon completing this book, I fear that I may have acted rather like the incautious young fox running rashly over the ice: I have perhaps gotten my tail wet.

The chapters' words

It is difficult to write about change. How can one write a book that will be a correct yet fluid rendition of phenomena that emerge, recombine, and crisscross nonstop? My anchorage has been words. Indeed, I believe that words are still at the root of all the changes.

Fortunately, my scrutiny of Chinese words, as used today, by women and men, has helped me realize that there is no such thing as the terrifying "mot juste," 'zheng ming' ('correct designation'). Words are on the move, all the time. Every single work I have examined is an attempt at "saying" things otherwise, from within and without Chinese culture. Language is the most vital common denominator of all the works discussed in this book: literature, television, film, art, music, theater, and performing arts.

I have divided the book into two parts, both starting from the most organized form of word ordering, literature. Chapter 1 is dedicated to literature, while the next two gradually open up the written word, speak it out, act it out. Chapters 4 to 6 also deal with literature but as condensed images, as sounds, and end up with telling portraits and the yelled-out lyrics of rock.

Chapter 1, "Literary Experiments: Six Files," is a close reading of narratives written by three men (Ma Yuan, Ge Fei, Yu Hua) and three women (Can Xue, Chen Ran, Xu Kun). I show the particular agenda of each one, by examining their respective narrative techniques and idiosyncratic effects. These writers provide a sampling of most of the problematics and themes to be discussed in the rest of the book: commentaries on other cultures (non–Han Chinese, European, American) and on their own culture; revisions of Chinese history and of Maoist politics; positions on the private and the public and on sexual difference, as well as on consumerism and Americanization.

Chapter 2, "Away from Literature I: Words Turned On," studies literary works in transition. The focus is on one writer, Wang Shuo, simply because Wang's signature is manifest all over China, in all cultural forms: literature, television, music, film, art, theater, and most important of all, in people's mouths. I examine how Wang Shuo with his partners, notably Feng Xiaogang, but also Jiang Wen, have literally turned on words, put them "on the box." The key to Wang's popularity and financial success is his invented lingo, a combination of subverted political formulae with streetwise slang, always adapted for a light-hearted effect. The rest of the chapter stays light and cheerful, notably with women's works in film, music, and literature (Ning Ying, Liu Sola, Xiaoyen Wang).

Chapter 3, "Away from Literature II: Words Acted Out," focuses on theater experiments. In the first section, I distinguish between what is called or marketed in China as experimental and what is to my mind experimental, namely Mou Sen's work. Mou works with collaborators from different cultural spheres, notably Yu Jian (a poet), Wu Wenguang, Jiang Yue (both video producers), and Wen Hui and Jin Xing (dancers). The second section covers more experimental, independent, and underground productions, from Zhang Yuan's to Jia Zhangke's, which struggle like the theater performances to make, in China, the invisible (quotidian actions, politically sensitive sites, marginals such as migrant workers or those stricken by AIDS) visible.

With chapter 4, "Colorful Folk in the Landscape: Fifth-Generation Filmmakers and Roots Searchers," there is a return to literature, but of yet another kind, linked to a certain kind of cinema. Novels of the "roots-searching" school (including those by A Cheng, Mo Yan, Liu

1. Detail of *Here, There, Anywhere*. Installation by Gu Xiong, 1995.
Photograph by Vancouver Art Gallery.

Heng, Han Shaogong, and Jia Pingwa) have much in common with the films of the famous "Fifth Generation" (with Chen Kaige and Zhang Yimou as main representatives), whether they have been adapted for film or not. One common trait is their use of basic images of China: its land, its peasants, its written system, its mode of naming, and its taboos. These writers and filmmakers invent from enduring indigenous conventions, and I investigate their works from one of their pet paradigms, the animal. The 1980s ox evolves into a butterfly in the 1990s.

Chapter 5, "China's Avant-Garde Art: Differences in the Family," is an attempt to make sense of the paradoxical condition of Chinese avant-garde art, which is virtually invisible in China. With Hal Foster's authoritative critical work on American art as a background, I draw a picture of the complexities specific to an art that is not American, does not want to be American, yet does not care to be labeled Chinese, either. These are the main differences with the big "family" of avant-garde art, which is shedding its ethnic, sexual, cultural features and moving more and more toward what I call an immanent anthropology.

Chapter 6, "Rock Music from Mao to Nirvana: The West Is the Best," focuses on the West, as in North America and Europe but also as in China's western frontier, specifically Yan'an, Mao Zedong's revolutionary base. I show how China's rock spans both registers, with Cui Jian at one end of the spectrum and the No group at the other, with a full range of popular styles, by both male and female performers, in the middle.

The conclusion, "A World Wide Web of Words," reiterates the importance of language in my scrutiny of contemporary Chinese culture. I replay some words as they are used today by women and men, in gangs and cliques, and in the advertising world. Spoken Chinese is richer than ever, written Chinese is spotted with letters from the Roman alphabet. My concluding words are for poetry, which not only participates in the linguistic dynamic but also undertakes what I call an ongoing vivisection of language, allowing for a full manifestation of the temporal-spatial relations within words—lest we forget.

References

Although there are innumerable links among the various expressions of Chinese cultural production and although most of it is language-specific, it is not a closed circuit. It is moved by concerns traceable throughout the planet. In fact, the emphasis on language, the critical examination of its instrumentalization, is one such global preoccupation. Other endeavors are linked to language: for example, the desire to deny human beings a special status as Homo sapiens. This deanthropomorphisizing of human beings is at work in Chinese cultural productions as it is elsewhere. There is also no humanistic notion of creativity in the current work of many Chinese artists. The authority of the author, or the confidence of a unified subjectivity asserting truths about a self or about China, is virtually nonexistent.

The ways in which Chinese cultural producers deal with representation (of self, nation, others) are also not exclusively "Chinese." I show how they position themselves in various ways: from inside and outside, with new and old referents, and with references from other cultures, which are already part of today's Chinese culture. Thus this book holds many heterogeneous references. It is good to be in culture shock.

1 Literary Experiments

Six Files

Setting right what has been spoiled by the father.

Hexagram 18, "Work on what has been spoiled," *Yijing*

Literature is the least transitive medium. It is basically untranslatable because it is an assemblage of the words of a particular language, as spoken and read by people in a particular culture. (Even when the writers are following foreign models, such as Beckett, Borges, Duras, Kafka, and Robbe-Grillet) Chinese literature is a particularly indigenous, context-specific enterprise. Translations of Chinese literary works are of course possible (and they are increasingly available), but without linguistic commentary they don't yield much more than a storyline with a certain unfamiliar air. The nonreader of Chinese will necessarily turn the works into some form of out-of-the language interpretation, something akin to what Jameson called a "national allegory" reading.[1] This opening chapter is to be taken as a linguistic commentary on some Chinese literary works that have rather slim storylines but heavy textuality.

Such literature is not a popular cultural phenomenon. Its production is a most private affair: between one writer to one reader, from one individual to other individuals. It is not only individualistic but elitist too, like it or not. Not everyone reads, and those who do don't necessarily want to read convoluted twists on their familiar words. Thus the reader of literary experiments is an intellectual who has a feel for words at large but who cannot be personified or clearly identified. She or he remains ex-centric and anonymous. My commentary attempts to highlight some of the possible positions of this reader.

I will give few details about the six authors' circumstances, because (literary) experiments are not translations of a single person's life, nor of his or her culture. The selections I have made, however, are guided by a desire to show various individual options which, taken together, constitute a certain sampling of literature. These files are to be read like documents found in a filing cabinet, where many more are waiting to be read.

The files are presented in a loose chronological order (Ma Yuan is the old hand, a sincere hippie, while Xu Kun is the newcomer, a mocking yuppie), but that's of little importance, since my aim is not to move historically from one school to another and since the works themselves shun realistic conventions of storytelling and of historical time. No cause and no crescendo will be found in the following pages: all cases are extremely different and point to different problematics, which are all crucial, whether they are writing another culture (Ma Yuan), writing today's culture (Xu Kun), writing a (woman's) point of view (Chen Ran), rewriting history etymologically (Ge Fei), personalizing the collective (Can Xue), or collectivizing the personal (Yu Hua).

Literature experiments with culture between the lines and is a refraction of it. The works under scrutiny here are like subtexts of what will be discussed in the following chapters. They render new, in their own idiosyncratic ways, language and representation. Words are questioned, discourses are doubted and rerouted. Referentiality is skewed and no assertions are made, except ironically. Reality is also a word, and it has different meanings for, say, Ma Yuan, who writes unreal things about the forsaken; Ge Fei, who demonstrates the unreal of the accepted concept of reality; or Xu Kun, who derealizes the idioms of today by repeating them out of sync.

The serious, deep question "why" leads nowhere. It is better to scrutinize the ordering of words.

"Now I must give you this fictitious ending. I'll tell it to you under my breath. Here lies all my sorrow and satisfaction" ("Fabrication," 141).[2] Ma Yuan writes in earnest. He is a fiction writer (or was, in the eighties), and he experienced extraordinary, hard-to-believe things while living in Tibet, between 1982 and 1989. Born in 1953, he is not Tibetan but of Han origin, and from the north of China, near Shenyang in Jinzhou.

Ma contends he is not a Hemingway type of writer; that is, one who contents himself with just imagining things and who can thus ease his pent-up feelings of sadness (103). Nor is he one to let his imagination roam like the proverbial "celestial horse wandering across the sky," which would be the typical and traditional Han Chinese way. But Ma needs the horse and the sky as prerequisites. Since leaving Tibet in 1989, he has written very little. He has been working since 1992 on a film project "Xuduo zhong shengyin — Zhongguo wenxuemeng" (Many different voices — China's literary dream), among other things. It consists of interviews with at least one hundred Chinese writers, from Ba Jin to Ge Fei. It's a serious project that attempts to trace this century's living writers and their work.

Ma Yuan's stories seem to be the far-fetched products of a fertile mind. His experience in a leper colony in the short story "Fabrication" ("Xugou") (1986) is a fine example. In "Fabrication," we are told repeatedly from the start that we are reading a "fiction." "Ma Yuan" is the name of the narrator; he is a writer who concocts the tale, who boasts about his literary masterpieces, offers a sensational dénouement, and the ensuing "satisfaction."

But "Ma Yuan" might also be someone who actually lived the leper colony experience of the story. I say "might" because, if the ending is fictitious, that is, if it undoes the true narrative, then "Ma Yuan" never lived through this trauma. However, if the ending is just a fictional dénouement for the sake of fiction, then chances are that "Ma Yuan" did love a leprous woman, did befriend a Loba sculptor, did become the old Guomindang soldier's confidant, and so on. And this presents us with a cruel reality, thus the ensuing "sorrow."

Ma Yuan has been hailed as the pioneer of experimental writing in whose footsteps have followed Yu Hua, Ge Fei, and many others. I suspect, however, that he might only accidentally be part of a literary trend. For Ma Yuan is not a trendsetter. He is, rather, very much a bohemian, for whom the expression "accidental tourist" might be more appropriate, since he stayed in Tibet for a long time by chance and to this day has no fixed address.

His short stories all take place in Tibet, where he was assigned to work as a journalist in 1982. Tibet overwhelmed him, but also bored him. Writing became a means if not of overcoming then at least of coping with both states of mind. His writing took the form of a personal diary, of a travelogue, of a newsletter to friends, as one can see from "More ways than one to make a kite" ("Die zhiyao de san zhong fangfa").[3] "But I have my own way to kill the boredom. Reading novels is one of them. . . . Or I draw the curtains (my own spare bedsheet, that white-blue checkered one you all remember), shut the door, turn on the desk lamp, sit at my desk with the three drawers in a horizontal row, and make up stories for you" (246–47).[4]

The aside to the reader is not necessarily a postmodern, Calvino-like game. Nor is giving the narrator his own name a willful crisscrossing of meganarrators with nanonarrators, an endless ludic *mise-en-abyme*. Yet the first sentence of Ma's short story "Fabrication" caused a great sensation when it was published: "I am that Han guy called Ma Yuan, I write novels" (101). This flouting of a basic convention of fiction propelled Ma Yuan's work into the category of experimental writing and opened up metafiction in China. Most of his works also have a narrator called Ma Yuan, which refers to Ma Yuan, the experiencing subject, the narrator, and the actual writer. As Wu Liang notes, the ambivalent reality effect relies heavily on "Ma Yuan."[5]

This "Ma Yuan" the subject is a tall, bearded man (the real Ma Yuan is also tall and bearded) who carries a knapsack, a camera, a map, a pen, and sometimes a harmonica, and who encounters strange people in Tibet. These people—beggars, prostitutes, ex-highwaymen, lepers, and strays from the Guomindang (KMT)—all tell him their incredible stories. He, in turn, befriends them, and, if they are women, he makes love to them. He is a benevolent tourist. The writer side of "Ma Yuan" transcribes the stories and adds a little spice; for example, something to at least end those everlasting stories. He also comments on his own status as a writer of fiction, of what is called "creative writing."

"Ma Yuan" mocks himself constantly, either for his art or for his ways. He is never as sexually potent as the natives. He is the logical one, who asks questions where there are no answers to be had. He represents the predictability and pragmaticism (amiableness and hypocrisy) of the Han Chinese. He is a typical Han Chinese in Tibet, a subject who does not acknowledge that he is in culture shock. Ma Yuan recovers from this drawback in his art by putting his craft (his literary artfulness) to the fore: educated in the Han language and literature and also versed in foreign literature, he can remap things with both accuracy and imagination. In jest, he compares his ability to write (in Chinese characters) to the deities' faculty of creation. The epigraph he gives to "Fabrication" is a comment on the deities' styles.[6] It reads that deities, forever self-confident, actually all narrate genesis in the same way: they all repeat the same fiction. Singular things may have occurred, but they are all recast in one mold.

The epigraph has an ambiguous status. If Ma Yuan the writer is like a god, then his narratives should also be uniformly the same. That is both true and false. Actually, Ma Yuan is extremely conscious of language, of the fact that he is transcribing events (and nonevents) into the Han language. His lexicon, unlike that of the complacent gods, is that of doubt. "What is left ruling the whole narrated world [of Ma Yuan] is the uncertainty principle. . . . So the true-false switch is subjective, depending on the acceptance of the receiver."[7] I would add that Ma realizes the effects and the limitations of the Han language on Tibetan reality. He warns his readers, probably Han Chinese like himself, that he will use sparingly verbs of action such as "to occur, to take place" 'fasheng' and privilege verbs such as "to be, to have" 'you' along with the tentative "possibly" 'keneng' to yield a nonauthoritative, conditional mode. He also calls attention to his avoidance of terms used by anthropologists and adventurers referring to the discovery and observation of so-called natives.

The narrator figure, "Ma Yuan" is forever conscious that he does not speak the natives' language and so must rely on his own culture to understand them. He makes mistakes — "mistake" is a term highly recurrent in Ma's works (there is even a short story entitled "Mistakes" ["Cuowu"], 1987).[8] His mistakes are caused by his desire to understand, to penetrate mysteries: he makes presumptions and asks too many questions. He relies too heavily on analytical logic and on his sense of sight. The fact that he wishes to take photographs is indicative of these traits. The following passage neatly exemplifies his mode of inquiry and interpretation:

> "Hold the child," I said. "I'll take a picture of you." "I don't take pictures. I don't understand pictures." I took a photo album from my knapsack and showed her a color photograph of me. She said without flinching, "That's you." I explained to her that I could preserve her on a thing like that. She shook her head. She said, "I understand. I don't take pictures. I don't understand pictures." Her words were contradictory, but I sort of guessed what she was saying. What she was saying was that she knew (understood) what pictures were, but she didn't understand how pictures could move people onto a thing (paper) like that. She didn't want people to take her picture. I remember reading in a book that people who had not been exposed to modern civilization thought photography was a kind of soul-snatching; that their soul would be captured in the little box of the camera. I'd like this detail to appear in my next masterpiece. It seemed that she must have seen people taking pictures or shooting a film or a video. Time would show that I had made another error of presumption. I forgot that people here had seen movies. Photography was by no means beyond their understanding. When she said she didn't understand, she didn't want her picture taken, there were other reasons. But more of that later. ("Fabrication," 110, with modifications)

"Ma Yuan" is by turns an obnoxious tourist who wants to take pictures of every sensational thing or person, an understanding interpreter of the natives' peculiarities, and a dupe. He tells us at the very end of the story—when the tourist "Ma Yuan" attempts once again to photograph his prize trophy, the leper woman—that she didn't want to be photographed because of her devastated looks. "Suddenly I realized why she didn't want to be photographed; she knew that with this disease she was no longer good-looking. After all, she was a woman" ("Fabrication," 142). In the end, if there are realizations or understandings—can the comment "After all, she was a woman" be termed a "discovery"? They are limited to "Ma Yuan," both subject and interpreter. Because the reality out there, the people out there—the forsaken 'qi'er'—remain inaccessible ("Xugou," 88).[9]

"Ma Yuan" gets to photograph only the usual tourist fare: women walking around sacred trees, a sculptor creating Buddhist statues. He returns from his stint in the leper colony with a statue in his backpack and this "sensational story" with a "knock-out subject matter" ("Fabrication," 102). But in confessing his fallibility, his inability to transcend his culture and improve anything out there, he makes his narration more effective. "I was nothing more than a Lhasa resident who wrote novels, inspired from time to time with excessively romantic notions. . . . No one could be more useless than I was" ("Fabrication," 137). And at the end of the story he reverts to an authoritative, rational voice—he asks for the date, he declares the old KMT officer "mad," he says he "loves" the (leper) woman's body. Especially given the array of sources for his tale—archeological, geological, medical, scientific literature—these features of the story defeat its "natural" purpose, which is to convince the reader that only a madman would have lived through this. When "Ma Yuan" claims that he is not crazy, although the story's facts point to the contrary (he claims he is institutionalized in a psychiatric hospital in Beijing), we tend to believe him. He may not be in such an institution at all (this may just be poetic license—"Ma Yuan" being so intimately connected to Ma Yuan that he could easily play such tricks), and he may be feebly taking a "rational" stance to end this damned story of the condemned. The dumping ground in Tibet that the Han Chinese use for its contagious, unwanted ones connects metonymically, therefore, to a very real situation. "They may share the same planet as we do, but our worlds don't connect—they are the forsaken" ("Xugou," 88).

Ma Yuan seems to have problems ending his narratives precisely because they are all interconnected fragments of life and heavily intratextualized, like one never-ending story. "Fabrication" ends with the total disappearance of the leper colony in a mudslide—a deus ex machina finale—but that same village reappears, verbatim, as an epigraph to another short story, "Heart-to-heart tale" ("Qingshu," 323):[10] "The leper colony had no wall or fence of any kind. No patient could be prevented from leaving, and no outsider hindered from entering" ("Fabrication," 106). In other stories such as "An old Himalayan song" ("Ximalaya guge"),[11] Ma starts by locating the place (in Tibet, naturally) where the story will occur, lest one should doubt the existence of such a place later on. In "A wandering spirit" ("Youshen"),[12] the narrator says he won't deal much with one particular character's personality because he's already written about it elsewhere (275).[13] Indeed, Ma's stories are closest to stories told to a live public with whom he would play tongue-in-cheek games and for whom uniqueness would be irrelevant: "Any of my readers who are interested can have a look at the *Spring Wind* literary collection, 1986. Remember my name is Ma Yuan — that's my *magnum opus*" ("A Wandering Spirit," 275). These authorial cross-references to the world out there undo the fictional self-containment.

Repetition also points to the artificiality of Han Chinese discourse. For example, a conversation with the KMT officer is given twice, once in chapter 2 without "Ma Yuan"'s retorts, and the other time in chapter 16, with "Ma Yuan"'s reactions made implicit by the officer's responses to them. This "dialogue" begins the same way both times, with the impossible utterance "I'm a deaf-mute. (People here take me for a deaf-mute)" ("Fabrication," 103, 134). Similarly, the accounts of "Ma Yuan"'s attempts to convince the woman to be photographed has her reiterating simple statements such as "I don't take pictures," "I don't understand photography" ("Fabrication," 110). Ma Yuan tells stories of nonevents, of gazes gone askew, of disturbed certainties. For a little longer than the time of the story, the normal and nonnormal worlds are rendered disturbingly coeval, after he has demonstrated how, in reality, they are worlds apart ("A wandering spirit," 274–75; "Fabrication," 130). All of Ma's stories are also stories about narrative time colliding with "real time." In "A wandering spirit," there is a section entitled "A story about telling stories" (275) and another, the closing one, entitled "An end or a beginning?" (281), where a character is mentioned "racing towards ["Ma Yuan"] at high speed, racing toward the end of the story" (282). "Fabrication" covers some five days (or is it three? or seven?) in 1986; it was also written in 1986 (the story ends on May 4; Ma actually finished writing it on April 25). The artifice of fictional time is constantly upheld in Ma's stories. He resorts to old narrative devices, such as "more on that later," gives way to digressions and to new tricks to deceive the reader's expectations. For example, in "A wandering spirit," Ma writes: "This may be a short story, but it covers a long period of time" (264).

In "Mistakes," when the narrator goes up to his thirteen roommates to find his cap, we read the same phrase thirteen times: "Hey, get up" (31). That same narrator at the onset had stated: "I really can't stand using flashbacks. Why should I be obliged to start my story with 'at that time?' I don't know either the origins or the consequences of this affair" (29). Uniformity, not singularity, is also stressed, whether it be a disease such as leprosy making all the contaminated look alike ("Fabrication") or a seductive woman, turning all men's gazes into the same ravished expression ("A wandering spirit," 269). By reading Ma Yuan, the reader learns to navigate around the fictionality of his stories, to feel the thrill of the "knockout subject matter" of the enthusiastic novelist "Ma Yuan," but especially the despair of the "unlucky bastard" that "Ma Yuan" is ("Fabrication," 140–41) for being stuck with this experience to put down in words, an experience that will be rendered utterly fictitious and therefore highly credible. When "Ma Yuan" says to his readers: "I am sure you will forgive me, I cannot finish this story. I am tired" ("More ways than one to make a kite," 251), once again fiction's time collapses with storytelling time and the real time of the reader.

Ma Yuan requires much patience and perspicaciousness from his readers. He is an author who feels no duties toward them; on the contrary, he jests with them. He prevents his reader from taking the stories too seriously, but he also frustrates a reader who needs explanations, or symbols, or a neat conclusion. Ma leaves "Ma"'s experiences raw. Ma doesn't write much these days, perhaps because he has returned to the Han Chinese world and feels he has no "real," unbelievable experiences now.

Ge Fei, the eraser

Ge Fei (pen name of Liu Yong) was born in 1964 in Dantu County, Jiangsu. He is the archexperimentalist of literature in China.[14] His writing is experimental on many levels: narrative voice, plot (de)construction, characters turning into objects or into signs and vice versa, the obliteration of boundaries such as those between history and fiction, public and private, past and present. His work, indeed, appeals foremost to the intelligence of the reader. Ge Fei's works consequently are often

2. *Filing Cabinet.* Oil painting by Mao Xuhui, 1993.
Photograph donated by artist.

compared to Luis Borges's,[15] because they are labyrinths and puzzles to be figured out.

However, for Ge Fei, the immediate model is the nouveau roman writer, Alain Robbe-Grillet.[16] Ge Fei writes a subtext of seduction into his narrations, thus engendering a pervasive sexual atmosphere much akin to Robbe-Grillet's. Ge Fei's work also appeals to the senses because, like Robbe-Grillet, he pays attention to the slippings and slidings of words, of their coatings.

"A flock of brown birds" ("Hese niaoqun")[17] uses what at first glance would seem to be a "Ma Yuan"–type narrator; that is, himself, a writer. But his "Ge Fei" puts such emphasis on his status as a writer that he is closer to "Borges" in *The Other*. "A flock of brown birds," in which is embedded another story, tells of the writer "Ge Fei," who has isolated himself in the countryside in order to finish a novel that he is dedicating to his wife, who died on their wedding night. A woman, named Qi 'Chess', visits him; they spend the whole night together talking and looking at painted portraits of herself that she has brought along. Their conversation centers around a story he tells her: his own love story (with his deceased wife). The plot of the love story develops thanks to Qi's questions, but it also wanders from flashbacks into different periods of "Ge Fei" 's past to insistent descriptions of the loved woman's boots and gait. Although it does have many interruptions, the story can be pieced together. But it is a most disquieting story, with violent deaths, sexual brutality, and fetishistic fascination. Moreover, it is a most unlikely story, because "Ge Fei"—or is it Ge Fei?—turns his beloved into a ghost: her hand is like an eel (147); her skin is as cold as a frog (149); she disappears without a trace on a snowy night and dies again on her wedding night.

This attempt to undo all realistic conventions of fiction is omnipresent in "A flock of brown birds." Ge Fei here experiments with the reality effect in literature. The reader does believe in the strange love story, even though there are too many coincidences, unexplainable events—such as the abrupt vanishing of the loved woman, or her unconditional love for a brutal husband. We adhere somewhat to the tale because we have Qi who straightens out the narration when it goes awry. She explains why the text is circular and repetitious. "Your memory has been annihilated by your novel" (128), she says; elsewhere, she thinks she can guess the development of the story, "because it follows the formula of love" (131); she asks for the meaning of the symbols (127); she eggs him on: "And then [what happens]?" (129). But Qi is rendered an incompetent and unreliable "reader" at the end of the story: a woman approaches "Ge Fei"'s abode, "Ge Fei" recognizes her as Qi, but Qi—exactly like the loved woman in another situation—denies ever having been there and claims she does not know him and is just passing by. The story has thus gone full circle: at the beginning of the story, "Ge Fei" claims he does not know Qi; at the end, it's her turn. The investigative reader then understands the lure. All these characters, "Ge Fei," Qi, and the deceased lover are mirror images of one another. At the end, "Qi"—whom we mistook as a friend-cum-mediocre psychoanalyst—comes not with portraits of herself but with a mirror showing us the labyrinthine structure of the tale. The name "Qi" is the name of the strategy game that calls for players and good tactics, but it is also the homophone of "wife." Qi could just as well be "Ge Fei"'s beloved. The guessing game of homophones is almost endless: *qi* can mean "other," "weird," and last but not least "deception."

Compared to Ma Yuan's self-portrayal, Ge Fei's inscription in the text is rendered totally fictional. "A flock of brown birds" is a play with time, people, emotions, objects, all conflated into pawns, or signs, to produce an experimental tour de force. "Ge Fei"'s memory and time lapses—he is unable to tell time if the migrating birds don't come round—are lures for this highly constructed tale where no detail is left unaccounted for. For example, upon Qi's (first) visit, "Ge Fei" says that Qi is carrying a painting album or a mirror. On Qi's first visit, it turns out to be a painting album; on her second visit, it is a mirror. But that second visitor may well not be Qi. She has been erased as a character. In a similar play, the loved woman utters a proverb meaning death, "The light has gone out" (151), and her death follows. Words, Ge Fei's words, kill her. Ge Fei acts like a magician who brandishes words, juggles with their meanings, all for his audience's intellectual pleasure.

The development of the story has all along been in "Ge Fei"/Ge Fei's control, as he makes clear (131); it has not followed any other logic, such as the "love formula" Qi refers to. It has been built with signs, some retrospectively purely aesthetic, such as the color brown for the birds, the loved woman's boots, Qi's attire, the earth, and so on. They mark the unfolding of the story, and its circular, self-contained logic.

Ge Fei creates an ominous atmosphere in all his stories by experimenting with obsession. He forges characters who have highly selective or faulty (hypo- or hypertrophic) memory, which freezes some blocks of time, which makes them insistently evoke the same events, who turn "reality" into an individual affair and focus on very private recollections. It is always as though their smells, their sounds, their visions colored and paced the narrative. Apart from "ill forebodings" 'buxiang de yugan,' Ge Fei's favorite term is "in the recess of one's heart" 'neixin shenchu.'

Such is what prompts the short story "The lost boat" ("Mizhou") (1989).[18] The term *mi* (lost, confused, fascinated) of the title recurs many times throughout the story and is linked to its homophone, *mi* (riddle, enigma, insoluble mystery). In one sentence, Ge Fei uses the latter homophone three times to render the mystery hiding deep in the protagonist's heart ("Mizhou," 305).[19] This story recalls those of Gabriel García Márquez (especially his *Chronicle of a Tale Foretold* [*Cronica de una muerte anunciada*]) and begins with a prologue in which a narrator tells of the mysterious disappearance of the main character, the commander Xiao. Xiao, commander of the 32nd Brigade under Sun Chuanfang (a historical character of the warlords period, circa 1926–27), has "ill forebodings" about the imminent war. By a curious—coincidental—set of circumstances (the death of his father), he ends up in his native town, where he encounters his childhood sweetheart, now a married woman. For him, she is a "fruity fragrance" 'guoxiang,' a fitting description for a woman whose name is Apricot 'Xing,' which is a homonym for "sex." This smell eventually guides him to the tea field where she works, then to her home, for more adulterous lovemaking. Of course, the liaison ends tragically for the woman: her veterinarian husband returns, smells something "fishy," gouges out her sexual organs, and sends her packing to her mother's. Xiao dies too, but not because of this love affair: his bodyguard, obeying higher orders, executes him for treason. No one could have foretold this outcome, not even the Daoist fortune-teller who had warned him against his "wine-cup" (83). Things just go awry.

Serious, dedicated military men such as Commander Xiao in

"The lost boat," or Colonel Younghusband in "Meetings" ("Xiangyu") (1993),[20] lose their perspective as a result of unexpected encounters (for Xiao the loved woman; for Younghusband, the head lama), or, rather, they lose the perspective they should have as military men. Xiao does not realize that his beloved's home is in enemy territory (under his brother's command); Younghusband, "the headstrong, rash and impetuous . . . young officer [who was] undoubtedly the most suitable choice to take command of a war in a mysterious country like Tibet" ("Meetings," 15–16) does succeed in his expedition to Lhasa on July 30, 1904, but he has lost all of his certitudes concerning the superiority of Western science. The story ends with something the head lama once told him: "The earth is not round at all; it's triangular, like the shoulder blade of a sheep" (49). Although "Meetings" has a real historical background, like "The lost boat," it is ahistorical and apolitical. What is told is the story of an individual's "innermost feelings," which the reader alone (with Ge Fei) can somewhat grasp. The "world outside [fiction]" knows nothing. We, the readers, have had access to these characters' intimate experiences, thanks to the meganarrator who reads or, rather, fashions minds. We read that the purposeful Colonel Younghusband, for example, is something of an aesthete, because, while traveling toward Gyantse, he sees the scenery as "unreal, like a painting in oils" (26).

Similarly, encounters, or lack thereof, all take place under Ge Fei's control and we are powerless to guess or interpret them. To interpret Ge Fei's stories symbolically or psychoanalytically is to run into a dead-end. Ge Fei, like a magician—he makes a cut-off pigtail continue to grow or a dead man unbutton his shirt, perhaps because of the heat—is experimenting with form, with words, with signs; he aestheticizes them and erases all referential possibilities.

The short story "Green yellow" ("Qing huang") (1989)[21] is an even more obvious case of stories constructed with a proliferation of signs, because here the pretext is a term: "green yellow" 'qing huang.' Obsessed by the lack of a definite referent for that term, an ethnolinguist, the narrator, surprisingly follows the tracks of an unreliable source, his own academic adviser, and heads, against the latter's advice, to the village of Mai in order to find "Green yellow," which he believes to be a book, a year-by-year record of the lives of boat prostitutes (designated "green" if young, "yellow" if old). Instead of finding the book, he finds stories, each one shadier than the other: Chang the ex-boatman is a wandering ghost; his wife has no vagina; his daughter gets raped; Li Gui is a somnambulist, and so on. Some stories are and are not related to the lure, those fishing boats turned brothels. Also, the possible meanings of "green yellow" become confused: it might refer to prostitutes, but the investigator also meets a daughter called Young Green and a second wife, Emerald; it might even simply refer to nature, because its cycle evolves from green to yellow, and the charm of Mai is purposely described with these two colors. The reader is literally dazzled by all the clues strewn about. Green Yellow is also the name of a type of dog, greenish back, yellowish belly. According to a Ming dynasty dictionary the ethnologist consults, green yellow is a plant. And so on and so forth. Ge Fei even adds a sequence where there is a yellowish coffin in a green patch! It would seem that the ultimate "green yellow" is indeed a book: Ge Fei's own fictional work, "Green yellow."

The narrator who tells the strange stories claims that he is affected by the air and loses track of and interest in his own linguistic investigation. Perhaps, but not the author. Near the end of the story, narrator and author unite in this avowal of the fiction of it all, which recalls Colonel Younghusband's statement: "The village—its quiet river, the red sand on the riverside, the people rushing around, their shadows—all this seemed to have been fabricated, or all this looked like the common objects one sees in still-life sketches" ("Green yellow," 40, with modifications).

Ge Fei's "Hushao" ("Whistling") (1990) [22] also illustrates this objectification of people and aestheticization of things, people, and nature. An old man—who is also a historical figure, Sun Deng—rambles on about his past, especially about his friend, the poet Ruan Ji (210–63), and views and comments on his surroundings, which comprise a painting and whatever he can see of the outside from his old chair. All fragments are given as views or details of sections of a painting. Nothing whatsoever happens in this story, where time and memories are frozen into pictures, which are constantly—like a simple jigsaw puzzle—being rehearsed, at different moments of Sun's life. It is an experiment with surface 'mian,' a term recurrent throughout: what's on the table (a chess game), the surface of the painting (which represents a chess game), the cracked ground of the atrium, (wrinkles on) people's faces, which are said to be like mirrors (44), and of course the "pictures" (45) 'tuhua' (220) of natural and pastoral scenes, as well as the surface of conversations he overhears. This is Ge Fei in his most semiotic manner: no events, no feelings of joy or sadness, but imperceptible transformations of sight, sound, or smell. There is no (special) meaning to be sought and no reason (such as waiting) for this exercise in recollection. Sun Deng may just be a senile insomniac who can't, for instance, take a nap while all others are doing so. Or else Sun Deng, a senile insomniac, is trying to attain tranquility. Yet the reader is waiting, expecting something to happen; what "happens" is a slow, brilliant writerly confusion among nature, art, and fragments of Sun's life. Myriad variations on a relatively invariable routine. Painting the same scene and scenery over and over again, with different lighting, at different times of the day and year.

As in most of Ge Fei's stories, dialogues (for example between Sun and Ruan) and written messages (for example the poetry manuscript on Sun's lap or the inscription on the painting) are undecipherable. What is more, the whistling, which gives the work its title and which alludes to the mode of communication between Sun and Ruan, is left unanswered. Sun attempts to whistle — to communicate by returning Ruan Ji's whistle — but he cannot produce a sound. As is customary with Ge Fei, the story then ends with a comment on the theme and on the writing of it. Replacing Sun "the poet who died long ago" (68) is a daydreamer, a living person; that is, Ge Fei.

If Ma Yuan's stories extend on to the reality of the world, Ge Fei's remain in the "deep recesses" of individuals. But this depth does not belong to them. It is the depth of words — multiple meanings, uses, connotations, sounds — which we readers are asked to fathom, to investigate, much like the ethnolinguist, the writer, or the etymologist. I cannot agree with Zhang Xudong's claim that Ge Fei creates by his experiment a "dialogical situation" that yields a certain sense of community.[23] There has to be a complicity, or rather an intelligence shared by author and reader; otherwise, the potentialities of the text would be left unexplored. Ge Fei's works are literary/aesthetic experiments, turning historical figures into signs like any other object.[24] When "Ge Fei" is involved, he shares the same fate: he is another character, to be mirrored into yet another object, to be added to another scene or scenery. Consequently, I also cannot agree with Jing Wang's position, which is to deny the epithet "postmodern" to Ge Fei (and Yu Hua) because "they in fact present various versions of that old bourgeois subject caught in the act of discoursing about itself. . . . [T]hey adhere to the modernist myth of the subject" (245).[25] Ge Fei remains an archexperimentalist in a self-contained world, resisting meaning, erasing all attempts at any unified subjectivity.

Yu Hua's method with the real

Yu Hua was born in 1960 in a small town near Shanghai. His parents both worked as doctors in a hospital, and he himself trained as a dentist. Emerging as a writer in 1984, Yu Hua has been at the forefront of China's experimental writing ever since.

If Ma Yuan experiments with his own life experiences, thereby opening up a space to the real world, Yu Hua experiments with collective experiences, or with "culture," and that opens onto the real, onto political space.

If Ge Fei's experiments remain a linguistic, literary, self-referential world of meaning, Yu Hua's literary experiments thrust us out of it. Ge Fei requires the (cultured) reader to go through the full hermeneutic circle. Yu Hua leaves us stranded, and terrorized. The reader is faced with an autonomous machine at work, programmed to destroy. There is no possible community with Yu Hua: we are inside the machine, forced to comply with the functioning of the process. We are confronted to a deadly logic, carrying out orders, from "nowhere." The reader is manipulated.

Hence, our unease when reading Yu Hua. The reader becomes part of the "collective assemblage of enunciation"[26] and is therefore involved in the text's ceaseless engendering of violence. Andrew Jones has asked a vital question concerning Yu Hua: How does a reader cope with such graphically violent texts ethically?[27] The answer most certainly entails a political positioning. Yu Hua's texts, like Kafka's, are eminently connected to the political. As Deleuze and Guattari have noted, the more individual the plight is, the more collective and political it is. Yu's characters become Every(wo)man.

Yu Hua's obsession is foremost with bodies, which he defamiliarizes.

Bodies are not envelopes for the soul, for a subject; nor are they machines that eat, walk, love, and suffer. All bodies are matter caught in the workings of an anonymous force, a compulsive drive toward physical mutilation and/or destruction. Like Kafka's bodies, they are not used metaphorically: they are flesh and bones to be broken up.

"One kind of reality" ("Xianshi yizhong") (1988)[28] is a deployment of the logic of dispassionate revenge. It is the logic of retaliation, where one part of the family is pitted against the other. A four-year-old child, Pipi, kills his younger cousin, whom he literally takes for a toy. At first, this family feud is "child's play":

> So he slapped the baby again, with all the might he could muster. No big reaction—just more of the same sounds, except that the crying became a little more drawn out. So he abandoned this tactic and, grabbing the baby by the throat, began to throttle him. The baby clawed back desperately at Pipi's hands. When Pipi finally let go, he was rewarded with just the kind of crying he wanted to hear. He did this over and over again, first choking the baby and then letting go, reveling in the explosive screams that burst forth every time. Eventually, though, when he loosened his hands around his cousin's throat, the baby no longer cried with the same intensity and passion. All he did was open his mouth and let out short, tremulous gasps. Pipi soon lost interest and wandered away. (25)

The dead child's father, Shanfeng, kills Pipi by hurling him into the air. Another skull is left open in the courtyard. Shangang, Pipi's father, then kills Shanfeng, his own brother, by making him die of laughter (a dog is made to lick his feet smeared with delicious stew). Shanfeng's unnamed wife reports Shangang to the police, who execute him. This killing is also a messy affair: they shoot three times, the first shot tears off an ear, the second hits the back of his head, and the third finally lodges into his head, while his buttocks are high off the ground. Shanfeng's wife—pretending she is Shangang's wife—donates the executed's body to science. A medical team, joking as they work, opens up Shangang's corpse; a high-heeled lady, the dissector, elegantly collects his skin, a urologist his testes, an oral surgeon the undamaged lower jaw, and so on.

This gruesome tale, sparing no graphic detail, leaves the reader cold and stunned. Although there are some funny episodes—when Shangang is shot the first time and he asks twice, "Am I dead yet?" (59, 60); when Shangang's wife realizes she has not seen the live-in mother-in-law in quite a few days; when the medical team exchanges smart-ass jokes in the morgue; when the dead Shangang appears to his wife with only half a head and says he's fine, perhaps he just caught a cold. But in general, what occurs is no laughing matter. Yu's humor is akin to Kafka's. It grows on you and is quite unsettling. "One kind of reality" even has a "happy end" of sorts: Shangang, who lost his own son, posthumously and by proxy impregnates a woman who gives birth to a male heir. Unlike Ge Fei's stories, Yu Hua's conclusions are open-ended, never circular. The nightmare can continue. The literary machine continues to burrow its way into the most unexpected domains of investigation.

No one is impervious to the workings of the machine. In "Shishi ru yan" ("World like mist") (1988),[29] all the characters have one-track minds or, more accurately, are the workings of a machine of doom. None of them has a name. Some have numbers, some are referred to by their job, some by their kinship with a "number." The body of the machine is therefore even more visible for the investigation into the contaminating power of fear, paranoia, superstition, and morbidity. There is no main character. Or any of them could be a main character: the fortune-teller who rapes, kills, kidnaps; the blind man who "sees" the intricacy of many trappings; the girl called 4 (Si), whose name and calling is death 'si.' Regardless of the power or influence at times that one might have over another, all these players are mere parts in the global design of annihilation. As in "One kind of reality," a chain of verbs of action sets one part then another into motion. For example, 7 has been ill since his son's birth: the fortune-teller tells them that their natal coordinates are at odds. The only way out is to expel the son, which is done by giving him away to the fortune-teller. In turn, the latter feeds off that foster son to boost his own vitality. This process is never entropic: as one part disappears (a son dies, for example), another pops up, replenishing the energy. There is self-engendering (engineering) at work. Yu's stories have branchings beyond the text's final period. There will be more lovely girls to commit suicide, more romantic men to follow them into the river; marriages will follow deaths, suicides and murders will follow marriages.

In other words, Yu Hua's experiments maintain the live immediacy of the present, never letting it pass to become a past, and therefore never allowing for a future. No one is an autonomous body; no one body is immune against torture, a most immediate experience, including ghosts, which mingle with the "living dead." They torture and are tortured. The story "1986,"[30] written in 1986, is an example of the presence of ghostly workings. In this story, the (nightmarish) dream world, the supernatural world, and the waking or real world are interwoven, as well as the past and future, conflated as 1986, the year the story was written and in which it takes place. After a disappearance of over a decade, a mad ghost that haunts the town returns to his home, where his wife and child have cut off all links with him, including erasing the family name. But their efforts are to no avail. Although it is said that "the disastrous years of the past decade or so have faded into the mists of time" (143, with modifications), and the Cultural Revolution slogans have been replaced by billboards, the past is still very present. The woman is overwrought with fear of her dead husband's return, and she lives in seclusion at home with her daughter.

Throughout the story, the madman/ghost repeats his performances of mutilation and self-mutilation. Formerly a high-school teacher who was interested in doing research on traditional punishments, he is now putting his knowledge into practice. Chapters 2, 3, and 4 of "1986" are so packed with graphic accounts of the severing of bodies (nose cutting, testis crushing, leg chopping, and so on) that the reader is trapped into an everlasting experience of a (hellish) present that never ends. For example, the madman after shouting, "Nose cutting!" starts to place the saw under his own nose; the cutting scene lasts for a good two pages, then the clinical account moves on to the legs, and so forth.[31] Kafka's *The Penal Colony (In Der Strafkolonie)* displayed torture machines; Yu displays the torture machinery in full operation.

The bodies are machines one works on, that one "fixes." Pain and suffering are incidental, because the goal is to dismantle them much like a machine, to break them up. Bodies in Yu's stories are machines with each part as significant or insignificant as another. Of course, "1986," by virtue of its timed setting, lends itself particularly well to a political reading: Yu is definitely dealing with the ghostly presence of the Cultural Revolution. But this is not the only possible reading of Yu, no more so than the stories of Can Xue, which are discussed below.

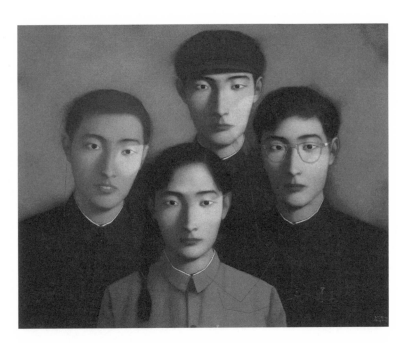

3. *Bloodline: The Big Family no. 2.* Oil painting by Zhang Xiaogang, 1996. *Photograph donated by artist.*

Yu's insistence on telling the procedures of bodily mutilation in many of his stories leads the reader into experiencing, through the proxy of words, the mechanics of torture. Hence, torture and the body become deterritorialized, become an immediate intense material experience with ramifications in each person's life. It could be termed an erotic experience, in that we become sadomasochists because we read on, because we proceed from one section to the next.[32] We thus comply with the story's logic, where distinctions such as victim and victimizer do not hold, past and future are totally senseless, where literary discriminations such as beautiful and ugly, clinical and lyrical, where moral and psychological judgments such as good and bad, sane and mad are indiscriminately eaten up by the body-time machine.

"Wangshi yu xingfa" ("The past and the punishments") (1989)[33] illustrates a dialogical situation where the reader can perhaps choose his or her position: a victim, called "the stranger" and a victimizer called "the punishment expert" are the characters. Highly reminiscent of the odd situation in Kafka's *The Trial (Der Prozess)*, the stranger, for no reason, is called by the expert to receive his punishment (the expert tells of an identical experience). The stranger complies and agrees to be sawn in two. But the victimizer, a very polite and erudite executioner, cannot carry out this plan and consequently disappoints the stranger. The expert cannot even carry out his own refined punishment, a ten-year project, and ends up inflicting the most degraded (note: not "degrading") punishment, that is, suicide. Throughout the story, historical dates — all of the Cultural Revolution period — are tossed about like wild cards, as if they were clues to explain the punishments. Both the stranger and the expert have knowledge of these dates. It is even suggested — but never asserted — that the stranger was the expert's victimizer. We are left in the end with one character, the stranger, who will surely keep the killing machine working.

What is striking in all of Yu's narration is its matter-of-fact style, which of course prevents the reader from feeling compassion for the "speaking parts" of the machine. But who feels compassion for machines? The only feeling other than sheer horror is occasional laughter, due to the hyperbolic description of torture. It recalls classical Chinese texts, such as *Water Margin (Shuihuzhuan)*, which are packed with gory murders. But the classics have been entertainment for the young and old since Yuan times. Yu's narratives are less stories than procedures or investigations into a logic that has many connections with today's reality.

It is therefore not surprising that Yu's discourse on fiction almost always deals with authenticity or reality or, indeed, with truth. Radically antirealist, Yu believes in the order of the world — an objective reality 'keguan de zhenshi,' and he is interested in the profundity of things. But such reality or truth is neither to be found in common sense, nor in one's experience. Yu has put it this way: "There is another kind of order and logic [of civilization] which makes the world go round. . . . I write to get closer to the real ['xianshi']. . . . Any event can in a literary work symbolize a world."[34]

When Yu Hua talks about symbolizing 'xiangzheng,' I believe he is talking about metonymical action. Novels must link up with reality in a metonymical way. Like Kafka, Yu Hua "kills all metaphor, all symbolism, all signification, no less than all designation." [35] The works are written without literary self-reflexiveness, as if no one was writing them. With Yu Hua, we are forever dealing with reality, a most profound thing indeed.

Yu is not a postmodern writer of "surfaces"; at the same time, it is true that there is no psychological depth, no motivation, no access to the inner recesses of the mind. His narratives are not soul-searching, nor heart-stirring. But Yu's quest is, as he wrote in 1989, "to grasp the 'real' ['zhenshi'] of the world," [36] an ongoing process. As he reiterated again in 1994, his aim is "to seek out the truth ['zhenli']," [37] the real order of things.

Between Ge Fei and Yu Hua there is a literary abyss. Although they both play with resurging time and both (for different reasons) pay homage to Robbe-Grillet, [38] Ge appeals to our aesthetic, literary competence to disentangle his network of signs while Yu—for whom the term "appealing" is preposterous—sticks our nose into the murk of a certain kind of reality and leaves us there, his words forgotten (gone up in smoke). This can perhaps account for the many varied interpretations of Yu Hua, depending on the political agendas of the critics: cultural nihilism, complicity with the official order, criticism of patriarchal order, and so on.

Yu Hua admires one modern Chinese writer, Lu Xun, and one contemporary Chinese writer:[39] she is Can Xue, a writer who also works with logic: not that of violence but of the violence within language itself.

Personally speaking, Can Xue

Can Xue (the pen name of Deng Xiaohua) was born in Changsha in 1953 and is the most radical and hence the most potentially disturbing writer in China. She calls herself a barbarian and claims to write in order to take revenge. Her work is a resistance against culture and language.[40]

Culture is an ordering of the world by man [sic]; it is what civilization entails: cities, institutions—such as marriage, work units, literature, medical knowledge—and last but not least, language. Can Xue's works make fun of all of these either by refusing to acknowledge them or by exposing their civilized pretensions. Stripped of their veneer, things and people become barely recognizable; language likewise escapes referentiality, the reader cannot comprehend.

It is somewhat miraculous that Can Xue has been published in China, manages to live there as a writer, and has been translated—before Ma Yuan, Ge Fei, Yu Hua et al.—into English, French, Japanese, and probably more languages. Abundant criticism has been written about Can Xue and her works. Most of it revolves around the question of madness (of all forms: perversions, schizophrenia, scopophilia, paranoia), either disclaiming it or attempting to prove it.

In my opinion, her world is not peopled by madwomen in the attic or Luxunesque lucid madmen (that is, people whose madness is sane); it is a ship of fools, with Can Xue sometimes at the helm (after all, she writes, publishes, and uses language, too). (Everyone, including her, puts on airs.) There is no single logic to be found in Can Xue's writings. There are, however, techniques that serve to counter logic and not only common sense—that which the fool or genius lacks—but any logic, that of a dreamer, of a hallucinating subject, of a madperson, of an autistic, of fairy tales. Her stories mix all of these with the actual state of the Chinese language and with the inherent logic (the visual, aural potentialities) of the Chinese language.[41]

There is a radical negation of systematicity in Can Xue's work, and Can Xue shies away from responsibility. She has no master and does not yield any master signifiers. Her works show a total disregard/disrespect of external reality, an indifference to anything, anyone, exclusive of her own person.

There is in all her stories a "voice" that is indifferently couched in a male or female body, young or old. This "voice" functions within a closed circuit, and is not even solipsistic because it does not master itself. It is a fool's voice that does not even own, let alone control a body.

In Can Xue's works, the human body is very present and visible. It is a public, malleable thing that undergoes constant alterations. Such transformations occur, haphazardly: (1) when another person looks at you and measles rash spreads on your nape or a bulge appears; (2) when you have a disease that "pops up," a nose cancer, a lung tumor, or a boil on your buttock; (3) when insects enter you and your leg turns the size of a lead pipe or your belly bloats like a pregnant woman's; (4) when—

simply because it is a living body—your nose runs, you defecate, you stink of garlic, you snore, you rot; (5) when you are fearful or terrorize others and you turn green, or black or white or any color, or your eyes bleed or the soles of your feet sweat; (6) when you are dead and your eyes are eaten; (7) when literary images—which are the same as clichés in Can Xue—become concrete: your chest is filled with bamboo shoots, blocking your breathing; (8) when you turn into an animal and grow a tail, get furry; become a howling wolf; (9) when you dream or are in someone else's dream; (10) all of the above, especially at night time; (11) for no particular reason, when you cough, gasp, puff, pant, or slobber.

Can Xue's fictional body is anarchy itself. No law governs it, not even its owner, and certainly not nature. It is "logical" that the human body would be at the center of Can Xue's imagery: the body is what is most inscribed as both "nature" and "culture." Can Xue stresses its rich physicality and downplays its noble humanity. For example, in "Shanshang de xiaowu" ("The hut on the mountain") (1986),[42] bodies are notably hearing bodies. The main character hears thieves, hears a locked-up man in a hut crying out, hears her father-turned-wolf howling at night, hears her own body freezing; her mother hears the bugs that come in at daybreak as they cross the floor. The normal activities of the characters are few. The main character tidies her chest of drawers, or sits with her hands on her lap in an armchair; she visits a hut behind the house, plays solitaire (to ignore her mother's stamping in the adjacent room), and eats dinner. Like all the characters, she is hypersensitive to sounds, but does not respond to conversations, perhaps because "everyone always says time-honored things" ("Shanshang de xiaowu," 97). (It doesn't matter what is said, it is always time-honored.) The father, for example, has been saying the same thing over and over again for twenty years, she claims; he talks about some scissors he dropped in the well a long time ago; he fears they have rusted. He says his wife says this is a figment of his imagination. But he goes on, "I've been troubled by this for dozens of years. The wrinkles on my face look as though they've been carved in" (96).

Here, worry for the state of the scissors and the scissors themselves have both "carved" his face. As in careless, or automatic writing, Can Xue likes to carry words over.[43] Scissors 'jiandao,' like knives 'dao,' carve. And figuratively, of course, worry does make a face furrow. But then the next image of worry is the familiar "whitening of hair": her father's hair has turned white, but on one temple only, the left one. (This, by the way, is no less incongruous than the transformation of the socialist iron girl, the "white-haired girl" of the play of the same name, whose vicissitudes under the old regime brought on the premature aging.) In answer to her father's lament, she complains of the cold. The cliché of the "piercing" cold is made literal: "Bits of ice are forming in my stomach. When I sit down in my armchair I can hear them clinking away" ("The hut on the mountain," 214). Can Xue uses catachresis and distorts idioms, much in Samuel Beckett's way. "I am no enemy of the commonplace," says Beckett's Molloy, who would rather call his mother "Mag" because "without knowing why, the letter g abolished the syllable Ma, and as it were spat on it." [44]

Shirking away from all authorial duties, Can Xue leaves us without a conclusion, except for a makeshift one. The main character — we can call her "Can Xue" (does it matter?) — goes for the second time up the mountain to inspect the hut and concludes by saying, "There were neither grapes, nor a hut" ("Shanshang de xiaowu," 98). This is a very different finale from that of Ge Fei: instead of showing off some literary prowess by describing the "circular ruins," she closes with a matter-of-fact sentence that abruptly ends whatever expectation the reader could have had — on the layerings of a word such as "the hut," for example. And it is also not an opening-up of the story, as in Yu Hua's fiction: Can Xue throws in a totally heterogeneous object, grapes. This is disturbing, since grapes have not at all been referred to in the text. The only possible explanation is the author's very free association of the mountain with grapes.

Grapes pop up again in another story by Can Xue, "Tianchuang" ("Skylight").[45] She is invited to someone else's hut, where there are grapes. Can Xue's recurrent excursions — her call of the wild — are very much in the spirit of Little Red Riding Hood. In "Skylight," she complies and follows the old man for a scary, convoluted walk through the woods. She meets with an eerie collection of fantastic animals, both winged and legged, and of course with big long teeth. But the "grandfather" is not such a bad monster after all. She recalls going to pick mushrooms with him a long time ago (317). And he is not a wolf, nor is he a member of her family. He makes his identity clear from the start: he is the father of her colleague A (306). To her direct questions, he replies that he is a cremator (311); he is the old man who digs tunnels in the cemetery (314). Yet, he is also nasty: after crushing her ribs with something like pliers, he makes her say "Please." She complies (313). And there is a cannibalistic side to him, since he eats the eyes of corpses, the "grapes" he enticed her with, in his written invitation.

The fairy-tale atmosphere is reinforced by the childishness in the narrations, both in style and in content. The attitude of the protagonist is often that of an observing child, such as in "The hut on the mountain." In "Skylight," although she is an adult — she says she is three years older than her forty-year-old brother — "Can Xue" is a child missing her mother, as the cremator makes apparent to her. Acting like a psychoanalyst for a minute — nothing is ever pursued in Can Xue's writings — he says to her, "You speak now." This brings her to tell of her family: "Me? As soon as I was born, I was thrown into the piss pot. Because I was steeped in urine, my eyeballs are always bulging, my neck is cotton-limp and my head's bloated like a balloon. I've spent so much time inhaling poisoned air that my ribs are ravaged by tuberculosis. My father is syphilitic, his nose has rotted down to two terrifying holes; as for my mother . . . my home is on top of ruins" (309). To this, he comments, "Mama, you want to say: Ma-Ma" (310). Later on, he mocks her, after she has described her mother lying in the bathtub, with her head flayed: "Oh! Ma-Ma" (314). The daughter's ambivalence toward her mother recalls Molloy and his dealings with his beloved "Ma(g)."

Fairy tales are domestic affairs and are fittingly Can Xue's favored structure. For Can Xue, it would seem that everything is (like) a family affair, where, however, no one has a fixed role. In "Skylight," the cremator, AKA her colleague's father AKA wolf AKA (grand)father, also talks of his mother. In the end, the old man is also herself. She has switched roles: from Little Red Riding Hood to the big bad wolf.

To a greater extent than other stories, "Skylight" is also riddled with onomatopoeia, which are the mark of nursery rhymes and other children's stories. At first, the old guy is the teacher. He tells her: "Listen: Bang, bang, bang, bang, bang! bang, bang, bang, bang, bang! She [his dead mother] jumps like this all night" (313). It allows language to become visible. Plain words like "mother," "please," and phrases such as "happy new year" are defamiliarized. As in a dream, they are not used in a communicational sense but for (un)sound purposes. "Mother" 'Ma-Ma,' as we have seen, is two lamentable sounds; "please" is inadequate as a response to abuse; "happy new year," one of those things one says only on the occasion, is here a wild card. Like the grapes elsewhere.

Of course, this is "free" association and it blends in with other rhetorical tricks that Can Xue pulls out. The Chinese saying "Xiong you cheng zhu," for instance ("Bamboo grows inside the bosom": a thought is first conceived in one's heart, as the bamboo is imagined before it is painted), is materialized into a progressive choking. At first, there is a bamboo bud growing in the woman's lung, then shoots, and then the growth hurts unbearably (314–16).

There is never any jabberwocky in Can Xue's words, though. She will not gratify us with such Carrollian entertainment. Her endeavor is anticultural, and any new construction would be a building of something. Can Xue detests clichés with a vengeance, especially of the highfalutin, inflated, sycophantic kind. In "Skylight," the female character scoffs at her father who uses the phrase "I admire" 'xinshang'; likewise, the term "to approve of" 'zancheng' often recurs ironically in her texts. Critics have shown how Communist language—ways of speaking that are pompous or banal—is turned on its head in Can Xue's work.[46] But there is a whole lot more than contemporary politics involved. Her attacks are always far-reaching but also never exhaustive. Can Xue does not aim to describe a system. She is not a theorist and will not be linked with philosophers or any other "comrades-in-arms," as she calls the critics.[47]

A more recent work, "Mingren zhi si" (The death of a famous person) (1991)[48] has the subtitle "Can Xue tan yishu" (Can Xue talks about art). The topic is the foolishness in the social use of language and in the ways of even famous people. She starts by mocking the pretentious wording of obituaries. She quotes the customary phrases used when people die: "Returned to the bosom of mother earth," "peacefully and serenely slipped into eternal slumber," "swam with even strokes into the silent depths of the vast seas." Then, she moves on to discuss the death of a famous person, which should be couched in such noble words. But the famous person dies ridiculously: imitating a bird, he flaps his arms and tries to fly from the seventh floor. The famous person had wanted to do an experiment: "You can understand that, you're a writer," he had said (361). As much as Can Xue mocks famous sayings, famous people, she doesn't spare herself and the artistic community—they are all *shagua* 'fools' (363). Imitation 'mofang,' a deep-rooted bad habit 'liegenxing,' is, along with death, every(wo)man's condition (363).

"The death of a famous person" is one of the few works by Can Xue that is relatively intelligible and that takes some moral stand. She clearly states her opinion on human beings. Language—spoken, written—is our worst enemy and our best friend. It is our clothing, our body, our camouflage. In "Canglao de fuyun" ("Aging Clouds") (1986) a pure sophist's dialogue unfolds (between a husband and wife):

> —Why are you laughing at me? (husband)
> —Because you are a fool. (wife)
> —What about you then? (husband)
> —How can I be a fool? If I'm a fool, how would I know that you are a fool? (wife)
> —So that's how it is. (husband)
> He had seen through her. But she didn't know; she was still playing the old game of tricks.[49]

Of course, the above statements are impossible, unverifiable; and none can alone carry any truth content. What remains consistent in all of Can Xue's stories is the "voice" within the anonymous recording machine of language, in the not-so-closed circuit. It is some "inner/outer voice" that "Can Xue" listens to, once the big bad wolf has been outwitted, as in "Skylight": "coldly smiling, warmly smiling, acridly smiling. At that moment the light went out, the bell rang. I have finally become fascinated by my own sound, that's a soft and graceful low sound, forever pouring out next to my ear" (318). Thus we find something like the grin of the Cheshire cat.

Can Xue is right in saying that "critics have not succeeded in penetrating [her] turf."[50] There is no territory to start with, no land of opportunity for systematic critics in search of an overarching logic. Can Xue's work is, in a very idiosyncratic, oxymoronic way, "personally" hers. It freely mimics the world and makes words break out, like pimples.

Chen Ran, born in 1962, is a Beijing "free writer" 'ziyou zuojia,' or so states her business card. She started writing fiction in the mid-eighties, at much the same time as Yu Hua, Ge Fei, and many of the experimental writers. But she is an outsider to that group; she has gained some recognition only in the past few years and as a feminist writer. She is *the* representative of feminist writing in China.

Within literary circles, Chen Ran's writing is not viewed highly. Her works are considered weakly structured, repetitive, and lacking scope. Chen Ran writes "little" stories about herself, about women much like her (that is, urban and middle-class), which focus on (female) sexuality. They are quite repetitive and seemingly autobiographical. There is an obvious conflation of narrator-author, since Chen's characters, and Chen herself, sometimes quote each other. What interests me in Chen Ran's work is how she incessantly rehearses the same theme, often with the same expressions, and makes much use of Western references in this ongoing performance.

Chen Ran's overt references are mainly to writers: female writers like Virginia Woolf, Marguerite Yourcenar, Marguerite Duras; male writers like Borges, Joyce, and Rilke. But her range of Western references is broad, from music to architecture to film, with director Ingmar Bergman as the most recurrent figure. Yet, in the midst of all this high culture, there is one very incongruous Western reference: to former U.S. president Richard Milhaus Nixon, her figure of the father-lover and *the* representative, for her, of the early 1970s.

Nixon's death in February 1995 may have been the catalyst for her novella "Pokai" (Breakthrough) [51] written in March 1995, which alludes to Nixon and the news of his death. "Breakthrough" is, however, not about (American) politics; it is considered a "feminist manifesto," as feminist critic Dai Jinhua has said: "Chen Ran's most radical work yet." [52] "Breakthrough"'s diegetic time is the beginning of March 1995, a week after Nixon's death, and its events revolve around a one-week trip from a southern town to a northern city. At the onset, the narrator, Daier (a protagonist name one finds in other pieces by Chen Ran, obviously referring to the neurotic but lucid character Lin Daiyu of the *Dream of the Red Pavilion* [*Hongloumeng*]), is traveling back north with her best

friend, Yunnan (homophone of the southern province, Yunnan trans-
latable as "dead nanmu tree" and evoking, by sound also, "dead man").
The narrator went south to meet her friend in order to establish, with
women artists, an association against gender discrimination that they
named Pokai, 'Breakthrough.' We don't get to know why Yunnan, who
lives in that southern town, travels back with the narrator, but, at the
end of the story, the narrator asks Yunnan to go home with her, and
Yunnan accepts.

While waiting for the plane and during the flight, the two friends
mainly talk about their feelings for each other and discuss gender issues:
there is an unfathomable barrier between the sexes, men discriminate
against women, women are scapegoats, and so on. This is very much
the standard feminist discourse based on the binary male-female distinction, castigating the masculinist economy. This discourse will resurface several times in the story, with an increasing radicalization of
the distinction between womanhood and all phallic constructions, and
the ever pressing need to break away from men.

Conversely, the inadequacy of language to represent new female
bonds is discussed. Refusing the feminine marker *mu* (mother and
female) to describe each other, they revert to fraternal and sororal terms
mixed together, as in "little brother-like sister" or "little sister-like
brother 'didishi de meimei,' 'meimeishi de didi' (94). As for the name
of the association, they prefer "Breakthrough" to "The Second Sex," for
they find Simone de Beauvoir's expression derogatory. The term "love"
'ai,' always referred to within quotation marks, is also rejected in favor
of the more egalitarian and less compromised "affection" 'qingyi.'

"Naturally," this story also thematizes the emancipation of women's
sexuality. "I firmly believe I am not a lesbian," declares another of Chen
Ran's protagonists.[53] In "Breakthrough" however, same-sex love (or affection, if you, like Chen Ran, prefer this term) is explicitly broached.
Indeed, there is from the start a mutual seduction strategy, of which
Yunnan is definitely the leader. She is the bold, talkative woman, who
forces avowals from the other and whose role is inscribed as masculine
in many ways. Daier even claims that Yunnan has asked more than once
whether, "if she were a man," would Daier marry her (115). Yet Yunnan
is the object-choice: she is the one who is physically described—and
more than once—by Daier at first and, in almost the same terms by an

old woman in a dream that Daier has. At the end of the story, it is not Yunnan who asks the other "to come home with her," but the neurotic and impressionable little Daier.

Daier, the protagonist and narrator and obviously Chen Ran's fictional self, is the one who "walks into dead ends," who says she's not anywhere as good as her friend, who has no sense of home. But she's the one who dreams. There are two dream sequences in the story: one a feminist utopian dream at the end of the story, the other a denunciation of the "daughter's seduction"[54] toward the beginning of the story. They are of equal importance in length, and, I would say, of equal importance as feminist statements. Together, they express the impossibility of breaking through the "heterosexual matrix,"[55] but also the possibility of exposing all fixed identifications as phantasms.

The second dream wraps up the "sisters unite" discursive sections and occurs at the end of "Breakthrough." This dream takes place after the establishment of the association, with Yunnan by her side on the plane heading back to the northern city. Yunnan has just told the narrator Daier that, were they to die now, she would kiss her — "Why should only men kiss women, kiss you?" (118). The dream is a magic reenactment of the imagined situation. The plane crashes, and Daier enters the underworld where an old woman tells her to remain with her friend, reminds her that salvation comes only through female solidarity, and sends her off with a gift of beads, "a sign" 'yi zhong fuhao' (124). The beads are luminous if strung together 'chuan zai yiqi' (124). Upon waking, the magic remains: the old woman is identified as Yunnan's mother, the beads are real—they spill out of Daier's pocket on the streets—and Daier is holding on to her friend's sleeve. This is a performance of feminist and lesbian fantasy. It doesn't fully work in "real life" though: it comes out of a dream, and the beads—which do spill, onto the dirty city street, are little white "teeth-like" beads, not the oneiric crystal. What comes closest to crystal are the glassy, phallic buildings of the cityscape, which both women find icily cold (126).[56] And it comes out of a fiction that leaves the last words to Daier, AKA Chen Ran: "My tongue stuck like a stiff tile in my mouth" (128).

Such irresolution at the end of a feminist manifesto is peculiar. But "Breakthrough" is not an expression of any kind of closure. The title might even be ironic, especially when one considers the first dream (actually a daydream), in which Daier reveals her problems with men, particularly with father figures, whom Nixon incarnates. I think that this story is an account of a breakthrough as concerns Daier's understanding of herself as a woman struggling against heterosexual norms, against fixed gendered desire, and all other forms of conventional identification. (Hence, I cannot agree with Wendy Larson's reading, which analyzes Chen's work in terms of a postmodern discourse of desire, which she of course cannot find. She writes: "Desire is unrooted, vague, variable and cannot really be called desire at all; it is mildly robotic, manipulated, and functional to the extent that it enacts itself to promote itself.") [57]

Chen has to deal first with the "daughter's seduction." The first dream or reverie, which features Nixon in the father-seducer role, takes place on the plane, on way south, before the establishment of the feminist association, before the explicit union with Yunnan. Obviously, it is a difficult story to tell because, Daier (Chen Ran) cloaks it and mixes it with assertive feminist statements and more resolutely lesbian declarations. Still, what is said is that, "until recently," Daier had been waiting all her life for a man ("intelligent, talented, and gentle-mannered") and that man, she realized, was someone like Nixon. But now she has dropped the gender requirement, "the sexually different prescription" 'xingbie yaoqiu.' It was "after traveling in old countries with modern civilized ways in Australia and Europe," that she realized it [same-sex sex] was not "abnormal" (102). As long as the relationship is fatal/vital 'zhiming'—like her phantasmatic identification to Nixon, she adds.

Daier exposes the strange connection in a very theatrical way. A newspaper, the official *People's Daily*, is given to her by the stewardess. She drops it on the seat next to her, but the cover story catches her eye: "Condolences to former U.S. President Nixon." She plays out a mock funeral for him: "I stopped looking out the window when the plane shook. I said to myself: 'Farewell, Nixon, Adieu.' It was as if this trip was especially to bid farewell to Nixon, at the gate of paradise, in space" (107).

This mock ritual is of course a self-mocking. Daier is criticizing herself for being bogged down in a fixation dating to her prepubescent self, which identified Nixon as a nice man, a kind father, and her own father as a stultifying monster. This is potentially a very subversive political statement: Nixon representing the better side of the 1970s, displacing all

Chinese fathers, the great Mao and her real one. The following passage is also a repetition of a family disposition, with the "normal" Freudian tensions between mother-father-child exposed.

> My relationship with Nixon is actually a relationship with the Nixon era ['shidai']. When I saw his name written out, what I saw was in fact the naïveté, the sadness, and the flimsy, innocent life. I was sitting in a large old-fashioned room with dark brown window frames and off-white window paper, sitting in my father's desperate, angry gaze of those red years ['niandai'], the gaze that stifled the child's clear and vivid voice in my mouth. I saw that girl child, both hands on her knees, scared eyes, yellowish hair like wild wheat in the wind, she does not know how to comb her hair, she waits for her mother to come home . . . she moves onto the street, stands on a rock to see her mother one minute sooner. A home without a mother isn't a home, a home without a woman isn't a home, and that little girl, one couldn't say she was a woman. (105–6)

The breakthrough for Daier, when it comes, is out of the heterosexual matrix of desire. The child waiting for her absent mother has now been replaced by the adult who longs for that woman Yunnan, for Yunnan to give her a certain sense of home, and the real aging mother is now the one waiting for her (128).

By reenacting such childhood scenes, Chen Ran has succeeded in displaying the phantasmal structure of identifications and to begin to construct new ones. As Judith Butler has said: "The rules that govern intelligible identity, that is, that enable and restrict the intelligible assertion of an 'I,' rules that are partially structured along matrices of gender hierarchy and compulsory heterosexuality, operate through *repetition*. . . . In a sense, all signification takes place within the orbit of the compulsion to repeat; 'agency' then, is to be located within the possibility of a variation on that repetition" (145).

But of course, Daier or Chen Ran doesn't achieve a full assertion of that "I." The end of "Breakthrough," we have seen, is not a resolution.

The Nixon obsession and the family drama are replayed in at least two other works, "Yu wangshi ganbei" (A toast to the past) (1991) and in Chen's long novel, *Siren shenghuo (Private Life)* (1996).[58] In "A toast to the past," Nixon appears in a narrative where the twin taboos of incest and homosexuality are performed. In *Private Life,* Nixon is still the ideal man for her: "There was only one exception [to both beauty and talent in a man]: former U.S. president Nixon, both handsome and successful. What attracted me to him was, I discovered, that his noble nose, wide shoulders, and benevolent attitude corresponded very much to my model of a father. I would superimpose ['fugai'] on my boyfriends this father image—this is a fault I have had till now" (152). Chen Ran said this last sentence word for word in an interview in 1995.[59] It is evident that all of her protagonists are herself, or else that she plays out alternately all her characters. The reality effect of Chen Ran's identifications is what matters, not whether she is heterosexual or homosexual, or bisexual. "Woman" here is an emerging "I" that struggles against congealed substantive identity, unceasingly and playfully rehearsing scenarios of sexuality.

Chen Ran has many Western feminist (and postfeminist) writings to back her up. Butler and Gallop, especially, but also Irigaray, Lacan's "daughter," are there, in the margins.

Xu Kun's theme parks

At the other end of the spectrum of female "gender trouble," there is the satirist Xu Kun, born in 1965 in Shenyang and now living in Beijing. Since 1993, she has been writing novellas that intellectuals, both male and female, love to read. If Chen Ran rehearses a person's multiple identifications, Xu Kun parodies society's diverse identifications. Unlike Chen's works, Xu's do not attempt to find alternatives; they play with what's there. Her characters are men, women, young, and old and she surveys the scene from afar, using different styles, different masks.

Yet her replications of today's trends are not uncritical. She operates critically within the heterosexual matrix of power and although no one is immune to her mocking, men are definitely the main target. They perform acts of bravura throughout her works, from seduction to suicide, and put up their own flagposts. Rendered larger than life, they and their exploits become "incredible."[60]

Xu Kun's caricatures evolve in a world of novelty and of replicates. "Regou" (Hotdog) (1996)[61] recounts the trials of a fiftyish-year-old

4. *Sleepwalking.* Oil painting by Yu Hong, 1993. *Photograph from exhibition catalog.*

man, Chen Weigao, to join the young crowd, "to eat, drink, and be merry." He is a theater critic who gets involved with a young woman, an aspiring postmodern experimental theater actress seeking fame. Of course, he will boost her career by shamelessly eulogizing her with the latest fancy expressions, riddled with "new" and "posts"; and of course, she in turn will sleep with him. Together, they will drink black coffee and eat hotdogs. Foolish Chen has only harsh words for his own wife of twenty years. Her odor of lard and pig pancreas is everywhere, on the sheets and on the towels, as well as on his shirt collar; when he burps, he smells the stink of his wife's garlic and dried shrimp dumplings on his breath (201). The pathetic Chen nevertheless returns to his wife's cooking, once the pretty starlet has dropped him. Xu here uses food as an indication of people's cultural level: if you are "in," you eat Western fast food, whether you like it or not.

If in "Hotdog," Xu Kun blends Western food culture with novelty in theater, in "Xianfeng" (Avant-garde) (1996),[62] she mixes Western figures and expressions with novelty in the fine arts. It is to my mind her most incisive work because the frame is broader, extending to questions of neocolonialism.

Her protagonist is Satan 'Sadan,' the name he has adopted as an artist; he was formerly called Foolish Egg 'Shadan'. Satan is a wannabe artist who suffers from delusion and megalomania. Both, or alternately, Jesus Christ and Zen Buddhist monk, Satan wanders at the beginning as well as at the end of the story in a theme park. This amusement park is an amalgam of the Garden of Gethsemane and Disneyland, and of the Imperial Summer Palace that was devastated by the European allied troops at the turn of the last century. The Yuanmingyuan ruins (as they are called today) were also until recently a haven for "free" artists. Xu's story starts in 1985, when the first wave of bohemian artists moved into run-down places that they rented from farmers around Yuanmingyuan.

Somewhat accidentally, Satan, along with his friends, is acclaimed the preeminent special avant-garde painter of the "Ruins" school. His school is entered in the Cross-Century Encyclopedia under *F* for *fei* 'ruins' and *H* for *houwei* 'post-garde.' Eventually, his work is bought by the Fine Arts Museum, and he can live off the royalties of postcards and reproductions. But Satan is a naive, tormented soul.

What Satan wants, as is discovered after his death, written on the inside of a picture frame, is "to write, in my momentous way, a chronicle of art history" (334). No less. The ways of his epoch 'duandai xingshi' are realized in a single work of art. This work is an empty metal frame, which in 1985 is entitled *Being (Cunzai)* and bears one vaguely Sartrean (or Buddhist?) inscription: "All nothingness is being. All being is nothingness" (281–82). In 1995, Satan adds a canvas on which he splashes red paint and throws himself (naked) down onto, then writes, between the outline of his legs, an inscription. The inscription reads: "I am copulating with my own image" (327). The 1995 work is retitled *To Live (Huo-zhe)*, in reference to Zhang Yimou's 1994 film of the same name. Indeed, Satan simply tries to "live as an artist." His own speech is almost as sparse (and crude) as his sole piece of work: He says "fuck" and "waa-ow!" and will not partake in any isms: "Let me be vanguard, stop these isms, OK?" (288).

The problem is not the quality of Satan's work but the unwarranted reception it receives. Satan is whirled into all sorts of discourses, all ill-fitting. Like a gardener becoming president, Satan is upheld by the art critics as a new cultural phenomenon. "The critics who'd studied abroad and were desperately thinking of ways to link up with the world ['jiegui'] were all excited: that was it! They took up their bilingual dictionaries to dress [him] in new clothes" (283). But they also have problems importing concepts. The custom machine is blocked on the word "avant-garde" because the only available definition of vanguardism is the "red and expert" one, forcing the critics to use instead a soccer term, "frontline" 'qianfeng' (284).

A woman, the "oriental beauty," also coopts him in order to get back unto the cultural scene. At the same time, she makes him his sex slave; Satan must yield his brush to serve her with his virile "pen." No one cares for his art, especially not the peasants. Once, in a field, Satan is kicked out by the owner of the field who calls his art "dick all" 'jiba wanyi' and forces him to leave.

Satan has romantic ideas about art. Xu Kun makes him resemble Jesus Christ with his unworldly airs, long hair, and pauper's clothes. On the other hand, when he goes to the big city, people simply take him for a migrant worker or a common beggar. Satan is forever longing for an ideal. That is why he leaves his wife—called, incidentally, Juliette—and child, and goes out searching, perhaps for his roots. Neither the Buddhist temple life—where all is commercialized with a rhetoric strikingly similar to the fashionable art world or again to the Christian mass ("Nibble this. Chew on this" [308])—nor the peasant life "works" for Satan.

In a wheat field, Satan becomes a cross between Holden Caulfield and Vincent van Gogh. In a moment of artistic inspiration—where he utters "Wow!"—Xu Kun describes him as "the catcher in the rye" 'maitian shouwangzhe.' This is a truly far-fetched and highly ironical reference.

For one, as Caulfield's kid sister tells us, the momentary tenderness and harmony with the world that Caulfield experiences derives from his misreading of a Robert Burns poem, which has nothing to do with "helping people through." What is more, Satan, a husband and father, is imitating a teenager from some American novel.[63]

As for the actual "feel" of being in a wheat field, Xu Kun guides us toward van Gogh, unrecognized genius, who for Xu and other Chinese was the Western artist par excellence. Yet how can Satan, who does not create but simply drags his picture frame to the wheat field, be twinned with such a figure as Van Gogh? This is another preposterous comparison, which, along with the comparison to Caulfield in *Catcher in the Rye,* is nevertheless the frequent positive (romantic) reference in China's current art scene. Xu Kun is therefore making a copy of a copy of what cannot be called an original.

"Avant-garde" is a parade of figures, Western and Chinese, that are tried like outfits on Satan the artist and that show the ground on which art in China stands. At the end of the novella, Satan, who has stolen his precious work from the museum and destroyed the canvas, bears his frame as Jesus bore his cross and wanders back to Yuanmingyuan. A peculiar carnival awaits him: the ruins have been metamorphosed into an amusement park recreating the imperial glory prior to the European invasion one hundred years before. Satan, in his delusion, sees the Qing dynasty emperors Kangxi and Qianlong coming toward him. With them are such female historical personalities as the empresses Wu Zetian and Cixi and the loyal eunuch Li Lianying (these historical figures have all been turned into household names thanks to television and cinema). Satan is taken aback, and steps back into yet another world: the Trojan horse, where beautiful Helen will kiss his feet so forcefully that he can't stand it and shies away, only to fall into yet another world: Disneyworld. Satan is now riding in the "Magic Mountain" roller-coaster. His innards want to spill out, he gets very excited and cries out to his image to come back to his body, as if his painted image, now destroyed, were an essential part of himself. That's when Satan, totally bewildered, not knowing heaven from earth, or his body from his image, undoes his safety belt, falls out of his seat, and dies.

So much for the romantic artist as a young man or as a madman. And so much for the imperial grounds now turned into a theme park. Xu Kun equates novelty in the arts with out-of-place copies of Western art and revived Chinese classical lore. Is Satan's work zero-positive ("oriental") or zero-negative ("Western")? She chooses a man as the ill-suited actor and the invaded grounds as the scene of the carnival. "Avant-garde" is a cartoonish roman-à-clef, in which many cultural public figures of the last decade could fit the roles (the popular Wang Shuo and the Jia Pingwa of *Feidu (Wasted Capital)* for literature; the Fifth-Generation filmmaker Zhang Yimou and the Sixth Generation Wu Wenguang for film; pop artists such as Fang Lijun, Liu Wei, Wang Guangyi, and many others for painting; the "oriental beauty" is Liu Xiaoqing, who, once her beauty had faded, became involved with the business world of cosmetics and real estate. Since the writing of this novella, China has acquired its American theme parks: on the outskirts of Shanghai there is the "American Dream Park," which replicates stereotypical American attractions.[64] Already in the beginning of the 1990s, Beijing had its indigenous "Dream of the Red Pavilion" theme park.

The recycling of roles does not end with people or with sites: the Satanic/foolish work of art is converted into a useful tool. After Satan's death, an anonymous character finds Satan's discarded frame, adds wheels to it, and turns it into a trolley for household appliances. He is granted a large sum of money for the patent. This episode ends the novel.

"Youxing" (Parading) (1995)[65] is Xu Kun's most outspoken novella on the division of roles according to the sexes. In this novella, everyone parades, everyone has a ground, a public place 'guangchang' to be more precise. Except for the female protagonist, who is a wanderer. Beautiful and talented, Lin Ge is a reporter who has three love affairs: one with an old poet whom she idolizes and who writes about gods; one with a progressive intellectual who worked twice in a "production team" 'chadui'—the Cultural Revolution and Oxford University (which is a "foreign production team" 'yangchadui')—and who seduces her with his discourse; and one with a young rocker whom she "packages" for success. After the old poet's silly baggy underwear, after the intellectual's peevishness in front of his own wife, and after babysitting the sulky youth, she simply disappears from the public sphere, from the text. "Some say she's dead, some say she got married" (27). The novella ends with the following: "The square, it is always open; and also, it is always closed" (27). Lin Ge has gone through what she calls various "explorations" 'tansuo': poetic idealism with the poet; seductive dialogue with the intellectual; and plain monologues with the rocker. These men have all managed to "raise their flags" in a public place. She, on the other hand, swims, wanders, conducts some symbolic guerrilla warfare, and parades through the square. The novella's tone is set with the term *you:* to float, wander, and so on. Under the title is the phrase "Guanjianci: youxing, youdang, yousi" 'key words: to parade, to wander; wandering thoughts' (4).

If "Avant-garde" deals with fine arts, "Parading" deals with literature, criticism, and rock music, in other words with more new cultural phenomena. It is obvious in the stories that such activities belong to men. This story is as wild and hilarious as the others but the fact that the point of view is Lin's, that is, a woman's, must mean something more. Here, perhaps, Lin Ge is—as Daier was for Chen Ran—Xu's alter ego. This fictional alter ego, though, has no agency whatsoever. Lin Ge is just a reporter, someone who takes on other people's words, one who is culturally invisible. She writes down notes on what's happening and what other people are doing, and it is only logical that she disappears from the text at the end.

Before her vanishing act, though, she has made us laugh at man's vanity, at his attachment to his pen/penis[66] and his desire for fame. She has compared a man's erection to the state of the stock exchange: nothing stays up forever, not even U.S. hard currency (10). She has also made us laugh at the romantic idealism of young women by commenting on her sexual adventures as "sacrifices" for the cause and comparing the way three generations of men use rhetoric when they want to have sex. Also, Lin Ge A K A Xu Kun can talk dirty, in Chinese as well as in English. She is adept at making the wildest associations: Confucius with Christmas greetings, Pink Floyd with the Berlin Wall and the Xidan Democracy Wall. She wants neither to be a Nüwa nor an Eve: there are already no gods in this world, she says (22).

Once the female protagonist has "done" the three men, has completed her mission, she can swim away. There are no places, let alone flags to raise, for women. Territory is definitely a masculine conception in Xu's writing. Men are the ones engaged in questions of indigenous things, of land and discourse, versus American or foreign imports. Like the shaky ground on which China's new art is built in "Avant-garde," the "flags" marking territory in "Parading" are heavily criss-crossed with local and foreign references. For example, the intellectual lover, although educated abroad and versed in poststructural theory as well as Freudian terminology, proposes to counter foreign imperialism through the dissemination of Confucian thinking: "In the twentieth century, foreign things have been pouring in madly, foreign guns, foreign cannons, color televisions, and all we have to send back, apart from our Chinese medicine, cuisine, *taiji* and *qigong,* is Confucianism. We should convert the world to it" (15).

Xu Kun's writings are about contemporary China as one big theme park: a Buddhist temple next to a Caulfieldian rye field, where a clone of Jesus might be seen sipping chrysanthemum tea with a Tao Yuanming look-alike. Xu, a satirist, magnifies China's desire to link with the world, which makes all the more evident the connection between modes of cultural identification and a masculinist economy.

2 Away from Literature I

Words Turned On

A spring wells up at the foot of the mountain. The image of youth.
Hexagram 4, "Youthful folly," *Yijing*

Wang Shuo's mimics and gimmicks

"Xu Kun is Wang Shuo's female counterpart."[1] This statement may be true only if one considers Wang Shuo solely as a writer: both are entertaining, both write about contemporary urban Chinese society, focusing mainly on young people's lives, and both have their characters say what one hears on the streets and in the media. The main difference between the two is that Wang Shuo practices what he "preaches" — entrepreneurship — while Xu Kun remains in the literary arena, as a writer and critic.[2] Xu Kun is writing now, while Wang Shuo has stopped writing novels. If literature is intransitive for Xu Kun — as it is for most experimental writers — it is in transit and absolutely transitive for Wang Shuo.

Wang Shuo, born in 1958 in Nanjing but living since childhood in Beijing,[3] is the foremost experimenter with the exchange value of words. He has written twenty-four novels (between 1984 and 1991) and has also participated in the writing of scripts for several television series. Since the end of the 1980s and increasingly so in the 1990s, Wang has been capitalizing on his own work: he has written songs derived from twelve of his novels' themes, has started to turn his own novels into scripts for television and film, and collected his novels in a four-volume edition. Everything he has done has been hugely successful. No one in China has packaged his own words and his media image as successfully as Wang, except perhaps for Mao Zedong. (Of course, the comparison fails if one thinks in terms of quantity reproduced: strictly on the numbers, Mao is definitely the winner: the number of square meters of floor space occupied by Mao's work in the repository building is *ba wan ba,* that is, 88,000).[4]

A comparison between Wang Shuo and Mao as concerns their play with words, or their "literary" fortune, could easily be pursued. People call the collected works of both writers the "Four Volumes" 'sijuan'; there is a Maospeak and a Wang Shuospeak; both have recycled old expressions for their own purposes. In 1993, Mao's speeches were sold on tapes and Maoist songs revamped, while Wang's novels, more famous than ever, were made into songs. Literature serves a purpose, and in this goal the two "leaders," of course, differ totally—unless one could say that Wang Shuo also aims at "serving the people" of his generation, a generation without a living Mao and in great need of entertainment. He claims to be "the secretary of his times," anchoring his stories in reality.

Wang Shuo serves his contemporaries with stirring narratives: romances, coming-of-age stories, detective stories, and political-social farces. And of course he serves his own interests by creating, every time, a bestseller. Wang Shuo is a public figure, a self-made man, who can write a mock autobiography with a title as self-assertive (and self-derisive) as *I am Wang Shuo,* yet another bestseller. He can easily say, "Just don't consider me a person" and "I'm a bum. Of course, I'm fearless."

Wang Shuo's commodity is language: more specifically, his art of repartee, his glib tongue. "Wanzhu" (Troublemakers), written in 1987,[5] and *Bianjibu de gushi (Stories of an Editorial Board)* (1991)[6] are both of the same recipe: smart-asses giving out advice to others and more often than not bringing trouble upon themselves or upon their clients. The former was the first work of Wang Shuo to be turned into a film; the latter was written by Wang (and others) directly for television. It was mainland China's first sitcom.

"Troublemakers" is an illustration of private entrepreneurship based on the word. It is the story of three young men who devise a fun way of making money: they act as surrogates, substituting their bodies—above all their repartee—for their clients'. The "Three Ts," their company name, refers to themselves, the "three substitutes/surrogates" 'ti' and also to their three areas of specialization: troubleshooting, tedium relief, taking the blame (26).[7]

In one instance, a young writer of pulp fiction, ironically named Zhi Qing ("Pure Wisdom," also a homophone for the Cultural Revolution's "rusticated youth"), badly wants a literary prize. The three entrepreneurs satisfy his demand by organizing an awards ceremony. Versed in simulation, they create a mock event that parodies literary experimentation and the literary institution. Phonies are asked to read "poems": a woman posing as a poet of the "Misty" school, the underground school of poetry noted for its abstruseness, stands staring at the audience and then places her long hair on one side of her body while reciting impassively: "People say this side of me is the Yangzi River." She then proceeds to place her hair on the other side of her body and ends her performance with: "People also say this side of me is the Yellow River." It earns her raving applause. As is especially evident in the film version, the evening is a spoof of what Chinese television tirelessly shows: that is, speeches. And what it holds at regular intervals; namely, evening galas 'wanhui.' One of the surrogates starts the show with the usual official phrasing: "Today . . . we are all here together . . . to hold such a meeting . . . that's very good" (33). Then another one continues with the typical blurb: "I was invited to come at the last moment, I've had no time to prepare anything, plus I don't speak well, in my opinion there's no need to give you the habitual phrases, I'd like to express my congratulations to the Three Ts company for their good work" (35). Once all the necessary speeches, and the ludicrous poems have been delivered, the scene turns into a frantic fashion show gone awry. On stage, dancing together to the rhythm of disco music, are workers, peasants, traffic policemen, female bodybuilders, old-Shanghai prostitutes, clowns and literati from the Chinese opera, Eighth Army and KMT soldiers, Cultural Revolution red guards, students from the May Fourth (1919) era, a bride decked in white as well as pretty fashion models. All forms of ideology are mocked here: different historical and political times are conflated, politics flirt with traditional and pop culture. Entertainment is the name of the game in the film, and it would also seem to be Wang Shuo's goal.

There is no particular social critique in Wang Shuo's work. As one of his protagonists matter-of-factly says to defend himself, when accused of seducing a client: "I only used words from the Xinhua [New China] dictionary" (49). Wang picks up from all discourses indifferently: political, economical (including black market jargon), social, intellectual, Freudian, and so on, and does not mind if his script is altered: "If something's got to go, then out it goes" 'yao gai jiu gai ba.'[8] The novel, which is almost totally made up of dialogues—banter on anything from sports to Oedipal theory, has an improvised quality, which the film version pursues by deleting and adding rejoinders here and there. (For example, the Misty poet adds a new jewel: "When I was born, I was already dead," or this disconcerting response to "I'm sorry I'm late": "So what, I'm not waiting for you.") As Liu Xinwu has expressed it, Wang Shuo's works are about the here and now ("this time, this place, this body, this intention") (202).[9] Any displacement, therefore, brings on modifications.

Quick wit is all that is required in the constant re(dis)placements the three stand-ins execute. Whether it be during their "social counseling" or during their leisure time, their tongues never rest. Even songs are not left without some rejoinder: to a People's Liberation Army song about a soldier leaving for the Sino-Vietnamese war, which comes on the radio with the farewell words "If this should be so, don't be sad," they retort in chorus: "I'm not sad!" (32–33). Indeed, there is no chorus of recrimination on their part. "We can stand anything because we know there's nothing perfect, everywhere's the same. We have no expectations, no recriminations" (50–51). "If you don't rely on anything, then you don't care about anything" (36). Consequently, the novella "Troublemakers" can end with the deictic nonauthorial phrase picked up from the radio: "And this ends our programming for tonight" (52).

The film, however, attenuates the radically dismissive attitude of the bums and turns them into do-gooders, much like the editorial staff of *Stories of an Editorial Board*. *Stories* is nevertheless of crucial importance in China's television programming history because it is China's first sitcom, "by far [the] most popular American prime-time genre."[10] The twenty-five-part serial comedy that Wang Shuo wrote with his now most frequent collaborator, Feng Xiaogang, made everyone, young and old, men and women, laugh heartily when it aired in 1991 and continued to keep people giggling at each of its reruns well into 1993 (at least 140 throughout all of China). The comedy's success rests almost solely on its linguistic games, covering a wide range of everyday situations. It has since become a prototype of the Chinese television series.[11]

The sketches revolve around the six staff members of a mediocre magazine with a pompous name, *Guide to the World of Man (Renjian zhinan)*. They are harmless fun, without any social critique, or as Feng Xiaogang put it, the idea is "just touching on social things, never dealing with the system."[12] Perhaps the most famous saying of the series is "Money isn't everything, but without money you just can't do anything," which is offered by the entrepreneurial middle-aged Yu Deli. As in "Troublemakers," the actors in *Stories* act as social counselors most of the time: to find a wife, settle a family dispute, help a fat man lose weight, a handicapped singer gain recognition. They never solve too many problems, and as editor-in-chief Chen says, "We're not too busy, we have time to do some in-fighting." As spectators, what keeps our interest up, apart from the goofy solutions, are the verbal exchanges between these very different members of the team, all of whom are rather prolix. Gender and generational difference create humour between the older Big Sister Bovine (Niu), a true "red," and the young journalists, Ge Ling and Li Dongbao. Big Sister Bovine finds ideological faults with them constantly; in turn, they retort with Maoist expressions. Li cries out: "How have I been less fervent than you, Big Sister Bovine? All the rules to follow, I have followed them to a *T*, including even the Party's calls to eliminate rats, kill flies, donate blood, study Lei Feng, marry later, buy national products, and to stay off the streets during the chaotic years: when have I ever lacked passion?"[13] Ge Ling, just as quickwitted, makes cracks at Big Sister Bovine's past by saying she can solve a fraud problem, because she was an iron hand during special investigations in the Cultural Revolution.[14] Big Sister Bovine still holds the torch and is rather proud of her former experiences as a (Maoist) "mental labourer ['sixiang gongzuozhe'] who's gnawed all the tough bones": when visiting a man who has marital problems, she bluntly says to him, as if she were an iron maiden still: "Just consider me sexless."[15] Young Ge Ling and Li Dongbao, while dealing with yet another marital case, speak as if they were veterans of the Long March. Li: "If we had abandoned [the cause] then, would there be today's happiness?" Ge: "*Fanshen* ['to emancipate oneself,' or, literally, 'to turn one's body around'] means to stand on one's own two feet, not to tumble on other people" and "We can't lose the big banner of the 'Five Talks, Four Beauties.' "[16] Ge and Li, who flirt with each other, nevertheless call each other "comrade" 'tongzhi,' and Li talks of the staff as a "troop" 'duiwu,' "dynamic as a mighty torrent."[17] To any viewer of the 1990s, this contemporary use of worn-out political phrases and applications of Maoist practices are just fun.

Their monthly magazine is a jumble of personal ads, two-liner advice to the young, comfort for the old, tear-jerking pulp fiction, test and contests, how-to tips on such topics as "with which blood-type to be united in wedlock" or "proper abstinence for couples during sexual intercourse,"[18] and other light reading, which they themselves concoct or solicit. Their publication criteria are plain and simple: "We don't want texts written in a sloppy hand, or those which are not written on standard graph paper; neither do we want letters to the editor which are too fulsome or too sincere. Nor do we want content which touches upon officialdom from the county level up, or texts without the seal of approval from the appropriate party committee."[19] When a writer submits a sentimental novel, they all find it too long and needing too much revision, and, finally, they even accuse him of plagiarism, without ever having read the work. Ge Ling offers this solution: "Does he have other works, or perhaps is he interested in gardening, fishing? In his free time, does he play tennis? Does he know how to play chess? Has he ever practiced splashed-ink calligraphy?"[20] When they have to write a speech for a children's gala, they show off their mastership of Maoist clichés: "Dear little friends, you are the flowers of the fatherland. Our future, the heavy responsibilities of Communism, will fall on your generation's shoulders. Today you are little grass blades, tomorrow you will be pillars."[21]

In the sketch "Shui bi shui sha duoshao" (Who's dumbest), Wang Shuo has created a female version of his troublemakers, a streetwise, female hipster. Her name is Nancy, she speaks some English ("What-

THE STORIES OF AN
EDITORIAL BOARD

總策劃：鄭　　世
導　演：趙寶剛
　　　　金　炎
美　術：李俊明
　　　　　　明

編輯部
的故事

北京電視藝術中心1991年攝製

5. *Stories of an Editorial Board.* Publicity material from
Beijing Center for Televisual Art, 1991.

you-name"), and she poses as a superefficient factotum who can run
their editorial board. This imposter uses catchy phrases like those Wang
has scattered throughout his novels, such as "swearing on Mao's head."
She is irreverent toward everyone and everything, hangs out with guys
'dawan' who drive Ferraris, wear large gold rings, and hold cellular
phones 'dageda.' She never eats (plain) Sichuanese food but goes for
Cantonese food. When accused of being a bum 'liumang' by — of course
— Big Sister Bovine, Nancy replies: "I don't know anyone by the name
of 'Liu,' except for him [Liu Shuyou, an older staff member]" (27).

The humorous, tongue-in-cheek crosstalk, with young people as the
star performers, are Wang's trademark in all his works. Whether he

Words Turned On   55

made them up or picked them up off the street, expressions such as "I feel for you like the masses do for the Party," proffered by a girl to a boy in the novella "Dongwu xiongmeng" (Wild beasts) (1991) have become standard jokes throughout China. As Geremie Barmé has stated, Wang Shuo "plays with Party language to an extent unprecedented in Chinese literature."[22]

Having said this, Wang Shuo is anything but a dissident. No one and nothing escape his mocking, from rock star Cui Jian to human rights. In the novel *Wande jiu shi xintiao (Playing for Thrills)* (1989), a man in a bar attempts to seduce a woman with Cui Jian's most popular song, "Yi wu suoyou" (I have nothing): "I'll give you my dreams and my freedom." On top of his dreams and freedom, the suitor claims he would also give her his democratic rights and earnings. But the tough chick refutes him: "Now you're pushing it. . . . I don't need those. Give them to somebody who really wants them."[23]

Suns and lovers on and off screen

Wang Shuo's work is not subversive, because he celebrates free-wheeling spirits (like himself) who are not involved in anything social or political but in their own enterprise. Furthermore, for Wang Shuo, literature is the art of concealment, of counterfeit, not of revelations. "My first experience as a writer, when I was 12, was a 5,000-character essay of self-criticism. It was a good piece of literature."[24] Apart from his very early work, any sentimentality or tinge of genuineness is erased by his literary brio. "Dongwu xiongmeng" (Wild beasts)[25] is exemplary in this sense. A coming-of-age story, it tells of a fifteen-year-old boy's summer in the mid-1970s from the point of view of the same boy as an adult. The protagonist is a juvenile delinquent who breaks into homes with a master key, is rough with girls, cruel with other boys, skips school, and cheats at exams. He is perhaps a little bit worse than the other boys in his gang who are probably also beaten by their parents, hang out eating ice cream, fantasize about girls, and about war against the imperial powers according to Mao's design. But we, the readers, can't know because the story is written by master illusionist Wang Shuo who, from the very first lines, tells us that he just can't be honest 'laoshi,' that he's created his own "neat persona," and that he's fallen for it (406). Throughout the story, the adult narrator corrects his teenage impressions, frustrating any reader who wants to know the "truth." The constant conscious distancing from his younger self also preempts any nostalgia trip. For example, the object of the boy's desire is the well-developed ("like a white girl") Milan, whom he compares to Western food: "Later, after much consideration, I found an appropriate comparison for her: she was like the rich taste of a thick cream of tomato soup" (432). Milan's "every frown, every smile, became the equation [he] assiduously attempted to solve" (447) could be a more understandable image for the obsession of the high school boy, but it is followed by an unbelievable hyperbole: "Those were the happiest days of my life. The wrinkles on my face come from all the smiling I did in those days" (447–48). Every time readers think they are hearing Wang Shuo's "voice," they are being conned. For example, the end of the novel is a total deconstruction of the plot: the boy never personally knew Milan, never beat his love rival Gao Jin, and so on. After exhorting us to "forget about truth and keep on lying," he proceeds to tell us he raped Milan, beat up Gao Jin, and so on. He puts the blame on literature, on fiction, on the connotative power of words. "There is no way to render truth in art. Each word I choose surpasses the concrete meaning I want to give it, even when you use the most precise adjective it always yields more, like a hat that fits your head but always has some give. . . . I have never seen anything that adores self-expression and fabricates lies as easily as words" (482).

This sounds like an earnest writer putting his cards on the table. But Wang's cards are poker cards, and he, who doesn't want to be "taken for a human," certainly can't be taken for an earnest writer struggling with reality/fiction/fantasy/memory. Consider the ending of this other false statement: "When has the word 'honest' ever been mine? If I don't leave literature, this job, I will keep on fooling . . . but if I shatter my rice bowl, how will I survive? I have a wife, a daughter, and eighty-year-old parents" (484).

Still, "Wild beasts" contains emotionally strong moments, which, were they not constantly sabotaged by the narrator/author, could be quite intense. Jiang Wen, the famous young actor of *Red Sorghum*, made such a film from the novel and tellingly entitled it *Yangguang canlan de rizi (In the Heat of the Sun)* (1994). In the film, although the borderline between fiction and personal memory of the events is also muddled (and effectively visualized), it contains a share of angst and guilt that no work of Wang Shuo admits. The film can be seen as the story of a fifteen-year-old rapist who is embellishing his deeds and is, therefore, a rather pitiful creature. The majestic ending in the swimming pool—where his friends are ducking him each time he tries to emerge—yields an atmosphere of pathos, beautiful and cruel, enhanced by the 19th-century music of Mascani's *Rustic Cavalier,* the (romantic) musical motif of the film.

Indeed, Jiang Wen's film version appeals to the emotions and did extremely well in China with young viewers. It is a fine film, with an excellent cast, an excellent photographer (Gu Changwei), smart artistic direction, and a very crafty use of music. *In the Heat of the Sun* is China's first film celebration of the Cultural Revolution. Seen through the young boy's eyes, with an adult (Jiang Wen's) voice-over, it is a very personal, subjective rendering that millions of young Chinese—who didn't live through the Cultural Revolution—adopted immediately. In this sense, with this first film of his, Jiang Wen realized for cinema what Wang Shuo realized for fiction: inventing a positive feeling for a whole generation. Aesthetically, the film is a jewel. We are repeatedly faced with Cultural Revolution relics of all sorts: Mao's red-sun portrait hangs in the immense Moscow restaurant, little girls sing and dance to Mao love songs, a fight is heightened by the "Internationale"; seventies television shows us raving crowds of Mao idolaters, scenes from the *Red Detachment of Women* are screened outdoors, the gang impersonates the most often shown Soviet film, *Lenin in 1918,* or *Lenin in October* ("Vasily, quick, go save Lenin!"). At the same time, *In the Heat of the Sun* mocks China's award-winning films: the teacher is not perspicacious like the hero of Chen Kaige's *Haiziwang (King of the Children),* but simply a foolish, acned young man; the young protagonist, shot in full zoom reminds one of the bereft son in Zhang Yimou's *Hong gaoliang (Red Sorghum).* But, unlike that son, who cries out for his mother (in a ritualistic rhymed chant, amplified by plaintive *suona* sounds) — "Mother, Mother, ascend the Western Palace" ("Niang, niang, shang xitang") — Jiang Wen's hero sobs for his puppy love (without pretty lines): "Milan, Milan, Milan, Milan, Milan." This new generation of filmmakers does not so much deal with generational issues, but rather with their own generation's preoccupations, namely with fun and teenage love.[26] What is more, their music is no longer folkloric, but a blend of Western styles and Chinese pop music.[27]

The film is not pedagogical like its predecessors; instead, it creates a generational solidarity amongst those who were too young to have participated fully in the Cultural Revolution. Instead, they remained in the deserted cities and, according to Jiang Wen and Wang Shuo at least, had a great time. In interviews, Jiang Wen has said more than once that the Cultural Revolution was great fun: "like a rock 'n' roll concert with Mao as top rocker and the rest of the Chinese as his fans."[28] It was "a profound and salutary puberty crisis for the Chinese people."[29] In other words, the Cultural Revolution brought on the emergence of individuality for a generation.

Such is the import of Jiang Wen's very personal film and of Wang Shuo's novel: Mao was great, we are great too. As the protagonist (AKA Jiang Wen, since it is his voice-over) says: "August 23 was Rumania's Liberation Day. It was also my birthday, and Liu Yiku's [his friend's]." Unlike the Fifth-Generation film *Lan fengzheng (The Blue Kite)* by Tian Zhuangzhuang, where the parents' marriage is delayed because of Stalin's death, political events only run parallel to incidents in the main character's life. *In the Heat of the Sun* gives a cameo role to Wang Shuo as the "greatest bully in town"; he is shown sitting at the end of a very long table, with the two fighting gangs on opposite sides, one dressed in white, the other in black. Above Wang's head hangs Mao's sunny-head portrait. When the crowd of youngsters carry him off in jubilation, Wang's head even blocks Mao's. This is the "forgotten generation's" coming-of-age.

In Wang's novella, "Wild beasts," there is a long passage comparing the merits of ice cream with the food associated with the older generation ("rusticated youths" who include the Fifth-Generation film-makers), that is, *wotou* (a corn grit scone). Wang takes time to describe the kind of cheap ice cream they ate then, where they could get it; and, when they could afford it, swirled soft ice cream for five mao, or better still the delight of an ice cream with fruit mixed in: "That was quite an outstanding luxury, comparable today to going to a fancy Japanese restaurant, drinking British liquor and enjoying a Finnish sauna. . . . I admit, ice cream may not have the importance of 'wotou,' but for some people, they would rather not eat 'wotou,' go hungry and have an ice cream instead. At that time, the capitalists were outside our country's door, on the threshold, casting greedy eyes on us" (465–66). His generation is the fun-loving, consumerist generation.

For Wang Shuo and his partners, Jiang Wen and Feng Xiaogang, the sky's the limit. *In the Heat of the Sun* ends with the now grown-up protagonists, played by Jiang, Feng, and others, in a white limousine, drinking Rémy Martin cognac while circling around Beijing's Muxidi district, now full of skyscrapers. They are the kings now.

In the Heat of the Sun is a privately funded film, and it had the greatest publicity campaign ever. All around Beijing, ads for the film—and for Stag Beer, a main sponsor—could be seen. Beautifully designed promotion material, free T-shirts (with color stills of the actors and lines such as "Film mogul Jiang Wen moves the world with a powerful work of international quality"). Private funding for the film was possible because of Jiang Wen's reputation as a first-rate young actor; Jiang found money in Hong Kong and Taiwan (Golden Harvest), managed to get superstar Liu Xiaoqing's name as a supervisor 'jianzhi,' and created with friends his own company, Sun Film.

The film company has an office in Beijing and is making television series, hopefully films later too.[30] China has many such cultural companies, and everyone in the culture industry—the average citizen as well as serious, engaged literary critics and avant-garde painters—seems to want a place in the movie business.[31] Such a move is termed "electrification" 'chudian.'

Money, fame, freedom: Wang Shuo grabbed the recipe before any one else. His partner, Feng Xiaogang,[32] followed him shortly after and adapted a great number of stories, including of course Wang's, into exceptionally popular films or series for television. Wang Shuo and Feng Xiaogang created their own film and television company, called Haomeng (Good Dreams) in 1993. Without the shadow of a doubt, their *Beijingren zai Niuyue (A Beijinger in New York)* (1993) has incarnated the formula of (financial) success for television.

In terms of storyline, *A Beijinger in New York* is as much a milestone as *Stories of an Editorial Board*. If the latter continues to be the basic (as yet unrivaled) model for a portrayal of Chinese social problems, *A Beijinger* tapped into a new field, that of China in the world. As the title indicates, *A Beijinger* is the story of a Chinese man emigrating to New York to live his American dream. Since it aired, there have been several series based on a similar theme, namely, *Xin dalu (New Continent,* 1994), about eight students from Asia in the United States; *Yangniu zai Beijing (Foreign Girls in Beijing)* (1995), and so on. None has had the favor or the success of *A Beijinger.*

Like *In the Heat of the Sun, A Beijinger* was also fully financed privately. A total of $1.5 million was amassed from bank loans and from American and Chinese companies. Understandably, this twenty-part series, filmed outside of China, in New York and the surrounding area, abounds with "soft publicity" 'ruan guanggao' and dual marketing. Preceding each episode, Coke and Sprite ads are run side by side with ads for Chinese products, such as the local alcohol Kongfu jiajiu, which is advertised by the actress playing the main female role of Achun, or Dannel shirts from a joint-venture modeled by the American actor playing the part of David, the Irish entrepreneur. Chinese commercials had never been so deftly made and used. The series, airing in autumn, also contained ads for timely cold remedies like Wahaha. Furthermore, inside the episodes themselves, luxury consumer goods like xo Cognac, Simmons mattresses, "555" brand cigarettes, and Ray-Ban glasses, were all very obviously displayed.

In contrast to the first Chinese experiment in filming Chinese nationals abroad, *Zuihou de guizu (The Last Aristocrats)* (Xie Jin, 1989), *A Beijinger* is glamorous and convincing. The first scene of each episode is a commanding aerial view of Manhattan supported by a dramatic melody, with half-English, half-Chinese lyrics, "Time and time again" ("Qianwanci de wen") (sung by popstar Liu Huan). Feng Xiaogang, the director of the series, who had never been abroad before, gathered around him an excellent team: advisers living in the United States as well as in China, first-rate actors such as Jiang Wen for the lead role (his first for television—Wang Shuo linked Jiang, his ardent admirer, to Feng, his partner), the well-known actress Ma Xiaoqing (who played in *Troublemakers*) as the difficult child, and an expatriate who had lived in the United States for six years, Wang Ji, to play the mistress–business iron lady.

It was very much an improvised system of filmmaking, where everyone did more than one job, where deals of all sorts had to be struck in order to shoot this or that scene.[33] For example, renting a helicopter at a low price—for aerial shots of the city, of a burial, or a boat outing when the character Wang Qiming, by then a millionaire, takes his daughter on the Hudson in his personal yacht—and coaxing people into getting permission to film in sites that were off limits (for example, in a cemetery unavailable for film shootings since *The Godfather*) required exceptional connections and diplomacy. Director Feng is quoted as having said: "In the whole world, no place is better ['niu'] than the United States, and no place in the United States is better ['niu'] than New York. We Beijingers were able to shoot there, so we are the best ['niu']."[34]

Whether this statement was made in earnest or not,[35] it is telling in terms of the scope and hope the project inspired. *A Beijinger* is technically a very well-made television series. It is perhaps the first Chinese show with a brisk pace, created by fine editing that allows many different scenes and sequences to be viewed in one episode, and sustained by music of all sorts, such as an African American guy's drumming on garbage cans mixed in with Western classical music. The narrative is quite unpredictable: the storyline does not follow the habitual Confucian moral one, no character is fully good or bad, and China does not win over the United States (or vice versa). New York is both great and awful: "If you love him, take him to New York, for it's paradise. If you hate him, take him to New York, for it's hell."[36]

Based on the novel of the same title by Glen Cao (Cao Guilin), the television series—as is characteristic of most adaptations—leaves more room for hope than the book does: the daughter Ningning is still alive (and living somewhere in Africa with her white boyfriend); divorced Achun is reunited with her child; twice-estranged wife Guo Yan returns to China; Wang Qiming carries on his business, with his mistress backing him. *A Beijinger* is, nevertheless, not a representation of the American dream. It could even be regarded as a nationalistic, anti-American production, predating the anti-American fever reflected in a 1996 book, *Zhongguo keyi shuo bu (China Can Say No)*.[37] Five years after the extravagantly praised "azure civilisation" (weilanse weiming) of the United States in the television documentary *Heshang (Deathsong of the River)*, *A Beijinger* criticized the racism of white Americans and showed the anger of the immigrants, in this case the Chinese immigrants who must confront such racism. In the last episode, the hero

Wang Qiming vents his anger by directing obscene words and gestures at policemen and anyone who happens to be there. Of a fiery nature, he beats up quite a few people throughout the series. They are all white: a gas attendant, his own daughter's boyfriend, that boyfriend's father, and his business and love rival, David. In one episode, Qiming verbally and physically assaults a prostitute, also white. This violence is at times coupled with his love of Maoist songs, now set to disco rhythms in the 1993 album, *Hong Taiyang (Red Sun)*. Free and debonair, he yells out these tunes while driving on 42nd Street in his Mercedes, wearing Yves Saint-Laurent clothing and Ray-Ban glasses. There is nothing pitiable or laughable in Wang Qiming's bearing: he's cool and rich, with a good wife and an able mistress. He's made it to the top and can tell anyone off.

In a roundtable on the television series, the actor Jiang Wen claimed that he had not exaggerated in any way the rage and frustration of being a Chinese abroad, that on the contrary he had greatly downplayed the negative feelings freshly arrived immigrants usually harbor: "Americans are perhaps quite nice toward Americans, but with foreigners they are not so nice. They differ a lot from us Chinese." As for the director, Feng Xiaogang, he simply said: "The Americans can make a film like *Year of the Dragon* and give a totally distorted representation of the Chinese. When we made *A Beijinger,* all we did was to show some of our feelings." [38]

The debate around the series mainly dealt with verisimilitude. *A Beijinger* was the first convincing Chinese film representation of the United States, and, consequently, viewers watched it for more than the story: they also watched it for what could be seen. In the first episodes, Wang and his wife live in a dingy basement. Many parents of Chinese students living in the States phoned their offspring pleading them to come home, while younger viewers thought the pad was not bad at all. The sexy Taiwanese businesswoman, Achun (played by Wang Ji), became the most lusted-after female prototype in marriage agencies. [39] Achun, who speaks Chinese and English fluently, is a remarkable character: fearless, fierce, and passionate, she is also elegant, sexy, and an international jetsetter. Unfortunately, enamored of the hero, Wang Qiming, she lets go of her own career to attend to his.

All in all, Wang Qiming is the hero and very much a macho figure. The songs opening and closing each episode focus on him, the new hero, the Chinese musician turned millionaire who can have his pick of Chinese and white women (as well as beat up white men). The opening song, "Time and time again," tells of the change he's undergone, whereas the woman (his wife) has not moved on; the closing song, "Baoying" (Retribution) (also interpreted by a pop superstar, Na Ying) tells of the plight of the woman who waits fruitlessly for better days to come.

As concerns gender roles, the television series is in line with the novel by Glen Cao, who presents this work as autobiographical. His alter ego, the male hero, is definitely the focus, and women mere accessories. In his preface, Cao writes that, after spending ten years in New York, he returned to China with "nothing but a broken dream and a heavy manuscript. . . . I've made a fortune all right, but morally I'm zero. . . . I've become a whiner." [40] Yet his Wang Qiming is presented in a positive light, and it is clearly gendered: as the "greenwood hero of the new era" (166), as a "young forty-year-old who is particularly curious, loves to be energetic and throw himself into action" (178), or as "a wild bull who's been goaded in a corrida" (217). One is lead to think that this virile energy might come from the sun, the American sun: "The sun, ah, the American sun! . . . I can also get my share of the sun. . . . Ah! the sun, the fair sun [for one and all]!" exclaims a newly arrived Chinese national in the novel (79–80).

In and out of China: Do girls just wanna have fun?

Ultimately, the novel as well as the film presents a new Chinese male hero, one who is invincible anywhere, even abroad, but who maintains Chinese characteristics, namely, a profound love for the reddest sun, Mao Zedong. This would seem to be a common denominator of many of the works analyzed above. But for the other gender, for women, can they, under such circumstances, also become queens of the road? To his wild daughter, Ningning, Wang Qiming, says: "We're Chinese, try as we might, we can't become Americans. . . . I think that, for family concerns, for social relations, the Chinese way is better." To which Ningning replies: "You want me to keep Chinese ways. . . . What do you want me to become? An American? A Chinese? An American with Chinese ways? A

Chinese with American ways?" (128). Ningning is killed by an overdose in the novel; in the film, she runs far away.

Some women writers, filmmakers, have been offering other options, less dramatic ones. Even the female counterpart to Glen Cao's *A Beijinger in New York*, Zhou Li Fochler's *Manhadun de Zhongguo nüren (Manhattan's China Lady)*,[41] which has its share of patriotic statements and gooey sentimentality, does not carry the same heavy overtones. The pictures of Ms. Fochler that appear among the book's illustrations show her (and her Caucasian husband) smiling and quite relaxed; two pictures show her "before and after" (making it in New York): again both are "nice" pictures, the difference being that, in the latter one, the lady wears three rows of pearls and is signing a business contract. Compare the picture of Glen Cao, in his book looking rather glum and slightly aggressive as he stands by a Steinway piano—which has a picture of him "before," when he was a musician—and who does not even fuse his two names: first, he writes the Chinese characters and then underneath them, the English.[42]

Jiang Wen's *In the Heat of the Sun* also has some sort of a female equivalent, *The Monkey Kid (Hou San'er)*, made by Xiao-yen Wang. Wang was born in Beijing in 1959, is a graduate of the Beijing Film Institute in 1982, and left China for the United States in 1985. Technically, Wang belongs to the Fifth Generation of filmmakers; but, perhaps because of her younger age or because she left China after graduating, or again because she is a woman, she shares none of that generation's outlook. Wang returned to China in 1994 to independently shoot her first feature film, a film about her childhood during the Cultural Revolution. A low-budget, noncommercial film ($30,000), *The Monkey Kid* does not have the technical refinement or the authorial complexity of *In the Heat of the Sun*. It is a simple, sweet rendering of a nine-year-old girl's life during those "sunny days." None of the violence of *In the Heat of the Sun* is to be found there, and the Cultural Revolution artifacts are merely present, not lavishly exhibited. In fact, *The Monkey Kid* just happens to be set during the Cultural Revolution, when parents were away and all that was taught at school was the Little Red Book and Mao love songs. It is a precocious coming-of-age story where the local bullies are mischievous little boys peeing in Thermos bottles. Shi-wei, the heroine, learns how to make her way in life. In the last scene of the film she is seen, all

6. "Trying out Mom's Soviet-style bra." Film still from
Xiao-yen Wang's *The Monkey Kid,* 1995. *Photograph from
press kit.*

smiles, riding her bicycle in the rain. The sun, the heat of Jiang Wen's
film, is totally absent in this film, which starts with a snowfall and people
swaddled in heavy, unrevealing clothes. Shi-wei is empowered by small,
insignificant things, and that is thanks to her mother who, though often
away, takes time to educate her daughter in various ways: culturally (listening to Bizet's *Carmen*), streetwise (defending oneself but also attack-
ing when necessary), and simply on how to have fun (climbing trees). It
is she who unhesitatingly lets Shi-wei ride her bike in the rain, to which
the little girl comments: "If Papa were here, he'd say no." The female
connection is visible throughout the film: Shi-wei is fascinated by her
teacher, first pregnant, then breastfeeding; she stares at her big breasts
in class; at home, she tries on her mother's Soviet-style bra in front of
the mirror; with her girlfriends, she wonders about menstruation and
whether her brain will go soft. But most of the time, the little girls are
having fun: they play blindman's bluff together as well as skip rope or

put on make-up, don veils on top of military costumes, and execute minority dances. Before the final credits, a line appears on the screen, in English: "This film is dedicated to my mother." In an interview, Wang confirms the autobiographical elements of *The Monkey Kid:* "Each day my mother was forced to crawl through a dog door in and out of her school because she was the daughter of a landlord. But I was too young to know any of this. So, ironically, the years of the Cultural Revolution are the source of my happiest memories."[43]

If *The Monkey Kid* is perhaps a little too sweet (and the music, relying on the Chinese flute 'dizi' gives it a rather exotic, Oriental flavor), then there are other renderings by women of the Cultural Revolution with more of a bite. For example, Liu Sola's *Hundun jia ligeleng (Chaos and All That).*[44] Liu Sola, born in Beijing in 1955, and presently living in New York (after living in London), is both a fiction writer and a music composer. She wrote *Chaos* in 1991. It is a twofold story, with the female character Huang Haha as the focus. Haha's name was chosen by her father, who hop[ed] that with such a name she would rise joyfully above the ordinary" (11), in contrast to himself who "ahs all the time" (45). She is a student living abroad, in London. *Chaos* goes back and forth between her present life, told in the third person, and her childhood during the Cultural Revolution, told in the first. Haha mocks her boyfriend, Michael, a Caucasian, who finds her "exotic and inscrutable" (26) yet who also keeps a (rich, white) fiancée, but her wit and irony are mostly aimed at herself, now and during her Cultural Revolution days. Haha wants action, for example a satisfying love relationship, yet she spends her young adult days writing letters to people in China. The narrator reports that Michael calls this habit of hers her "contraceptive device" (93). Similarly, at the age of eleven, Haha wanted to become a red guard, but all she gets out of the experience is to learn how to talk dirty and eventually to guard her friend's cat. "The most essential qualification for being a red guard was that you had to be able to say to people's faces the kinds of things you usually only find written on toilet walls" (19). After having said "Fuck it," she is rewarded by her brother with a genuine khaki uniform and she gets to wear a Mao badge the size of an alarm clock (32–33). Haha demystifies and makes ludicrous the red guards and the whole era. She talks about what was anathema: "Long hair and high heels, like cats, dogs, and rabbits, were all class-enemy stuff" (12). We learn about how the teacher devised various versions of the gaze for exposing offenders, about Uncle Lei Feng, about the "Little Red fucking Book," about the unlikely yet very coded fashion of those days,[45] about embroidering portraits of the Great Leader, about the songs they sang concocted from quotations from the Little Red Book, of Russian ballads, and so on. Of course, sex is intermingled with the "political aspirations," but it comes nowhere close to, for example, Wang Shuo's depiction of sexual arousement.[46] The girls talk about tits and sex in a very naive way, like Xiao-yen Wang's sweet protagonist.

Liu Sola writes lightly about everything, an expatriate's struggling life and the traumas of the Cultural Revolution. Young Haha and a friend brag about their families' experiences:

> "Our house was searched by the Red Guards!"
> "Fantastic! Great! Ours was searched too!" . . .
> "My mom and dad's salaries were cut off. They're down to living
>   expenses!"
> "Same with mine!"
> "My mom and dad got locked up!"
> "Mine, too!" (94–95).

There is no trace of tragedy or of any form of grandeur hinted at in *Chaos*. It is an irreverent novel, which puts an expat's life and a Cultural Revolution experience on the same plane, a life in Beijing and a life in London. Liu added an afterword to the English translation:

> Forget about the distance between China and the rest of the world. Please don't get upset with this book, and ask me whether it's true that the Chinese kill cats and insult each other. And don't ask me if this is the story of my life. I can tell you this: the Chinese kill everything, just the same as you do. Cursing and insulting each other in all sorts of different ways is part of the Chinese civilisation. And this is certainly not an autobiography, or some historical epic. It's just a collection of scenes and verses, dancing hand in hand in circles large and small. When the circle is complete, the dancers laugh and call it a day. (127)

The same is true of Liu Sola's music. Somehow, it is impossible to classify it. It is neither Chinese nor Western. It isn't "world music," although in music stores that's where one finds Liu's CD, *Blues in the East/Landiao zai dongfang.*[47] What is more, as she herself remarks, one can't tell whether it's "popular music or classical music."[48] *Blues in the East* is a blend of different schools of Chinese operas, already something quite peculiar—the north not usually mixing with the south—but also of pieces based on African American sounds and with English lyrics (intoned by African Americans). Some compositions also include Japanese percussion. Liu Sola is a cosmopolitan: she speaks (or rather writes or sings) at times as a Chinese and at times as a world citizen. She refuses any kind of packaging 'baozhuang' from the United States, but also refuses to return to China where she would no longer find the stimulation 'ciji' the United States offers. Ultimately, or so she says, Liu Sola likes to be an "unclassified" person, to stay in the United States, where experimentation 'shiyan' is always possible, as opposed to England and China, which are both empires and very conservative.[49]

At the end of *Chaos,* the protagonist Haha receives a letter from a friend who has just returned to Beijing:

> You want to know what it's like here? I'll give you a list, and you'll know: skyscrapers, fancy hotels, supermarkets, fast-food joints, joint ventures, new policies, epidemics, nepotism, nude art shows, superstars, door-to-door sales men, export permits, arranged marriages, perfect couples, rock 'n' roll, elopement, prostitution, black-market fiction, modernism, human-meat dumplings, private cars, female infanticide, prophylactic dentistry, tourists, money changers, black-market U.S. dollars, television ads, firearms, factories, wars, henpecked husbands, abduction and sale of women, female professors, female authors, single-parent families, Kentucky Fried Chicken, Coca-Cola, fashion, consumer durables, prizewinning movies, getting rich quick, tours, holidays." (123–24)

This portrait of Beijing is mainly one of change, of new phenomena that would understandably strike a native returning home after a prolonged stay abroad. Yet this is not what fascinates Ning Ying, a woman filmmaker who left China in the 1980s and who has returned in the 1990s. Like Xiao-yen Wang, Ning Ying is technically of the Fifth Generation, but she is at odds with their deep and heavy ruminations on Chinese culture. Ning Ying has made two important (or, we should say "unimportant but great") films: *Zhaole (For Fun)* (1993) and *Minjing de gushi (On the Beat)* (1995). Both are set in her home town, Beijing, and both offer a portrait of "residual" Beijing.

Ning Ying has the eye of a tourist, perhaps because of her prolonged stay in Italy. (Sent there to study film, she met Bernardo Bertolucci and eventually became his assistant on *The Last Emperor*.) Her films seem to bypass modernity, the attitude typical of the sightseer looking out for exotica. But that is simply a coincidence. Ning's films are neighborhood films (similar to Wayne Wang's *Smoke* and *Blue in the Face*, located in Brooklyn, far away from corporate and cultural centers), and they could not possibly be located in highrises. Her neighborhoods are out of the view of tourists because they are far too ordinary and because they cannot be known unless one moves into them, lives in them. Consequently, Ning's films have had great appeal at art film festivals.[50] They show us an unchanged, ongoing way of life out of the limelight: in *For Fun*, we see Peking opera as performed by old men, who live in old quarters of the city; in *On the Beat*, police officers and old-lady committees, keeping watch in a very unchanged part of town.

Ning's films offer a better-than-documentary look at Chinese citizens. There are no statements made, no cultural commentary or social criticism. Her camera lightly and coolly records these people's lives in their everyday routines and in their unchanging boundaries. The social groups Ning has chosen to portray are not (upwardly) mobile: Peking opera will most likely die out with its performers, all retired men; neighborhood surveillance will also die out without the policemen's allies, all retired ladies. Furthermore, the area where *On the Beat* was filmed, Deshengmen, looks like a postwar city, with its rubble of torn-down traditional courtyard houses 'siheyuan.'

Ning does not look nostalgically upon these groups and their environment. As she has said: "I've never been to Peking opera; it doesn't interest me."[51] And how could anyone feel deep compassion for policemen, who are called, in Chinese as in French, "dogs"? Rather, she takes these people and neighborhoods as curiosities, amusing remnants among whom light comedies take place. She gently mocks the characters' vigilance. In *For Fun*, a former concierge from the Peking opera is forced to step down. He had become the very official coordinator of opera amateurs, a delightful bunch of old men, who in the end reprimand him. They don't want his authoritative management; they're just out for fun.

As one says: "Opera is good for your health. It makes you move and it's far better than staying at home and baby-sitting the 'little emperor.'" The punctilious concierge obliges. After that, it is just for fun.

Apart for the main character in *For Fun*, all of Ning's actors are non-professionals. In *On the Beat*, she even got real policemen to play their parts. In *For Fun*, there is a mentally disabled young man who follows the leader around. He is playing his part, naturally. He participates in discussions by repeating others' words, performs in the troupe (even though sometimes he hits his head instead of the percussion). This authentic quality adds to the peculiar charm of these off-beat narratives. *On the Beat*, for example, shows us how policemen are made to run after stray dogs and consequently have to get rabies shots; how, at the end of their day, in their grungy little office they watch American cop stories. There is no introspective probing, no existential depth in Ning's films (the city is not hostile, nor is it cause for jubilation); conversely, the cityscape does not recede in favor of the protagonists, as frequently occurs in urban Chinese films.[52] We are given a gallery of local portraits, of people who cannot be dissociated from their background.

Ning Ying, the youngest of the Fifth-Generation filmmakers, offers no major female roles in her films and has never done a film with women's themes: "I think it is ridiculous to be thought different just because I am a woman."[53] Ning obviously delights in the position of the distant observer, poking fun at a very male-oriented society and enjoying herself while entertaining us.

It would seem that Chinese women, or at least the well-seasoned world travelers, deal most willingly with fun things, pleasurable things, and leave "higher" artistic expressions of desire and identity to their male peers.

3 Away from Literature II

Words Acted Out

In the hunt the king uses beaters on three sides only
and foregoes game that runs off in front.
Hexagram 8, "Holding together (Union)," *Yijing*

Against theater's antics

Filmmaker Ning Ying has no professional actors in her films, with the exception of one veteran theater actor, Huang Zongluo, who plays the tyrannical busybody in *For Fun*. Ning claims she was delighted when no professional actors wanted to work with her.[1] Her delight is understandable, if one looks at the stilted acting that Chinese theater usually offers. In the media, theater is discussed in terms of "crisis" 'weiji'; the situation is generally said to be "bleak" 'xiaotiao.'[2]

The Chinese have a very short history, less than a century, of "spoken theater" 'huaju'. People like Huang, now in their seventies, have played in all the Chinese "classics" such as *Chaguan (The Teahouse)* and *Leiyu (The Storm)*. The huge state theaters are now practically deserted and its former players and playwrights all dead or retired. Few younger people are attracted by the stage. One well-reputed man of the theater, director Lin Zhaohua, has been trying in the past years to revive interest in theater, to make theater more popular. Accordingly, he has chosen plays with direct social relevance, such as Guo Shixing's contemporary plays, which include *Niao ren (The Bird Men)* and *Qi ren (The Chess Men)*. The Bird Men was a relative success when performed in Beijing in 1993–94. Action is on- and offstage, since a psychoanalyst watches the action with the spectators and comments upon it. The characters in the play include some bird lovers who go for strolls with their pet birds and make them sing and boast of their talents. But there is also a panoply of other people, ranging from an ornithologist to a kebab vendor to a black marketeer, and to a bearded foreign tourist with his Chinese wife. As spectators, we enjoy the display of people, birds, and their interactions. We are made to gently criticize all of them. As the program informs us: "We understand more and more the nature of birds, but less and less [the nature of] human beings." Indeed, all the characters are slightly warped, even the folkloric bird lovers, who at one point yell out in dismay when a poor woman from Anhui province walks toward their birds: their darling birds may be frightened by the red of her tattered clothes.

Following this success, Lin produced a far more experimental show entitled '93 xiju kalaOK zhiye ('93 Evenings of Theatrical Karaoke). Also performed in the huge Capital Theater, the play was again on and off the stage, and inside as well as outside the theater space per se. The action comprised real actors doing skits, the audience appraising them, video cameras constantly sweeping the crowd and the stage action. The topics broached by the participants were all taken from real-world scenarios: hotlines where suicidal teenagers phone in, sex among the elderly, divorce for pre-Reform couples, court cases for the yuppies, and so on. What to me was the most intriguing and most pathetic part of this inclusive show was the part played by veteran actors who were there on display. Indeed, Huang Zongluo and many other respected old actors were there to be photographed and talked to, and theatergoers could even try on their stage costumes. Obviously, Lin wanted total accessibility of theater.

Unfortunately, in such a grand venue, and with the high price of the tickets, such attempts at undoing theater's make-believe and at reviving while popularizing a snubbed art are doomed to fail. Still, one person is quoted to have said, after enjoying Beijing duck on the theater premises (as part of the show): "It tastes better here. In a restaurant, you only have the food. Here, it's tradition, culture that you eat."[3]

"Culture," however is not in deserted opera or art houses. As Artaud said in the 1930s, if the crowd doesn't come to the theater, that's because the masterpieces have become literary, that is, fixed forms that no longer answer the needs of the time.[4] The omnipresent karaoke joints, fancy restaurants, arcades, and discos are the spots where the young hang out when they do go out. Otherwise, like their elders, they watch television or go to the movies. One particular crowd, however, does go to the theater: yuppies. In the past few years, it has become fashionable to attend what are called "experimental" 'shiyan' plays, usually performed in little theater houses. The plays are reflective of that group's preoccupations: couples' infidelity, separation because one partner leaves to go abroad or else is a workaholic, loss of family values, money versus true love, women's liberation, and so on. These are popular boulevardish melodramas with pretensions to some artistic quality. For example, Zhang Xian's *Meiguo lai de qizi (The Wife Back from America)* was publicized as "a great work of art in a little playhouse." The mise-en-scène can be tellingly austere—a few pillows. "But don't get us wrong. If we use a totally empty set, it is not for lack of money," claims the program of one such play, *Linghun chuqiao (When Conscience Speaks)*. The characters may be reduced to two, three, at the most four (young) protagonists. But the "experimental" aspect is, in my view, solely there for reasons of marketing: it sells. These are consumer products, machines reproducing conventional dialogues, giving the public what it wants: namely, a flattering mirror for them to see themselves in, designed to elicit their consent.

In a way, they are like glorified television soap operas or domestic film productions that offer the same current topics and box office appeal. For example, playwright Zhang Xian writes both filmscripts (*Liushou nüshi [The Woman who Stayed Behind]*) and plays (*Meiguo lai de qizi [The Wife Back from America]*).[5] In 1993 he produced a film entitled *Gufeng (Stock Craze)*, followed by a play, *OK, gupiao (Okay for Stocks)*. In the film a female bus ticket dispenser becomes enthralled by playing the stock market, to the point of forgetting her husband and child. In the play, a man who has lost his job throws himself into the whirlwind of the stock market with the hope of getting rich. The "social messages" are obviously sanctioned by the state: financial success goes hand in hand with some form of patriotism and attention to family values. Among the couples separating, the person to identify with is, of course, the one who stays behind, who remains in China. Such is the case in *The Wife Back from America, The Woman Who Stayed Behind, Dasaba (Freewheeling), Shangyidang (Taken In)*, and a score of other films, which, incidentally, turn men rather than women into the better halves, because the men do not leave China. Actor Ge You in this respect incarnates the hero. He is the protagonist of the last two films mentioned, who stays behind. Ge is also leading actor in Wang Shuo's television series, *Stories of an Editorial Board*. There is a difference however between the early-nineties series and the more recent film productions: nowadays, Ge You's celluloid persona is always living very comfortably, drinks cognac, invites his girlfriend to the best restaurants. As exemplified by *A Beijinger in New York*, recent television, film, and theater productions all attempt to create a luxurious environment, which adds spice to the viewers' pleasure: ogling at consumer goods and wanting them, too. In a play written by a woman, Li Jianming, *San ge nüren (Three Women)*,[6] the most impressive element was the elegant wardrobe of the women and especially the display of more than fifteen exquisite pairs of shoes on stage. In Wu Yuzhong's *Louding (Rooftop)*, the focus was on one woman's laced, lilac underwear, which cost two hundred yuan, a month's salary.

As befits righteous bourgeois theater, the enticement to buy more, to always want more, is cloaked in some sort of moral warning. The program of the play *Qinggan caolian (Feelings at Drill)*, which deals with adultery, announces outright: "Perhaps this two-person world is yours? Perhaps you're the one playing? . . . Theatricality does not exist solely in the movies or on stage, but in our lives." The plays can at times stir a little awareness, a twinge of "conscience"—"a term that usually belongs to the elderly, or to women when they have lost their wallet."[7] Some even have a nostalgic streak, accentuated by appropriate music, usually pop campus songs churning out feelings for the good old days. When the lights went off at the end of *When Conscience Speaks*, the 1993 top-of-the-charts song, "Xiao Fang" (Little Fang) was aired. That was a fine example of smart "packaging" 'baozhuang.' "Little Fang" tells of the twinge of conscience in a grown man who reminisces about his country sweetheart, Little Fang, a peasant, whom he left when he returned to the city after the Cultural Revolution.

Nostalgia sells well. Yuppies, now working for big companies, especially joint ventures, can allow themselves moments of selective retrospection, of pleasant reminiscing. The reenactments of the eight model plays (operas and ballet) of Jiang Qing's Cultural Revolution agenda fit into such a view. Lavish set designs and a huge cast revives, on a big budget, the now-imagined ambiance of "those days." The iron maidens of the "Cultrev" model ballet, *The Red Detachment of Women (Hongse niangzijun)*, become if not somewhat sexy, at least attractive; the choreographed movements are softer, the music too. Such expensive stagings take place before sold-out audiences in China, and also in Hong Kong and Florida. They are for those who can afford to reminisce. Cultural companies 'wenhua gongsi' that sprouted all over the country in the nineties are the sponsors of such artistic manifestations.

With Beijing opera definitively dead, with stand-up comic crosstalk 'xiangsheng' devoid of piquancy, with realistic "modern" theater devolved into verbose or Vaselined Cultrev plays, the situation of the theater in China does seem to be rather desolate. But there is another outlet, and that is for truly experimental, alternative performances.

With the end of the 1980s and beginning of the 1990s, young theater people started to stage Western plays such as Pinter's *The Lover,* O'Neill's *The Emperor Jones,* and Genet's *Balcony.* In the Chinese context, these plays take on a definite allegorical coloring, what Chen Xiaomei has termed "occidentalism."[8] Chen has described well the instrumental uses given to Western plays from Shakespeare to Brecht, when performed in China: they are read as stories presenting allegorically Chinese problems that could not be exposed otherwise; in other words, they are filled with political innuendoes. One can understand why the experimental director Mou Sen (who staged Ionesco and O'Neill plays) calls his own productions of Western plays a "compromise."[9] Few young people care for current political issues; and they are certainly not interested in reviving Beijing opera, let alone Greek drama. Another experimental playwright, Meng Jinghui, born in 1966, is perhaps the youngest proponent of Western plays in China. Not only has he staged many (from *The Bald Soprano* to *Balcony* to *The Kiss of the Spider Woman*), but his own creations are offshoots of this "modernist" tendency, for example *Wo Ai Cha-cha-cha (I Love XXX)* (1994) and *Sifan (The Tale of the Nun and the Monk)* (1993). "Experimentation" in his plays means polyphonic voices, criss-crossed temporal lines, postmodern references to classical works, a medley of citations, and a very animated stage not averse to technological special effects. For example, *The Tale of the Nun* is a blending of two stories from Boccaccio's *Decameron* and an anonymous Ming dynasty love tale between a nun and a monk. The actors mix Beijing opera poses with Cultural Revolution gestures; the program notes, in a postmodern positioning, follow bestselling author Jia Pingwa, who imitated a mode of censorship using little black boxes found in classical erotic texts. In a commentary on *I Love XXX,* Meng said: "Language per se is part of our life. . . . Peasants can love their beast of burden—why shouldn't we love language?"[10] In 1997, Meng attempted an adaptation of Lu Xun's *AhQ zhengzhuan (True Story of AhQ),* which he entitled *AhQ tongzhi (Comrade AhQ).*[11] Meng does not operate the same way as his contemporary and one-time director, Mou Sen, even though, in Beijing, people talk of the "two Ms." Meng is syncretic in his art; he does not venture into improvised performances and remains within rather conventional paradigms of theatricality. Meng does not have a taste for the radical moves that Mou favors.[12]

Indeed, Mou Sen has moved into the critical terrain of true experimentation, an area that would be more appropriately named "performance" 'xingwei yishu.' A student of Lin Zhaohua, who himself was a student of Gao Xingjian, Mou has succeeded in challenging the place of mild social critique (reflective, naturalistic) in China's theater and of the idealistic (allegorical, abstract) streak of traditional productions. Actually, he has liberated Chinese theatrical practice of all expectations. He has accomplished this in collaboration with the poet Yu Jian, the video artist Wu Wenguang, choreographer Wen Hui, and a dancer, Jin Xing.

What these people do is shocking to say the least.[13] Mou's productions aim at being "performances" that disturb actors and spectators, in a holistic manner, that is, they are not limited to a single psychological, philosophical, social, or political realm. Mou Sen's first such experiment, *Bi'an (The Other Bank),* took place in a classroom of the Beijing Film Institute for only a few days in 1993. It was the work of many months of physically and mentally straining exercises for the actors, all young men and women from the acting class of the Film Institute.

7. "100 words of action." Dance performance by Wen Hui in Beijing's Film Institute. 1995. *Photograph by Wu Wenguang.*

Following Grotowski's emphasis on the actor's liberation (from his/her role, him/herself), Mou Sen turned the young actors into nimble, animal-like humans, able to cry, yell, laugh, speak, dance and jump. The Chinese saying "Juben, juben, yi ju zhi ben" (The storyline, the storyline, all's in the storyline) could not be further away from Mou's practice, especially in *The Other Bank,* where words finally become just words, sounds divested of their signifieds. Adapted from Gao Xingjian's 1986 play of the same name,[14] *The Other Bank* has been completely reoriented toward the concreteness of the Chinese language, which gets performed physically by the actors. It is another form of *juben,* "concreteness" being a homonym of "storyline."

Although Gao Xingjian's work is described as "experimental," it is to my mind still within the metaphorical (in this case, European absurdist) register.[15] The poet Yu Jian has subverted Gao's play by including a grammatical discussion on the term "bi'an" 'other bank,' which is rife with symbolic meanings of the elsewhere: in Buddhism, it refers to Nirvana, the inaccessible country or paradise; nowadays, it means any foreign land (anywhere but China), and in general, any ideal to reach for (the moon, communist bliss, love).[16] By focusing on the physical traits of the word (the fact that it is made up of sixteen strokes, is a noun, has two syllables, one with a third tone, the other with a fourth) and by repeating it tirelessly (bi-bi-bi-bi-an-an-an-an), Yu erases the ultimate idealistic weight of the word. Yu's contribution to the text is to undermine the power of such words as "elsewhere," "life," "theater," "aspirations," "waiting." He undercuts statements, as in " 'There'll come a day,' but that's not now" (Zong you yitian ke bu shi xianzai). The word that matters in the end is *dong* 'to move/to act up.' To turn all words into (words of) action is the aim of his grammatical venture and Mou's performance. "To act, to move around, that's living, that's the other bank, I'm 'other-banking' " (78).

This very Chinese-language play on words and their referents loses much in translation because, for one, the word "to move/to act" 'dong' is also the word for "verbs" 'dongci,' which are therefore literally "action words." Yu Jian's work is highly situational and concrete. He is vehemently opposed to flamboyant, abstract discourse, which he aptly criticized by saying "Mao Zedong never wrote about a cup."[17]

Mou Sen's mise-en-scène further suppressed the allegorical thrust of Gao's play. The actors were so much in motion, were so loud and violent, that for example, the rope with which they were acting/playing, originally meant to evoke a river, a bridge, and other links between humans, remained foremost a rope, not a prop for our imagination's wanderings. In fact, it became a "word of action," too. As Yu wrote of *The Other Bank:* "To call it a play with a storyline ['juben'], would be a bit much. It has no characters, no set."[18]

The production took on immense proportions after its performance. There was a symposium, filmed by Jiang Yue, who produced a documentary on the play and its impact, also called *The Other Bank* (1995). The symposium participants were all ecstatic about the production: Dai Jinhua, feminist professor of film and literary theory, stated that she had never in her eleven years at the Beijing Film Institute seen anything as powerful; it forced her into critical introspection. Independent video artist Wu Wenguang spoke of feeling as if he had been "stripped." Postmodern critic Zhang Yiwu heralded the performance as the death of modern Chinese theater and the beginning of a new culture without idealism. Many articles were also written on Mou's *Other Bank.* In one, it was described as a "theater of cruelty" 'canku xiju.'[19] Indeed, Artaud's conception of a nonverbal theater is somewhere in the background, and his statement "All that acts is a cruelty" ("Tout ce qui agit est une cruauté")[20] fits these circumstances. But Beckett's *Waiting for Godot* is also in the margin in this Beckett-like conversation: "What are we doing here? We're going to the other bank. . . . At this very moment, on this very spot, we're acting this play. What kind of play?" (65)[21] Grotowski's conception of a "poor theater" is here, too, with its emphasis on arduous physical training of the actors. One statement by Grotowski particularly resonates with Mou's *Other Bank*: "For me, a creator of theatre, the important thing is not the words but what we do with these words, what gives life to the inanimate words of the text, what transforms them into 'the Word.'"[22] Still, Mou and his collaborators have their own signature, specific to China. All in all, Mou's work belongs to the laboratory-theaters that have been emerging worldwide since the fifties. It is a form of resistant theater, resistant to classification, to all conventions of the theater, including China's.

The Other Bank has had many sequels. Mou Sen produced, again in collaboration with poet Yu Jian and to worldwide acclaim, *Ling Dang'an (File 0)* in 1994; they also produced one "flop" *Yu aizibing you guande (Things related to AIDS)*, in 1995. Performances of *Things related to AIDS*, like *The Other Bank*, were very few and were inaccessible to most people, since they were publicized only through word-of-mouth. *Things* has in fact nothing to do with AIDS. The people on stage simply prepare a meal and talk, some of them mentioning AIDS in passing, to remark how it was totally outside of their preoccupations. Many spectators—who had wanted finally to see a Mou Sen show and be part of the in crowd—were turned off by its untheatricality and lack of luster. No text, no actors, just people cooking and migrant workers bricking up some kind of a wall then eating dumplings, with the willing spectators.[23]

As for *File 0*, first performed in Belgium[24] then throughout the world (zigzagging from Eastern Europe to Japan to South America up to Canada, then back to Western Europe), it also exhibits typical Mou Sen characteristics: improvisation, minimal set and accessories, no individualized characters, and a lot of noisy interference. Yet, unlike his other works, it has a story to tell, or rather three stories to tell. *File 0* tells what Every(wo)man, but especially a socialist-country citizen, has:

a personal file that grows thicker and thicker as the person moves along in life. As Milan Kundera put it: "Our only claim to immortality is in the police files." [25] But because the main text, which is the heart of the performance, is a poem by Yu Jian, it is quite specific to the Chinese situation. The poem begins like this, with numbers:

> The Archives Room: Fifth floor of the building   a padlock and behind the padlock in a secret room   his file   stored in a file drawer it is the proof that he is a person   separated from him by two floors he works on the second floor   this box   separated from him by 50 meters 30 steps   a room unlike the others   in reinforced concrete on six sides 3 doors   no windows   1 fluorescent lamp   4 red fire extinguishers
>
> 200 square meters   more than 1,000 locks [26]

Yu's poem is taped and is turned on and off. It is somewhat reminiscent of Beckett's *Krapp's Last Tape* since it is an account of a person, a life of Every(wo)man. But in this story, the "I" is eradicated. A chilling authorial voice describes matter-of-factly a life: from the person's nondescript birth in some dreary hospital, to his (her) learning words such as "mother," "father"; to sexual initiation in a school lavatory; to present-day premature old age at thirty. The tape interrupts the other two narratives, but then these two will also interrupt our hearing of the tape and of their narration. That is in order: no one can be heard out to the full, and is it not banal anyway? Another "personal" narrative is that of the video artist Wu Wenguang performing in this show, who tells his own story, via his father's story. That's only normal because a file not only follows you; it also precedes you. As critic He Yi expressed it: "One is written up by the file, and not the other way around." [27] He Yi underlines one particular passage that totally eradicates a "self," any personal trait. This is an anonymous (Chinese) body:

> Name: horizontal stroke vertical stroke curved stroke to the right curved stroke to the left   Sex: the south will be yang the north will be yin Nationality: there's a pretty place   Family background: if the old man's a hero the son will be a good guy   if the old man's a revisionist the son will be a bum Profession: whatever

Heaven gave I shall use   Salary: a small dish of snacks not enough
to get stuck in the teeth. ("File 0," 56)

He Yi also makes it clear that Yu is parodying the Cultural Revolution's
formulas. Still, I find that Beckett's love-hate of formulaic language and
his use of very concrete things for vital matters resonates with the poem
"File 0." Also, Beckett's play on memory, time, and intemporality is akin
to the experiment here. One more narrative emerges at the end of the
play; it is Jiang Yue's account of his first love. This time, Wu steps in and
recites with him, the tape also plays, and it becomes a chorus of disso-
nant sounds, a noisy finale to an already noisy play, where a monstrous
ventilator is switched on and off, a welder (Jiang Yue) welds on and off,
a woman (Wen Hui) stridently screams, actors run in and hurl apples
into the fan. "Words are sent to the guillotine, ka-cha, ka-cha, off they
fall," says Yu Jian of his contribution to File 0.[28]

The enthusiastic international reception of this play was astound-
ing. It was widely read as an allegory of the Tiananmen massacre and
also as a direct criticism of ogrish China devouring its youth. The benevolent foreign public read the play much as they read Zhang Yimou's
films: the actors became representative victims of a dehumanizing system. Notwithstanding the evident social critique — or, rather, the evident assault on the system — in Yu Jian's poem, could File 0 have been
read otherwise in the international sphere? Nothing is more removed
from Mou Sen's goal than theater as a reflection of reality, or worse,
as allegory of an oppressed China. "Forceful stories about the Chinese
people and the mother country don't interest me. Nor do heroic political
deeds. I want to break through the cliché that China can be reduced to a
purely political phenomenon, to the Cultural Revolution, to Tiananmen
events, etc."[29] Against his will, his production became an autoethnographic performance.[30] What is more, File 0 offers no grand narrative or
any sort of conscience-raising Brechtian parable. Yet, it does "interfere
with reality," which is Mou Sen's aim.[31]

Other word-of-mouth performances

Being there. With File 0, Chinese artists were for the first time present on
our ground, in the West, showing themselves without an ID tag. For me,

their presentation was completely unallegorical, and unpsychological. It simply stated their "being here." During many long moments in the play we are face to face with an actor who just stares at us or speaks to us, but in a language most of us don't understand.[32] Robbe-Grillet has discussed the reception of Beckett's plays in the fifties with a discourse on presence, of the characters simply being there and not accountable in terms of psychology or ideology.[33] The discomfort we feel in the presence of the Chinese performers is enhanced by the fact that the people facing us are from another nation, another culture, another race (for most of the spectators), yet they deal with things that concern us all, as George Orwell, Noam Chomsky, and many others have attempted to tell us. On the question of racial difference, Genet's reply to an actor suggesting he should write a play to be performed by blacks is significant: "But what's a black? And first of all, what color is it?"[34] Hanif Kureishi's protagonist Karim in *The Buddha of Suburbia* offers another ironic counterpoint. Because of his ethnic and class background, Karim is chosen as an actor in an alternative play; he is told to go and research a real character, that is a 'black' character, "though truly I was more beige than anything" (167). Karim ends up playing a role that portrayed the "sexual ambition and humiliation of an Indian in England" (219).[35] Does "racial difference" necessarily supersede other differences on stage?

Chinese artists are moving on, and doing things everywhere. Even women! The concrete, physical credo of Mou Sen and Yu Jian has its counterpart in the work of an occasional collaborator, Wen Hui, who is a choreographer/dancer. In 1994–95, she created a work-in-progress 'zuopin zai jinxing zhong,' entitled "100 ge dongci" (100 verbs/words of action). Wen Hui first performed this dance alone, in New York City and in Washington. Upon returning home, after participating in Mou Sen's play *Things Related to AIDS*, she performed it again in Beijing, but with a difference. This time, Mou Sen, Wu Wenguang, and many other nonprofessional dancers, mostly men, also participated. The idea was simple: dance is not only on a stage: dance is life itself; all our ordinary actions are dance, too. Consequently, the other dancers performed everyday actions: they stood up, sat down, rested on one another, blocked others, took their clothes on and off. The performance had no set beginning or end. People just left at some point, with their props (a broom, a television set, a bucket, rice). Wen Hui's dance itself, though, was explosive, frenetic, as terrorizing as the best Louise Lecavalier dances. Lecavalier, who dances with the internationally known Canadian dance company, La La La Human Steps, is a platinum-blond, muscular Hermaphroditus, and she has an equivalent in this tiny, black-haired Chinese woman, who, when dancing, is as tough as anyone, of either sex. She simply immersed herself in water, then proceeded to dance from the tub of water all over the Beijing Institute floor. The performance of "100 verbs" oscillated between mechanical, daily gestures and wild frenetic motion; between sight (part of the performance was in total darkness) and sound, silence (except for the shuffling of feet) and noise — from buckets and brooms used in the banal yet strange quotidian activities.[36]

In Mou Sen's *File 0*, Wen Hui's dance role was rather passive, at best reactive. At some point in the play, she was completely enveloped in gigantic silky cloths. Perhaps this silent role should be reconsidered as pivotal in the play? Similarly, another person, also choreographer and dancer (Jin Xing), played a silent part in Mou's other production, *Things Related to* AIDS. If I understood well,[37] she incarnated the mystery of AIDS. All the other people were participating in some menial activity (cooking a meal or building a wall), while she made occasional appearances. Jin Xing has attracted much attention since she had a sex-change operation in 1993 to become a woman. Her mere presence in the play performatively acted out the issue of uncertainty, instability, but also of pertinence: Who can get AIDS? what does a woman stand for? what does a play need to be a "play"? and so on. In all interviews with her, Jin Xing claims that she cannot yet attract support just on the merit of her performances.[38] Perhaps Jin should stop trying to establish herself as a "natural" woman and instead concentrate on problematizing sexual identity.

One person who does precisely that, when he is not behind bars, is Ma Liuming. In his performances, he precedes his name with *Fen* (Fragrant). Ma presents himself as both man and woman: a woman's made-up face, a nude man's body. Ma believes that the specificity of his performance art is precisely the work on his body, because his body is "something no other medium can replace," and because it eliminates all mythic processes of art.[39] He refers to his art as "practical art" 'shijian yishu' that makes each human being a synthesis of elements 'zongxing'

(119). Ma alludes to Michael Jackson, who interests him for his special blurring of racial and sexual boundaries; he intimates that humanity's packaging of itself is all fake (and irrelevant, one could add) (119). Ma's position is therefore not autobiographical; he is not out to tell the truth about himself (or humanity, for that matter!) but to show the falseness of any assertions on the essential nature of biological sexual difference, on the fixity of object-choices, on the separation between life, art, artifice, and the rest (120). Yet, much like the crusading cops in Ning Ying's film *On the Beat,* the police deem his live works pornography and regularly lock him up.

The authorities don't look well upon independent filmmakers either and have blacklisted many of them several times. Making "independent" 'duli' films in China means that one has no recognition whatsoever in China. No funds come from Chinese film-related sources, and no distribution permit is allotted. The films are literally "closet works" 'chouti' since they are only shown as video copies to friends.[40] Perhaps the term "underground" 'dixia' is more suitable, given the recognition these days of so-called independent cinema in the United States.

The characteristics of such cinema in China are, first, very low budgets;[41] second, its blurring of boundaries between documentary and feature film; third, its thematic concern for the fringe of urban (especially Beijing) society (the mad, the bums, the alcoholics, the migrant workers, the vagrant artists). All three elements combine to produce films that are generally black-and-white and with nonprofessional actors. Zhang Yuan is the main representative of China's independent cinema and the most successful.[42] To date, he has made five feature films. Only his first film, *Mama (Mama)* (1990) has been shown in China, but to a very limited audience, there existing only three copies in circulation.[43] Zhang also was the first to make videoclips in China (for pop singer Ai Jing and rock star Cui Jian). None of the stunning and clever clips he made for Cui Jian has ever been shown on local television. He also occasionally does ads for television (they of course serve their purpose!). Funding comes from friends, from previous films, and from foreign countries or institutions, such as France's ministry of culture or the Rotterdam Film Festival.

English-language articles on Zhang use the term "gritty" to describe his style. A typical Zhang film has a slow, steady pace and no closure (like life). When there is violence, such as domestic violence (a son beating his father in *Erzi [Sons]* [1995], a mother pushing away her retarded son in *Mama* [1990]) or sexual violence, (a bum raping a woman in *Beijing zazhong [Beijing Bastards]* [1993]), his camera does not shy away from the indeed gritty scene. What makes Zhang's films poignant is the real life story behind the violence, as we see also in his *Dong gong xi gong (East Palace, West Palace)* (1996).[44] In *Mama*, the actress Qing Yan is in fact herself a single mother who cares for her retarded son on her own; the film includes archival interviews of mothers in the same situation. In *Beijing Bastards,* the protagonist is indeed a "bum" since Li Wei is in real life a rock music promoter and has no steady job; the rock stars Cui Jian and Dou Wei play themselves. In *Sons,* the Li family members play their own roles in a dysfunctional family, where alcohol and verbal abuse are everyday scenes. For the shooting, the father was taken out of the hospital for the mentally retarded where he is institutionalized and returned there afterward. *East Palace, West Palace,* a story about a policeman interrogating a homosexual, has as a start a real story, that of policemen searching gay parks and toilets in order to find homosexuals for a survey for which no one was volunteering. The only film without a storyline, *Guangchang (The Place)* (1994) treats perhaps the most sensitive of all topics: Tiananmen today.[45] This documentary film gives us a twenty-four-hour presentation of what goes on at the currently most infamous square in the world. All is quite serene, except for the chilling guards here and there (but they are watched by people who are sucking popsicles): we see kites flown by sweet old men, provincial tourists taking photographs, a businessman on his cellular phone, an old lady yawning while sweeping, and cute children with toy tanks. As if nothing had ever happened there, as if life just kept on flowing, as usual, which is pretty much true. Tiananmen is Beijing is China. As in all of his films, Zhang does not step in with authorial commentaries on what is seen and heard. *The Place* is also particular in his filmography in that it is "out in the open": all his other films, dealing with the oppressed and repressed, take place in claustrophobic environments, such as basements or dingy hangouts under staircases. *Beijing Bastards* is a fine demonstration of the absence of space for subcultures: guys smoke pot in the john, runaways find squatholes to make out, painters can't find studios, musicians don't have a hold on any rehearsal space (and certainly not on a performing place, except for underground fire-traps or anywhere outside, on side streets).

Zhang has a way of making his "actors" expose themselves frontally to us. In *Beijing Bastards,* Kar-zi (Li Wei) vents his anger in a long monologue to the viewer (about his pregnant girlfriend who left); Dou Wei writhes in front of the camera while he sings a song. In *Mama,* the retarded boy cries, staring at the camera.[46] Somehow, Zhang wants to give space to these people who cannot otherwise be seen and heard. It is another sort of autoethnographic filming. Zhang also considers himself a "bastard" and, in *Sons,* plays a madman. All the independent filmmakers make films about people around them, who are somewhat like themselves.

This secondary trait, that of self-representation, is most obvious in Wu Wenguang's documentaries, *Liulang Beijing: Zuihou de mengxiangzhe (Bumming in Beijing: The Last Dreamers)* (1990) and its sequel *Sihai weijia (At Home in the World)* (1995). In both films, Wu follows the same five artists, all from the provinces, who decided in the mid-1980s to remain in Beijing at the end of their studies. As critic He Yi notes, this refusal to take on an assigned job, to snub the work unit and to make it on one's own, was quite a rare phenomenon at that time. He adds that the decisive factor was Beijing itself: the city as political and cultural capital, as old and new, sacred and profane, as a living contradiction was the main attraction.[47] Beijing still holds that phantasmatic power for most artists today: it's where you are recognized by peers; it's where you make it.

But the irony in Wu's films is that, apart from Mou Sen, whom we see staging a play, none of the other artists is now engaged in any form of art. As He Yi puts it, "The most ironical thing is that these 'last dreamers' are bogged down by everyday living."[48] Thus the term "ethnographic" documentary is apt: we see one brushing his teeth outside, another cooking outside, yet others having a mad spell or marrying, and so on. I would say that the most ironical thing is precisely the marriages, a very antibohemian move. In the sequel, *At Home in the World,* all, except for Mou Sen, are living abroad and have married foreigners (an Italian, a Frenchman, an American, an Austrian). Only two of them practice some form of art. The women bear babies, and one wears a pearl necklace. The most striking feature of the sequel is the cynical reasoning they give. Photographer Gao Bo is paramount example. He tells Wu that he would like to go back to China, to be like him, having time to shoot the breeze; here (in Paris), all time is time used to make money. Making portraits on the street, Gao Bo is a slick salesman who knows all the best spots to lure clients. Good weather means good money-making days. Painter Zhang Dali, at the onset, seems successful both in family matters and professional life. But what does he do at night? He steals away with a spray-paint can and scrawls graffiti on Bologna's old buildings.

So what of Beijing as utopia? Obviously it is not one for the actors in Wu's documentary. Beijing was a springboard for meeting foreigners and making contacts to get scholarships to go abroad. Although Wu is a friend of all these "actors," they don't come across as particularly sympathetic, nor as "dreamers," nor as interesting world citizens. Wu's films are interesting in that when read against the grain, they show the aporia of artistic life in China.[49]

Another facet of this dreary picture of art, artists, and living in Beijing/China comes out in Jiang Yue's documentary *Bi'an (The Other Bank)* (1995). This film is an exposure of, I would say, dirty laundry.[50] Starting with the strenuous rehearsals for Mou Sen's play of the same name, the film then follows Mou's life and improved lifestyle, but especially it follows those left behind, that is, the fourteen young actors who acted in his play. After the week of performances, all of them stayed in Beijing with the hope of acting again in Mou Sen's plays. None ever did; after six months, except for one who stayed to study in another field, they were all forced to go back to their provinces. Jiang's camera shows them waiting for a call from Mou Sen, having barely enough food to survive, playing cards, keeping fit, and so on. At some point, they all have to work. One girl becomes a hostess for a restaurant; her job is to stand outside the door dressed in a *qipao* and smile at prospective clients. "No one remembers us," she says: "they only remember Mou Sen." The poet Yu Jian, whose "grammatical discussion" was a key part of the script, is shown saying, "The play dealt with a deconstruction of utopia. But these kids created another form of utopia." That is, sadly, what Jiang's documentary shows us. The most striking example ends the film: a peasant boy returns to his native Hebei (not very far from Beijing) to produce his own play. Performed on farmland, attended by Mou Sen, his girlfriend, and the villagers, it imitates slavishly the spirit

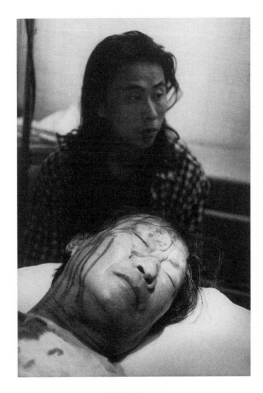

8. Film still from Zhang Yuan's *Sons*, 1995.
Photograph by Rong Rong.

of the play, *The Other Bank:* the "actors" say such lines as "What are we doing here? We're performing a play. What play?"

Beijing makes everyone dream, but not everyone gets a share of it. A small film group, Qingnian shiyan dianying xiaozu (Youth Experimental Film Group), was created in 1995 by eight young graduates from different departments of the Beijing Film Institute. Born in the 1970s in various Chinese provinces, they have chosen to remain in Beijing and make films specifically about non-Beijingers in Beijing. Their first work, *Xiao Shan hui jia (Little Shan Goes Home)* (1995), although a fiction, has the allure of a weird documentary. It looks like rough shots one sees in the evening news: one sequence follows another without necessarily being linked. The theme music that introduces China's televised news (Xinwen lianbo) is heard now and again. Subtitles in Chinese, vital unless one understands the dialect, follow the style of investigative reports but they generate here eeriness. The vital difference with official coverage is that *Little Shan Goes Home* is not about some colorful folk from faraway places. Little Shan is a migrant worker from Anyang, Henan, who has come to the big city. On the eve of the New Year, on the eve of his departure to go back home for the holidays, he is fired from his restaurant job. Penniless, without gifts for his family, he seeks out his provincial compatriots in the city: racketeers, prostitutes, university students, construction laborers, all to no avail. Left alone, he has his long hair shaved off and leaves Beijing.

There is a seven-minute-long sequence of Little Shan walking. Director Jia Zhangke claims that the group's aim, in such slow and long sequences, is precisely to make themselves and the viewers go through other people's miseries.[51] "Not averting one's gaze" seems to be their motto. Their films intentionally develop in a linear, newspaper-like fashion, because their aim is to report on the other side of Beijing, peopled with losers like Little Shan, who is pretty much like them: "We are migrant workers ['mingong'] in film."[52] The film group showed *Little Shan* to migrant workers. Ironically, one worker came up and said he was willing to act for free in their films anytime.[53]

This closeness to life, this displacement of art into life, which characterizes all the endeavors analyzed here, does not have the same meaning in China as, say, in the blasé United States. They are all forms of "closet art" or, to use a term from a Cultural Revolution practice, "manuscripts" 'shouchaoben' handed from one person to the other under the table. In China, such art is considered very threatening from the point of view of the authorities, and it is not diffused. Hence, it is invisible. When exported here, in the First World, its meaning moves on: the words, the gestures, become representative of China, though they are in the first place assertions of people simply "being there," where "there" is never in the (lime)light.

4 Colorful Folk in the Landscape

Fifth-Generation Filmmakers and Roots-Searchers

Revolution means removal of that which is antiquated.

The great man changes like a tiger.

Hexagram 49, "Revolution (Molting)," *Yijing*

A generation of Chinese grew up step by step, stride by stride, with the People's Republic of China. They went through the different stages of life during the country's different socialist and postsocialist stages: infancy during farm reform and collective nurseries; childhood during the antirightist movement and the first labor camps; preadolescence during famine, iron-smelting, and the rupture with the Soviets; adolescence during the Cultural Revolution; preadult days at the onset of reform; and finally adulthood during the current reform era. Their bodies and minds are inscribed with the great happenings and great catastrophes that their nation and they, as citizens of that nation, underwent. Understandably, this generation's artists are both worse and better off: their unique experience and opportunities have no match in the older generations, nor in the younger generations. Only they have emerged as Chinese from the People's Republic of China and matured as Chinese in-the-world.

In cinema, they are the so-called "Fifth Generation" 'diwudai' of Chinese filmmakers, that is, the first class to graduate after the Cultural

9. "The Fifth Generation at the Beijing Film Institute, ten years after graduation."
Photograph by Song Yuanyuan, 1992.

Revolution, in 1982.[1] My interest in contemporary Chinese culture was first aroused by these cineasts. The main representatives, Chen Kaige and Zhang Yimou, made Chinese films interesting to the world. They adapted their contemporaries' literary works, collectively called "roots-searching" 'xungen' literature. This chapter is dedicated to the study of this particular generation's evolution, in particular the male of the species.

Earthy creatures

Eating beef, one certainly doesn't become beef.

Lu Xun, "Concerning the Intellectuals"

The Fifth Generation's film products are fine examples of "grabbism" 'nalai zhuyi,' a term used and a mode proposed by Lu Xun to pick things here and there, from the past as well as other cultures, where and when needed.[2] As students, they viewed indigenous film (from all previous generations), Asian film (from Ozu to Oshima), and diversified foreign film (from the French New Wave and Eastern Europe artfilms to Hollywood's Oscar winners). There is no generational style unifying them, but there is definitely a common will, which, simply said, is to break new ground technically and thematically by exploring both their medium and their culture.

In this sense, the Fifth Generation echoes the new literary tendency of the mid-1980s, the so-called roots-searching school, their generational and artistic peers. No more than their filmmaking counterparts do these writers share a common aesthetic. For example, there is Mo Yan, who deftly combines old indigenous poetic devices with foreign techniques, such as Gabriel García Márquez's magic realism and Claude Simon's baroque painterly descriptions. And there is A Cheng, who recycles a Daoist-like attitude and a discourse of detachment and sparsity.

Perhaps, when Colombia's Gabriel Garcia Marquez, hailed as the preeminent practitioner of Latin-American magic realism, won the Nobel Prize in literature in 1984, this Chinese generation learned a lesson: cultural specificity at the very grassroots, especially from a Third World country, can lead to recognition. Then again, the lesson could have sprung from the excitement, controversy, and heated debates surrounding Luo Zhongli's hyperrealist oil painting *Fuqin (Father)* of 1980: a gigantic, extreme close-up of an old shabby peasant (with a ball-point pen behind his ear). Perhaps the lesson just came "naturally," in 1984, when *Huang tudi (Yellow Earth)*, with Chen Kaige as director and Zhang Yimou as cameraman was lauded, first in Hong Kong, then internationally. *Yellow Earth* cannot be more culturally specific. It contains all manner of details that can be read as distinctively Chinese within a Third World cinema, that is, as Teshome Gabriel described it in 1985, cinema "with a discursive use of medium and an appeal for intellectual appreciation," which privileges space and community over temporal manipulation and individual destiny. "Third World films are heterogenous, employing narrative and oral discourse, folk music and songs, extended silence and gaps, moving from fictional representation to reality, to fiction."[3] In a nutshell, *Yellow Earth* makes visible China's geography, folk, their customs, history, and philosophy, past and present.

Tellingly, the film opens with text, to situate the viewer (not necessarily [mainland] Chinese). We read that it is the end of the 1930s, where Mao Zedong, now based in desolate northern Yan'an, is consolidating his Eighth Route Army. In order to recruit the peasants to the revolutionary camp, a soldier is sent to the villages to collect songs, which will be adapted for the cause. This preamble announces a documentary, but *Yellow Earth* is anything but a documentary, if by "documentary" we understand a straightforward presentation of a certain reality. *Yellow Earth* is in fact a feature film, with a melodramatic plot — a young girl, forced to marry, commits suicide because the soldier did not come back in time to take her to Yan'an. Yet this narrative is buried in the material details, the excessive sights and sounds, of the film. The screen is at times all yellow loess, at times all sky or yellow river. The appearance of an old peasant with his buffalo at the very top of a high plateau also adds to the graphic quality. Some scenes are "copied and pasted" elsewhere. Some scenes of action are made to alternate with still-lifes. The camera, with wide angle shots, in long takes, also moves slowly, panoramically, across the scenery and becomes the visual complement to the young girl's off-screen singing. (These techniques go against the Hollywoodian trend of "invisible" narration and, taken together, weaken the melodrama, while yielding an ideological point of view.)

Few words are uttered on screen, yet sound effects are frequent. The microphones are nearby when the characters slurp their meatless porridge, or when the buffalo lows; the camera shows their unspoken understanding, their habitual mode of communication (or lack of it) through gestures; it goes into their dark shabby homes, without much lighting equipment. Faces are not made up, and most of the time they are expressionless. Cuiqiao, the daughter enthralled by the idea of socialism as presented by Gu Qing the soldier, looks like the celebrated victim-turned-heroine, the white-haired girl of the Yan'an era. She has that same obstinate, naive look retrospectively given to the pre-Communist heroines of the 1930s and 40s in the film, painting, and model plays of the Cultural Revolution. However, deprived here of the smiles and rubicund cheeks of those earlier representations, the peasants simply look like earthy creatures, with tanned skins, like their beasts of burden. The concluding scene, a rain-invoking ritual to the gods, secures in the viewer's mind images of primitiveness, both seductive and repulsive.

Yellow Earth can be read as a critical exploration of socialist Chinese culture supposedly based on peasant forces: peasants, it implies, have remained untouched by Mao's revolution. Or it can be read as a positive recycling of Chinese values kicked out during the socialist era: people live according to nature's seasons, not political upheavals; their lives are punctuated by folkloric songs and customs such as red weddings in palanquins. It is a most ambivalent hymn to China and its people.[4] In this sense, it is much like an ethnological documentary that leaves the viewer, including the indigenous viewer, contemplating (the pros and cons of) an alien culture. Such a sweeping critical approach to Chinese culture is typical of the generation born with the People's Republic of China. In 1988, forty-year-old Su Xiaokang edited and brought to the television screen the six-part documentary *Heshang (Deathsong of the River)*.[5] It seems that all of China watched it during its two airings (in June and August) and discussed its issues. Put bluntly, *Deathsong* is a devastating critique of Chinese civilization, of its sinicity, through long-standing and more recent icons: the Yellow River, the Great Wall, the Dragon, the Red Flag. Unsurprisingly, footage from the film *Yellow Earth* (for example, the waist drummers jumping up and down) is used to exemplify the backwardness and immobility of China.

Deathsong, however, is not made up of ambivalent statements like *Yellow Earth*. On the contrary, it presents the "national treasures" as totally negative, as fetishes of a primitive and stagnant society. A fetish in its first sense was "the name given by white men to cult objects and religious practices of people and civilizations from Guinea and Western Africa in the fifteenth and sixteenth centuries."[6] During the peak of the colonial period, fetishes became, for the West, signs of cultural backwardness among all nonwhite peoples, from Guinea to America.[7] Logically then, fetishes are/were tangible proofs of the orientalist distinction between the West and the non-West (the Orient) and the superiority of the former. (As if only barbarians would anthropomorphize gods, inanimate objects, and animals.) As Edward Said and many others have pointed out, orientalism is a discourse of exteriority and, consequently, so is the discourse focusing on fetishes.

With *Yellow Earth* but more unequivocally with *Deathsong,* the Chinese positioned themselves outside of their own culture, as ethnologists do, searching for their own civilization's fetish objects (and their own self-debasement). *Deathsong,* with its evolutionist subtext, ultimately depicts the Chinese as animals of a lower species. To wit, the beginning of part 6, "Weilanse" ("Azure Blue"), which divides the primitive and the advanced civilizations in terms of red/earth and blue/space: "Human blood is red. Almost all animals have blood that is red. Primitive religion defined the basic color of life as red. Early man daubed the corpses of the dead with red pigment from iron ore in order to summon back the life that had been lost. The blue sky is deep and mysterious. . . . When mankind left the earth's surface for the first time and *gazed back at his home from outer space,* [they discovered that] the planet Earth was a blue planet" (203, my emphasis).

The color red in *Deathsong* is viewed as wholly negative, as bloody: it is the color of the setting sun (another image of decline), of Mao's era, of the flag of the People's Republic of China, both indirectly evoking bloody turmoils, and of primitive customs such as painting corpses with ocher. Yellow is also undermined as the Chinese symbolic color: The Yellow River, "the most brutal and most unrestrained river in the world" (106) has even "dyed" 'rancheng' the Chinese people's skin (104); the yellow earth is "branded" 'laoyin' into Chinese people's culture and psychology" (119, my translation instead of "imprinted"). Emperors and despots wore yellow with clawed dragons inspiring terror, and so on.

The semiotic ways of *Deathsong* are manifold: the Yellow River is an aquatic Great Wall; that is, it is useless in preventing invasions and successful only in fencing in its own people. Icons are seen as totems, like the dragon, of a civilization burdened by endless floods, earthquakes, cyclical internecine wars, and revolutions: "once in every seven or eight years," claims the politically oppressed protagonist of the film *Furongzhen (Hibiscus Town),* quoted in the text/image. This recycling of old icons can in fact be considered an unearthing of fetishes deftly woven together. The authors probably consciously played on the timeliness of their production: 1988 was the year of the dragon, the first one to fall after that of 1976—a year marked by the official end of the Cultural Revolution, the death of Zhou Enlai, the Tangshan earthquake, and Mao Zedong's death and the end of his leadership. Would their critical inquiry bring about any blueness for China in the next year of the dragon, that is, in the year 2000, the year of the Olympics that China wanted to host?

Deathsong is now easily dismissed because of its manifold inaccuracies[8] and its "fixation on the Western model of development."[9] Yet, in 1988 and 1989, it reached people nationwide because it was televised, and so it is recognized as a "milestone in Chinese television."[10] The at least century-old questions of national salvation/doom were now exposed in images, in imagistic objects to be appraised for their symbolic value, as if from the outside.

To question a civilization such as "China" in a visual medium is necessarily to reify it. To question at the same time the possibilities of the medium, in this case, film, also entails a maximal use of sights and sounds. Among the early Fifth-Generation films, Chen Kaige's *Haiziwang (King of the Children)* is exemplary of this approach. Chen chose to talk of China's greatest all-time cultural fetish, the written word. He presented it in a clashing "natural" environment of oral traditions, with non-Han speaking woodcutters and cowherds, with the sounds of their singing, woodcutting, and shooing, of cowbells tinkling. *King of the Children* (1987) is an adaptation of the 1984 novella of the same name by A Cheng, a proponent of the roots-searching school, with incursions into A Cheng's other works, "Shuwang" (King of the trees) and "Qiwang" (King of chess), both of 1985.[11] A Cheng emerged in Greater China and subsequently in the Chinese diaspora with his trilogy of kings. His simple stories struck a (nostalgic) chord, undoubtedly because of the specifically Chinese traits of his texts—chess, written words, Daoist oneness with nature—and because of their apolitical nature. The style is spare and simple—in the positive, classical sense—and the stories, told in a gently humorous way, are basic lessons of life. Set in the Cultural Revolution, with teenage protagonists narrating, they tell of the apprenticeship of friendship, of individuality, of lasting values such as the natural world, applicable to the Chinese context at large. The tone is that of gentle detachment (from politics, from official authority, from the worldly). Probably, all these elements contributed to its literary fortune, inside and outside China.[12]

Chen Kaige chose to adapt the story "King of the children," which recounts the rise and fall of Lao Gan, a rusticated youth 'zhiqing,' who becomes a teacher in a remote Yunnan village. Chance, it seems, has chosen this unlikely candidate, who is just like his camp fellows from high school: rowdy, fun-loving, and nothing of an intellectual. Initially, his pupils scoff at him and the more serious ones reprove his frivolous attitude. Lao Gan gradually realizes the folly of teaching children useless and incomprehensible texts that smack of propaganda and decides to teach them basic words and then have them write compositions based on their own experiences.

Chen Kaige offers from the beginning to the end of the film visual images of the written word: one appears on the blackboard before the film even starts ("shang xue" 'to go to school') and another, also written on the blackboard, closes the film ("niu + shui" 'cattlepiss'). The written word is also presented as a fetish object, in the form of the dictionary. All these writerly elements exist in the novella, but Chen, working with sights and sounds, completely reorients the meanings of writing. In A Cheng's novella, Lao Gan's model student copies the dictionary and learns, like all the others, how to write after events have taken place, that is, to transcribe/copy in a proper way. In other words, Lao Gan's students learn the exchange value of the written word.[13] In Chen's film, however, all copying is decried: "Don't copy anything, not even the dictionary" are his last words to his pupil. But will his pupil heed his advice? One must answer no; after all, Lao Gan is dismissed from his teaching position, and Wang Fu, now beholder of the prized dictionary, will most likely continue his cumulative recording of characters. Chen Kaige aims to attack the written code at a symbolic and philosophical level, not for its down-to-earth, practical value.

The film *King of the Children* offers an iconoclastic view of the Chinese written code, as perverted by Lao Gan, who has himself gone to the school of life while he is stranded at the remote village and learned to doubt the system. He invents a written word: the combination of "ox-cow" with "water-urine" (niu + shui), which becomes a visual condensation of a lesson he has derived from grazing cattle. That invented character is also present in the novella, but there it has a metaphorical meaning, implying the kind of enticement one needs to offer in order to be obeyed: cattle like salty fluids, if you urinate for them, they will follow you. The film, by insisting not only on the anecdote but on the visual representation of the character (on the blackboard at the very end), presents characters at their simple face value. Thus, the film ironically ends with a written "word" turned into a symbol, a new fetish.

Chen has also added a protagonist absent in the novel, a young cowherd, and he has given prominence to the animal world. Left on his own, Lao Gan encounters strange creatures. The first is an old man who sings in a language Lao Gan can't understand. The (Han-Chinese speaking) viewers understand this first encounter to be with a national minority of some sort. Lao Gan laughs and leaves the scene. The second encounter is with a young cowherd, who will never utter a word, even when the protagonist asks him questions such as "Why are you not in school?" This dark-skinned boy, whose face is partly hidden by his straw hat, is at times accompanied by an ox or cow. Cattle are aurally present from the very onset of the film, contrapuntally with the scratching of chalk on blackboard, or of pencils in notebooks. Similarly, the cowherd is visualized in alternation with the pupils. A cow even becomes a protagonist in what is the third encounter: at night, Lao Gan opens his door and is brought face to face with the creature, which, like the cowherd, gazes at him, then leaves.

Progressively, this "humanimal kingdom"—nonspeaking, from the protagonist's point of view—becomes magisterially important. All scenes with them are eerie, mysterious, and left uncommented on. Lao Gan behaves less and less like a conventional human: he squats and looks like a rock or an animal; he stands up, like a scarecrow. A scene nearing the end of the film shows him contemplating gnarled tree stumps, and the cowherd. This strange scene, with the stumps anthropomorphized, appearing like combinations of objects, people, parts of humans, animals, segues into the one presenting the invented word on the blackboard. Lao Gan has somehow invested them with talismanic value, turned them into totems, into his own fetish, which counters the conventional one, the three-thousand-year-old written word.

With *King of the Children*, Chen attempted to deconstruct a fetish by confronting it with realities of the natural world and of peasant knowledge. But he only succeeded in showing his own ambivalence toward the written code, by transferring the fetish onto the other, that is, the nonwriting "animal" kingdom. Kings are fools, faulty words are correct, and vice versa. The Chinese written word, though convoluted, remains the root of all fantasy.

Few people have seen this film, inside and outside China. *King of the Children* was the very first Chinese film ever to be part of the official competition at Cannes. But the Film Festival jury of 1987 granted it its Alarm Clock prize for the most soporific film of the competition. Why? It could be sheer insensitivity and ignorance, or it could be that *King of the Children* was solely geared to a Chinese audience — those who can read Chinese characters, who know the right ones from the faulty ones and know that it works by combinations; who know that there is a Han culture and many other Chinese cultures, and so on and so forth. *King of the Children* could not (and was not intended to) work as an international cross-cultural commodity. Rather, it is a cultural investigation within one civilization.

Lessons of survival, in order to survive in the international arena, need more bite. And more convention. Zhang Yimou showed the way, with his own artful combination of Chinese fetishes. Although the statement that "fetishes are supremely culturally specific"[14] may not be altogether true, some have been classified as specifically "Chinese"; for example, foot binding (by none other than the father of sexual fetishism, Freud).[15] If one combines the initial meaning of the fetish (that which is primitive from an outsider's point of view) with its later meaning (as transference of the sexual upon objects), then the success, domestic and international, of Zhang Yimou's films can be understood. His blueprint is a combination of the Chinese countryside, Chinese old things, Chinese traditional arts and crafts, and attractive Chinese women.

His first film as director, *Hong gaoliang (Red Sorghum)* (1988) was immensely popular at home and abroad. At home, it became a cult film, all young men singing on the streets the theme song, "Little sister, keep on moving"; abroad, it first won the Golden Bear award in Berlin and then numerous other titles throughout the world, for its production crew, its photography, its actors, and of course its director. *Red Sorghum* is the adaptation of a part of Mo Yan's novel of the same name, which also became a bestseller following the film.[16] The story is a tale of love and independence, set during the China-Japan war in the late 1930s. A young couple meet, a sedan-bearer and a young woman promised in marriage to a leper who owns an alcohol distillery; they will manage the distillery, have a child, and all will be bliss, until the Japanese invasion, whereupon they resist in their distinct, daring ways. The film follows the novel in

10. "My grandpa, the pallbearer turned distillery owner." Film still from Zhang Yimou's
Red Sorghum, 1988.

its choice of point of view: an omniscient, off-stage, present-day male
narrator whose own life is gray and "small as an insect" compared to the
heroes of his clan, especially the grandfather and grandmother in their
prime. It starts with that voice, on a blank screen: "I will tell you the
story of my grandpa and grandma. . . ." "Grandma" then appears: instead of the expected old granny, we see a beautiful, twenty-something
woman (played by Gong Li) who, though clad in ancient fashion, looks
very contemporary.

The camera throughout the film takes in human bodies in detail: the
woman's eyes, breasts, open mouth, and yes, her feet (decked in red);
the man's nape, shoulders, back, and strong legs. All manner of fantasies are exposed in the film: sex in nature (the famous "wild union");
urine transforming liquor into the finest brew; women carried off like
big sacks of cereal; meat eaten off the carcass (a cow!); the flaying of

a person, and so forth. These scenes are presented in vivid, primary colors, where red stands out as beautiful, gushing blood. Zhang Yimou forcefully reorients the color red from its Communist value toward its material and traditional meanings: red is the color of marriages, of life as birth and as death, that is, of blood. He stresses the intensity of red by dyeing the alcohol red, by dressing the woman in red, by filming the fire that feeds the distillery and their home-made bombs, and by reddening a sunset sky.

The photography provides an album of beautiful, vivid, "Chinese" snapshots: the full moon over the deserted plateau, vast expanses of green fields interspersed with close-ups of beautiful, happy-go-lucky people, such as the youthful grandparents. Music intensifies the dramatic moments: harsh folkloric songs and the suona 'reed flute' for the heart-wrenching moments.[17] Nothing could be more "Chinese." Yet, as Zhang himself has said, the music is not, as it is in *Yellow Earth*, ethnographic in any way: it's a mixture of southern tunes with northern airs 'nanqiang beidiao'.[18] The customs presented—from the jolting of the wedding sedan to the red sorghum wine—are all inventions, as Zhang himself admits. But they are read as Chinese. And they are eminently legible cross-culturally. Two more examples can be provided here. One, in Zhang's words: "I think that for humans in general the color red excites passion; no one would say red is cold."[19] Another example is Zhang's Hollywoodian use of woman: woman is the suture, intra- and extradiegetically. She is the fulcrum of all projections, she is the hinge on which the narrative is played. The first image is "woman," speechless, exposed as matter, and her exposed dead body (under Japanese fire), brings on the closure of the film. Zhang works with conventions, many of which are common to non-Chinese, as well.

It is ironical to me that Zhang Yimou's films are unilaterally read as national allegories outside of China. They rather nicely tap into "our" own fetishistic fantasies. *Judou*, his second film, makes the point even clearer. It is a successful mise-en-scène of visual "pleasures." *Judou* is also an adaptation of a novel, this one by Liu Heng, who is also of the roots-searching school.[20] The story is set in prerevolutionary times. It is (once again) about a beautiful woman who manages to ease herself partly out of a bad situation by having an affair with another man. Judou is married to a sadistic and impotent old man who has a dye factory and who tortures her because he wants a male heir. He gets a son eventually, through his wife's affair with his nephew, Tianqing, a man of her age. The son, Tianbai, grows into a murderous monster who kills his two fathers. In the film, the woman immolates herself, setting fire to the whole factory.[21]

The film, beautifully draped in tints of blue and yellow, shows human feelings at their base level: a woman is brutalized; a man (Tianqing) looks at her/at her body through a peeping hole while she is bathing; she eventually finds out that he is peeping, and she willingly shows him her bruised yet superb body; she comes on to him while he is eating a phallic-shaped vegetable; they make love in dirty hideaways. The viewer is forced to become a voyeur, much like the donkey in the pigsty where she bathes, or like the son who catches the lovers in flagrante. It's exciting and traumatizing (a pitiful, exhilarating sight). One cries for Judou's fate, for Jiu'er (the female protagonist in *Red Sorghum*), for the death of these oppressed women. Woman is exposed to us in separate, fragmented parts: her face in a full-blown look at the camera; her (piglike) squeals off-screen; her full breasts clad in yellow, against a yellow ream of cloth; her foot in an embroidered red slipper peeping out of the sedan. The camera forces us to gaze at such an exhibition. In this sense, I partially agree with Rey Chow's statement that Zhang Yimou's (first three) films are "about the affect of exhibitionism rather than (as is often assumed) that of voyeurism."[22] Chow makes her point convincingly by focusing on the scene mentioned above, when a battered Judou knowingly allows the peeper Tianqing to look at her body (again, not her whole body, but a statue-like bust) thereby forcing him into an alliance with her and preventing both his and our voyeuristic pleasure. However, I would not rule out the spectator's voyeuristic drive in *Judou*. (Melo)drama (*Red Sorghum, Judou*) works to create such emotions as gasps of horror in front of sadistic acts, tears of joy in heterosexual reunion, and so on. All expressions of passion are embedded therein.

On the other hand, Zhang's third film, *Dahong denglong gaogao gua (Raise the Red Lantern)* (1991), is definitely about exhibitionism and its affect. Constructed like a Western classical tragedy,[23] *Raise the Red Lantern* freezes our fantasies and turns them against us. The final affect is a sense of the tragic, when exposed to unresolvable dilemmas. The story, also set in the 1920s, is an adaptation of Su Tong's novella "Qi qie cheng qun" (Wives and Concubines).[24] The story is one of conflict: four wives in a four-winged mansion 'siheyuan' fight against each other. Captive in their husband's home, they are at his mercy and their struggle is in vain. The fact that he is virtually absent from the screen reinforces his role as the Father, or the Hidden God of tragedy. There is therefore no suspense in this tragic machine, which unfolds mercilessly from Fourth Wife's arrival one summer, to Fifth Wife's arrival the next summer. Zhang here offers no (partial) nudity, no sex scenes, but a display of four types of human design, the four women. Like tragic figures, they have no psychological makeup: First Wife is an "antique" object; Second Wife is a "Buddha face with a scorpio heart" — note the use of tragedy's linguistic trademark, the oxymoron; Third Wife is an actress; Fourth Wife is a modern, educated girl. One could even categorize them in terms of their appropriate Chinese element, respectively: water (base of the household), earth (malleable matter), metal (sharp and piercing), and wood (youth itself). No fire, though. Zhang revives tragedy by preempting its "modern" content: the fire of love/passion.[25] *Raise the Red Lantern* is formalistic in all aspects: titles, appearing on an otherwise blank screen, announce the seasons and mark the changing acts of the drama. It is rigorously timed: act 1 (summer): Songlian (Fourth Wife) arrives and learns the basic customs of the house; act 2 (autumn): intrigues are deployed by all the women; act 3 (winter): the die is cast, severe punishments are carried out; act 4 (summer): Songlian (Fourth Wife) goes mad and Fifth Wife arrives. The absence of spring corresponds to the absence of fire, of love/passion; the single conflict is deployed within a strict time frame and circumscribed place. Also, the mode of exposition of the situation, which is indeed "a morbid atmosphere with an erotic background"[26] is perfectly inorganic: the camera is resolutely static, the rituals (lanterns, foot massage, eating, and so on) occur and recur in their due time, the seasons following each other, the architecture standing staunchly symmetrical, reinforced by the stolid, archaic calligraphy.

The acting is also supremely theatrical. The words are few, terse, and untrustworthy. Silences are very heavy with no background music to alleviate them.[27] The main protagonist, Songlian (played by Gong Li), poses more than she speaks. At the very beginning of the film, she faces us while talking to her mother-in-law; throughout the film, she stands in front of the mirror or the camera but never looks at anyone.[28] All she does is to expose herself in a forceful way: she often holds a lantern, marking her body as an exhibitionistic site. As the husband says when he watches her hold a lantern, an educated woman is different indeed. There is no shame, or frivolity. It is the strange, ungazing look of the knowing beast, much like the bull in the corrida. After having fought till the end, after having (mis)calculated, after having instigated the death of two other women, and the mutilation of another, she is facing us again, absolutely withdrawn; as the tragic victim, she is now blinded by her madness. Abandoned by her father, she is a latter-day Oedipus — whose tragic flaw is arrogance;[29] and, because of that self-exposure, she is the scapegoat of ritual sacrifices as well.

Zhang Yimou's work appeals to both international and indigenous spectators precisely because he always operates within two compatible parameters, within local and global modes of representation that appear archetypal. The idea of the fetish is exploited to the full: it is both sign and object of totemic primitiveness, of specular sexual perversion, of import-export commodity, and it therefore becomes an archetypal signifier. Zhang's complex mode of fetishization [30] has its roots in the literary school aptly described as "roots-searching" 'xungen.'

The investigation of proper names

Anyone who can conceive of looking for roots,

should, already, you know, be growing rutabagas.

Gayatri Chakravorty Spivak, *Postmarked Calcutta, India*

The roots-searching school of literature fed the Fifth Generation filmmakers with fantastic images of colorful folk in the landscape. This movement of the mid-1980s was the first since 1949 to critically investigate Chineseness at its very roots, hence the designation "roots-searching." A sampling of fetishes at work in the novels of Mo Yan, Han Shaogong, Liu Heng, Su Tong, and A Cheng shows that the recurring root is in fact condensed in the figure of the animal. The positive is coded

Colorful Folk in the Landscape   105

as atavistic and anachronistic wilderness, which is pre- or nonlinguistic, violent, sensual, material, and also amoral, apolitical, and ahistorical. These are characteristics attributed by humans to animals, which of course include humans, all humans.

Instead of considering this collective tendency as the creation of a "new aboriginality"[31] and thereby remaining within the traditional anthropomorphic bias — which is then translated into an orientalist view if the culture it emerges from is "of the Orient"[32] — one can see it as reappraisal, readjustment of the human, from a nonhumanistic, nonanthropocentric point of view, just as one can in non-Chinese literary works from Kafka to Zaniewski.[33] That is, from an earthy point of view. Men and women don't become animals, they *are* animals (too).

This zoomorphic point of view reaches far into any civilization's roots. Liu Heng, author of "Fuxi Fuxi" (Judou), reexamines the Chinese way of naming by materializing the mythological, by turning the philosophical issue into a material affair, more precisely a sexual affair. Fuxi and Nüwa, the yin-yang archetypes of humanity, traditionally represented as man and woman, brother and sister with serpents' bodies, are turned into incestuous cave dwellers with reptilian behaviors. Although they have proper names — Yang Tianqing and (Wang) Judou — they are most of the time accounted for in generic terms of male/female. Still, the story — and the investigation around naming — revolves around the clan name, Yang, the ultimate "male" signifier. That name is progressively endowed with all possible male — animalistic — attributes, which can however be subsumed by its synecdoche, the cock. And that is the name under investigation.

In the 1940s, a peasant called Yang Jinshan buys a woman, Judou (Chrysanthemum Bud), with one *mu* of land for each of her twenty years of life. He wants a son to call his own, to pursue the family lineage, to worship the ancestors after him, and so on. Impotent, Yang cannot reap what he sows. His nephew, *Tian*qing, does it in his stead. Two boys are born, and are called by the clan *Tian*bai and *Tian*huang. This nominal ordering accords with their real father's generation and makes them not Tianqing's sons but his cousins. They are thus Jinshan's sons and so Tianqing remains a true bachelor where status is given by that name (*ming fu qi shi de guanggunr*) (153). Such is the custom where naming is believing.

Liu Heng's novel downgrades indifferently all males to their sexual organ, the "cock" becoming a totem for all clans (instead of the ancestor's stelae).[34] In a mock poetic flight, the narrator tells of little boys comparing their "tools" while urinating on flitting butterflies (169); he describes Tianqing at length after his suicide in a vat—it is an anatomic description, with emphasis on his "rag-like thing" and "turnip-like thing" (166–67). As the novel progresses, the penis 'jiba'—the image of the cock is the same in English and Chinese—is proclaimed the base of life 'ben,' 'benbenr.' Tianqing, having been revealed as a well-hung man, is now the talk of the town; children call his penis *benr benr* (168). That term resurfaces in a mock scientific postscript, "Wuguan yulu sanze: daiba jian dui yige mingci de kaozheng" (Three unrelated quotations: an investigation of a name in lieu of postscript) (170). The middle quotation tells a story, by a certain Wu You Wu (homonymic to "Without With-without"), who, while searching for a stele strays into the wilderness, and sees some huge grain growing. Intrigued, he asks a peasant woman how the grain came to grow to such an impressive size; to which she simply shrugs. Then he asks her the name of the plant: "The root of roots," she laconically states. Egging her for an explanation, she laughs and points with her hoe to Mr. Without's lower parts and then to her husband's. Mr. Without eventually understands and gives us a dictionary-like entry: "The base 'ben,' that is human being's fundament. The base 'ben,' that is also the root 'gen.' That's it, it's also the male root 'nangen'!" (170)[35]

Liu Heng's ironic equivalences are even funnier when placed beside the statement of the founder of the roots-searching school, Han Shaogong: "Literature has roots. The roots of literature must be deeply planted in the earth of national ['minzu'] traditional culture."[36] Roots-searching literature thus gives us upside-down totems, where the ancestors are groping creatures, incestuously copulating and inbreeding. Freud said that totems, which are generally animals, are considered the ancestors of a group for which they serve as protector and benefactor. But totems come with taboos, for instance, the taboo against incest among those under the same totem and therefore with the same name.

Freud added that names for primitives ("savages") are "an essential part of man's personality and as an important possession they treat words in every sense as things . . . our own children do the same."[37] Han Shaogong, the spokesperson for the roots-searching school, seems to have turned this thesis upside down. He illustrated his view of Chinese "roots" with a novella entitled "Bababa" (Dadadad) (1986).[38] In it, he created a protagonist that is some kind of generic creature: "Critter" is fatherless, born of a woman who is a midwife; he has only a first name, which is not a person's name but a derogatory nickname: Bingzai (Critter). The creature's status is unsure: villagers oscillate between considering him an animal or a god-sent medium. Critter has what humans, even his mother, consider to be a nonhuman appearance and behavior. Waif-like, with a huge head limply hanging from a soft neck, unkempt, with snot and food running down his face and shit on his ass, Critter can only utter two words or rather two sounds: "Ba-Ba-Ba" (Dadadad) and "X-Ma-Ma" (Your Mother's) and spurts them out regardless of the person's sex, age, relation to him, or context. In between the atavistic wars that two villages—tellingly named Head of the Cock and Tail of the Cock—wage against each other, it is decided that a scapegoat is needed, and Critter is chosen. In bad need of some direction to win the war, one village turns Critter into an oracle. Critter is indifferent to the consequences, goes along with them, much like one of the dogs, "their hearts full of hope on the trail of human shadows . . . of chancing upon a human corpse . . . [which] they would tear up, chew, and gnaw on the bones till they splintered" (30). Critter ends up, matter-of-factly, a man-eater; and also a necrophiliac and possibly a motherfucker. Upon bumping into a dead woman—who looks like his mother (33)—he first sucks her fleshy breasts but to no avail, then mounts her and, before falling asleep beside her, says: "Daad" (33).

Han Shaogong's bizarre novella presents a character who incarnates both totem and taboo. In other words, he is not a character but a textual fetish. The novel presents itself as an ethnographic exposition, rendered by an intellectual narrator who "dares not give his public the dirtier lines of ditties" (7) and who, unlike Liu Heng's narrator, is totally devoid of humor. Han has said that his novels cannot be adapted into films.[39] The reason for this intransitivity could lie in Han's intellectual commitment to portray archetypal primitiveness. This novella of his, and his following one, "Nününü" (Woman woman woman) (1986),[40] where the woman in question is an old aunt locked in a cage whose defecations no one wants to pick up, are accounts reminiscent of May Fourth intellectualist depictions of "little people" (Lu Xun's Ah Q, Ba Jin's Dog, etc.). Han's roots-searching works seem to me to be highly pedagogical. In "Dadadad," the narrator—who acts like an informant from within a realist convention most of the time, says that "the stones were like lenses that had taken thousands of photos that would never be developed" (39). Somehow Han's illustration of Chinese ways connects with documentaries such as *Heshang* (Deathsong of a River), which strive to investigate with a clear head Chinese symbols.

A Cheng, who has also been associated with the roots-searching school, remarked that the movement was not initiated by writers of peasant backgrounds (such as Jia Pingwa) but by young intellectuals (like himself, and Han).[41] It may well be that roots-searching as a willed commitment surged from young urban intellectuals such as the Beijingers A Cheng and Shi Tiesheng,[42] or from Han Shaogong, from Changsha. But the earthy descriptions, those novels with a sense of smell (with a flair), do spring from peasant-background writers such as Liu Heng (from Hongshuiyu, Hebei), Mo Yan (Gaomi, Shandong), and Jia Pingwa (Danfeng, Shaanxi).

Mo Yan's *Hong gaoliang jiazu (The Red Sorghum Clan)* also makes the demarcation line between humans and other animals very tenuous, but his mode of exposition is, one could say, performative. Mo's five-part novel gives as much space and energy and feelings to dogs as to humans. For example, the humans may be the main protagonists in part 1, "Hong gaoliang" (Red sorghum), but the dogs have the lead in part 3, "Goudao" (Dog ways).[43] Humans and animals, both species, are on a par in this earthy story, where all senses converge in an unearthly partaking of love, revenge, and other fiery passions. *The Red Sorghum Clan* is structured archetypally. The novel endows the dogs, as well as the earth and the red sorghum, with the special power of the fetish. Significantly, the novel ends with an imagined exhortation to the narrator by his second grandmother, who tells him that the stalk of red sorghum is his "talisman [protection: 'hushenfu'], our clan's glorious totem ['tuteng'] and a symbol ['xiangzheng'] of the traditional spirit of Northeast Gaomi Township."[44] It confirms my reading of the novel as a phantasmatic construction of the past as earth that fed and bred its inhabitants, human, vegetable, and animal alike, so that their fate and behavior are interlocked and largely indistinguishable. Performatively, Mo Yan uses the same terms to speak of all orders of life.

The narrator, a contemporary figure who lives in the city, is alien to that earthy way of life yet fascinated by it. He conceives the past, that earth, in fetishistic, reified ways. Consequently, his unfolding of the story dramatizes the space and turns it into a tale of transgression and fantasy. If "[a] fetish is a story masquerading as an object,"[45] and a story a fetishization of an object, then his narration play-acts at two levels: his own obsessions and taboos and his clan's magic powers, both circumscribed in concrete images of humanimal behavior. Throughout the novel, the narrator demeans himself: he is a "shriveled insect" (132); he is a "homeless stray [dog]" (169); his feelings are "a pale desert" (272) and his smell and look are those of "a pet rabbit" (357). Not so for his clan—dogs and humans—who have powerful earthy smells, precisely because they feed off the land. Grandmother, on her deathbed—the sorghum field, again—smells of sorghum wine (65); the dogs, after eating human corpses, were "passing dark-brown canine farts . . . the odor of the turds and farts different from any . . . ever smelled" (211). The land is the matrix in which they plant their sorghum, which then yields food (cereal) and drink (wine). In turn, their defecations, love-making, and decaying in the fields, the urinating in the wine and disinfecting with the wine, all combine to make the earth fertile and its creatures strong. They are what they eat. Dogs eat men, and men eat dogs that eat men that eat dogmeat: "Having fed on human corpses, the dogs were strong and husky; eating a winter's supply of fatty dog meat was, for Father, the same as eating a winter's supply of human flesh. Later he would grow into a tall, husky man" (271). The narrator can only symbolically offer his heart to eat in the epigraph: "As your unfilial son, I am prepared to carve out my heart, marinate it in soy sauce, have it minced and placed in three bowls; and lay it out as an offering in a field of sorghum. Partake of it in good health!" The novel performs the sacrificial rite and points at its (content's) facticity.

This textual bluff is consistent throughout the novel. Although occasionally the narrator tells us he is fabricating ("Father never knew how many sexual comedies my grandmother had performed on this dirt path, but I know" (6);[46] "Father was too young then to describe the sight in such flowery terms—that's my doing" (24). Still, he is telling us a genealogically impossible tale, and what is more, he tells it as if he were really there, smelling, seeing, feeling. Indeed, the novel operates by excessively sensory descriptions, such as: "A year later, the bloated carcasses of dozens of mules had been found floating in the Black Water River, caught in the reeds and grass in the shallow water by the banks; their distended bellies, baked by the sun, split and popped, released their splendid innards, like gorgeous blooming flowers, as slowly spreading pools of dark-green liquid were caught up in the flow of water" (39).

The world created by Mo Yan is a mass of details uncannily combined, synesthetically held together: testicles cut off (by a Japanese running dog) or bitten off (by the family dog), red ants crawling into Grandma's decayed eye sockets, her feet like goldfish in a bowl, vomited eggs and the bullet-like flies inside the jolted wedding sedan chair. The images' primitiveness and picturesqueness accentuate the fictionality of the account, while their vivid concreteness (their "finish") [47] mesmerizes, placing both author and reader in the ambivalent split position of knowing, on one plane, and believing, on the other.

Mo Yan has said that "literature without imagination [wild association] is like a dog who has been ablated of one brain hemisphere . . . a wasted dog." [48] If dogs are part and parcel of Mo Yan's discourse, they are also the privileged image in Su Tong's novels about women. But for Su Tong, an urban and a younger writer than Mo Yan, the dog is dependent on man, and so are the women. Two of his "women's novels" have been adapted to the screen: "Wives and Concubines" (Qi qie cheng qun) as *Raise the Red Lantern* [49] by Zhang Yimou, and "Hongfen" (Rouge) [50] by Li Shaohong. Both novels tell stories of women who cannot live without men and who cannot understand themselves. (That is the hard anthropocentrist's point of view on animals.) They, Qiuyi and Xiao'e in "Rouge," and the four wives in "Wives and Concubines," are willful representations of male fantasies. In "Rouge," Xiao'e elopes with a man and leaves her child behind; she says, "I can't help it. . . . I understand everything, but I can't understand what kind of thing I am ['ziji shi zenme hui shi']" (43–44). In "Wives and Concubines," Songlian, now quite versed in in-house fighting, reflects to herself: "Women are so strange; a woman can understand other people perfectly, but can never completely understand herself" (77).

Colorful Folk in the Landscape   111

Su Tong, in a postscript, "Zenme huishi" (What's this all about), writes concerning his "women's novels": "I picked up old [-fashioned] clothes, and put them on the bodies of characters. . . . I like to structure my novels with women . . . perhaps because one has more interest to them, perhaps because I find that women's bodies are better condensations of novelistic material."[51] One could say that, in the above novels, women are abstractions and concretizations of the animalistic, at least. They are to be used and disposed of at will. In "Rouge," Qiuyi rashly describes her own lot: "I'm the only slab of meat left; who knows on which cutting-board I'll end up" (37–38). In "Wives and Concubines," the most frequent derogatory term for women is "bitch" 'gouniang,' which women also use to curse each other, when they are not thinking of cutting out each other's hearts to feed them to the dogs. Songlian, upon choosing to become a rich concubine rather than a poor wife, discusses her own case: "What is status? Is status something people like me can be concerned about?" (19–20). She always describes herself, and "woman," in the negative. "But I just don't understand what women amount to anyway; what sort of creatures are women? We're just like dogs, cats, goldfish, rats. . . . We're just like anything, anything except human beings" (58). She allies with no one, including animals. Once, she even kicks a cat because it was licking its own ass (25). Indeed, Songlian is never even quite a dog, cannot play up to a dog-act. In one instance, the master, unable to have an erection, asks her to perform some special sexual trick for him. She complains, "Wouldn't I be just like a dog then?" (70). In another instance, she is inebriated and attempts to seduce him into sleeping with her but is rejected with these uncomely words: "How could I love you in this state? I'd be better off loving a dog" (91).

Su Tong's women are carousel animals or stuffed dolls that one pricks, like the voodoo doll in "Wives and Concubines," so that they become dogs or ghosts, or anything hollowed out. It is no wonder that the women are made to say that they cannot understand themselves: they are pure sex tokens, perennially surrogates of each other, fetishes to be feared and idolized. In both of the novels, men say they are at their mercy. In "Rouge," Laopu says to the first woman, "Qiuyi, I just see you and I lose my mind. You've robbed me of my soul" (9); to the second woman, "Xiao'e, you can really ensnare people: I can't tear away from you" (26). As for the husband with four wives, and other women on the side, he explains his skinniness by being "worn out" 'taode' by women (17). That is the same spirit as the Ming dynasty erotic novel *Jin Ping Mei (The Golden Lotus)* whose male protagonist expires from an excessive withdrawal of yang. As Lü Tonglin notes, women in Su Tong's novels are "contagious," "infect the men," "contaminate" their order.[52]

Su Tong's "Wives and Concubines" does recreate some of the overwhelming sexual atmosphere of the *Jin Ping Mei*. The intrigues between the female contestants move in the latter's shadow; even Songlian's name echoes the classic prototype, Jinlian (Golden Lotus). What is more, Su's novels, regardless of the female point of view, are likewise absolutely male-centered. Yet this is contemporary China, and Su is experimenting with textual archetypal images of femininity, impregnated by *yin* (shadows, wells, ghosts), which he drapes in the roots-searching idiom of bestiality. Hence his women, like animals, become radically different from men, become men's indifferent radical other.[53]

Butterflies gone wild

Quoth the Raven, "Nevermore."

Edgar Allan Poe

Another writer who uses *Jin Ping Mei* as his novel's "root" takes it in a completely different direction. He is the peasant-born, roots-searching author Jia Pingwa. In the 1980s, Jia wrote stories about macho men, and pure women.[54] Now Jia claims that his recent novel *Feidu (Wasted Capital)* (1993) almost wiped him out 'ba wo shaohui'.[55] This *Wasted Capital* is not only a postmodern literary experiment but a serious jab at malehood and especially at male writers of his kind. With this novel, one could say that if roots-searching was a "masculinist ode to life," then it has gone full circle. In *Wasted Capital,* the primary target is a contemporary Chinese, a man who is a writer. His name is Zhuang Zhidie, literally "Zhuang's Butterfly." In the novel, all names can be explained onomastically, especially the main protagonist's: it is a direct allusion to the sage-philosopher Zhuangzi's most famous anecdote, a man (Zhuang Zhou) who dreams he is a butterfly 'die' and who, once awakened, can't figure out who is who (what is what), butterfly or man, dreamer or dreamt. Zhuang Zhidie, Jia Pingwa's protagonist, often bemoans that fact, especially as concerns his appearance and being: he is a famous writer, celebrated and recognized, but he doesn't write and feels he is a sham 'wei' (351). Throughout the (very long) novel, Zhuang Zhidie fools around: he has several trysts, eats and drinks a lot, hangs out with his buddies, and writes occasional words for the mayor of the "Wasted Capital" (Xi'an) and for advertisers, in exchange of money or favors.

If Su Tong reconstructs the morbid, "feudal" atmosphere of sexuality reminiscent of *Jin Ping Mei,* Jia on the other hand used the structure of the classical novel. *Wasted Capital* starts with the typically classical, myth-making introduction: miracles with strange plants, the sudden appearance of four suns, and unnamed and seemingly irrelevant characters alluding to the cyclicity, the predetermined and recurrent events of life. Yet, the first words are: "In the year one thousand nine hundred and eighty" (1). Such a mingling of classical devices and contemporary references constitute the rhythm and allure of Jia's novel. Classical poems, divinatory sentences, Buddhist chants, people's almanacs, local operas, popular folksongs side with commercial ads, grocery lists, ditties of social relevance, and local 1990s slang. Much like poetry in classical novels, they interrupt the main storyline which is about Zhuang Zhidie's plight. (There are no such "boring" things in Su Tong's novels: the women, for example, don't just sit there, drink endless cups of tea, and compose poems, or have a contest in proverb-making!) In *Wasted Capital,* however, women compare themselves to famous historical concubines and play word games, when they are not shopping for elaborately described voguish outfits or the best alcohols and gourmet treats available.

In terms of its erotic content, the comparison with the classical *Jin Ping Mei* is more of a marketing ploy[56] since Jia's novel has few sex scenes and those are mainly suggested, when not simply deleted.[57] Still, one sex scene deliberately refers to one of the most famous sexual exploits in *Jin Ping Mei,* the playful "plums-in-the-vagina" scene of chapter 27. Zhuang Zhidie, AKA modern-day Ximen Qing, inserts a plum in one of his playgirls, Liu Yue (Moon Willow), to the delight of both (335). In fact, the sex scenes in *Wasted Capital* are more like bravado gestures.

For example, Zhuang's first adulterous affair, with Tang Wan'er (whose gracious name points to the homonym "Plaything of the Tang dynasty") is a pure phantasmic translation of the Tang dynasty's most famous concubine, Yang Guifei, through Tang dynasty poems, into a contemporary depiction. The reader witnesses Zhuang's graphic and gradual striptease of the woman. He directs the reader's attention toward her shoes, her beauty spots, her panties, and so on (84–85). Tang Wan'er is offered in fetishized fragments that point to literary sources and to contemporary fashions. Another sex scene, with A Can, is even more deliberately textual. Sex with A Can, (the familiar diminutive "A" combined with the sunny brilliance of "Can") is a combination of animalistic, historical, and "Western" positions. First, she falls onto him like "a butterfly." Then "they not only went through all the descriptive language ['yuyan'] of the old classical books, but also spoke them out. . . . All the acts they had seen in the foreign videos, and those they had read about people of bygone days in the classic *Sunüjing*,[58] and even the ways of the wolves, insects, tigers and leopards, and those of the pigs, dogs, cows and sheep, they tried them all out; once done, they concocted new ones, attaining together orgasm much at the same time." Then, A Can and Zhuang Zhidie lie there "like fish on a bank" (303). And little details like her removing a hair from his lip spice the account even further.

Pubic hair, beauty spots, lipstick all operate as nomadic tell-tale signs of sexual intercourse, and the bearers, the women, too. Another mate, Liu Yue (Willow Moon) has no pubic hair; Tang Wan'er, the favorite "concubine," sends her plucked pubic hair and lipstick smears on a love note, by way of a pigeon; Zhuang's wife, Niu Yueqing, cooks up the pigeon for the lovers to eat. Only Niu Yueqing is not parceled out. Her name can be translated as Lunar 'Yue' Purity 'Qing' of the Bovine 'Niu.' That link to the animal kingdom is a positive sign in *Wasted Capital*, especially the reference to the bovine species. The "butterfly" protagonist, Zhuang Zhidie, is himself a close friend of a cow, whom he regards as the highest species, as philosophers whose ruminations are of a different order from man's straightforward thinking: "A bovine's ruminations are a kind of thought, but they are also different from man's thinking process, because the bovine can go back in time and space; it can, in a diffuse way, resurrect ['chongxian'] archaic images ['tuxiang']" (140). In the novel, the cow is Zhuang's, and his author's, alter ego and memory.

The narrator tells us: "People say that dogs are sensitive, cats too, but in fact bovines understand humans best" (55). Zhuang declares: "We are linked, the cow and me, by a predestined affinity" (136). Intermittently but regularly enough, Zhuang drinks directly from the cow's teats. That same cow offers us her worldview, in interior monologue form: human beings are pitiful creatures whose only real difference from other animal species is that they live inside cities (142); humans are one grade below bovines, in the reincarnation process (55–56).

Zhuang Zhidie's very first appearance is with the cow, as one unit, since he is drinking from its teats. He is described as short, with a pot belly, wearing long, disheveled hair and a T-shirt that advertises "Hans Beer" in the front and "Beer Hans" in the back. The portrait becomes even less flattering and funnier when one learns that this ladies' man drives a ladies' Mulan moped (so named after the Chinese Joan of Arc). All depictions give a mocking view by juxtaposing the serious urbane writer of "feminist novels" (137) who attracts stylish and sometimes quite sophisticated women with the country bumpkin who is impotent with his wife. Zhuang, who is originally from the countryside, like Jia the author, forever asks himself whether he is still Zhuang Zhidie. He is ceaselessly belittling himself, wanting to make amends, to stop being a degenerate, a fake (30, 63, 108). His point of view, all considered, is like the cow's: life in the city is good for humans, but it wastes good animals; humankind is a lower species than bovines or even crickets (308). As befits this intimate relationship of theirs, when the cow, a central protagonist, dies near the end of the novel, Zhuang requests her skin and tail, which he hangs in his stylish living room instead of a calligraphy. Now he has truly turned the animal into a totem.

After having made much use of his "root of the dusty world" 'chen gen' (32), after the death of his cow (and the women's various unfortunate disappearances), Zhuang is truly left with nothing but his name. He is found inebriated on the road, with a dog licking vomit off his face (507). Shortly after, he decides to leave the city and the novel. What is left? A bosom friend, Zhou Min, whom he meets by chance. The reader now understands the very beginning of the novel: the two unnamed friends are Zhuang and this Zhou, and that they are in fact the same person. The name of the confused dreamer in Zhuangzi's butterfly story is none other than Zhuang Zhou. This adds an ultimate ironic twist to the story. Zhou Min, originally from the same town as Zhuang Zhidie, provoked the main storyline of *Wasted Capital*, a court affair, and also was cuckolded by Zhuang himself. And Zhou plays the melancholic ocarina on the city walls. The flute, definitely a phallic symbol, enigmatically closes the novel. In the train station, our hero expires, holding that very flute. *Wasted Capital* is thus a bitter if not ironic celebration of male identity, oscillating between a "prick" and an animal. "I often find myself in a position where I can't tell reality from illusion," admits author Jia, thereby clearly associating himself with his character's dilemma and the philosophical tale (526). For both writers, real Jia and illusory Zhuang, the main question is whether or not they have become totally degenerate, in a consumer society that offers brain-stimulating hats, magic chest enhancers, venereal-disease-preventing underwear, and opium balls in your soup. It would seem that "serious" roots-searching is no longer viable in the 1990s, Zhuang never writing anything but for-profit prose and Jia making big bucks with his best-seller, *Wasted Capital.*[59] Being close to cattle is passé.

It is said that Jia wanted his *Wasted Capital* to be "a real life portrayal of the Chinese at the end of the century."[60] If that is so, then the butterfly has won: well-grounded and solid convictions, invested in cattle, give way to ephemeral, flighty whims. The butterfly is also the quintessential symbol of cultural miscegenation, at least between Orient and Occident. To reuse a butterfly motif in Chinese cultural production today is to cross indigenous Zhuangzi with European Puccini. This grafts a philosophical question on the real with a sexually phrased stereotype of Asians (in this case, the Chinese). The hybrid lepidopteran born of this union is an "Asian butterfly," neither "Chinese" nor "woman."

One noteworthy recent configuration of the Asian butterfly can be traced to Bernardo Bertolucci's *The Last Emperor*. When little Pu Yi grieves on the departure of his nanny, he whimpers: "She wasn't my nanny; she was my butterfly." That woman caring for the child emperor is thus not reified—a simple servant serving a definite purpose—but symbolized both as a beautiful creature in his possession and as a protective shield, keeping him under the wings of her silky costumes. This line was added on the spur of the moment, by Bertolucci himself.[61] When older Pu Yi takes a wife, Wan Rong (Joan Chen), she smothers him with "butterfly kisses" (163). Both the act of covering the young

man's face everywhere with her very red-hot lipstick and the end result of the process — the butterfly traces — combine here to associate the
butterfly with seduction (its suctorial mouth, flittiness, and makeup).
Moreover, the overall texture of the film is that of a dream (excluding
most of the postimperial epoch). The emperor and his entourage's life
seems to be that of Zhuangzi's Zhuang Zhou butterfly; they are living
an "unreal" life in an ivory tower, the Forbidden City. In his diary on
the making of the film, Fabien Gérard constantly alludes to the whole
enterprise as that of a dream. "But the dream goes on . . . like Victor
Segalen's *René Leys,* perhaps one of the most perfect novels ever written
on the last days of the Purple Forbidden City" (82).

That Victor Segalen's name should pop up when discussing a European film on a splendid, imperial China on the verge of disappearing
is unsurprising. Segalen's novel (written in Beijing, in the 1910s), takes
place during the fall of the Qing empire and recounts the period through
a European relationship. An older Frenchman who fantasizes on Chinese imperial secrets becomes totally mesmerized by a young Belgian
man, fluent in Chinese and versed in Chinese ways, who has his entries
(both public and private) into the Forbidden City. *René Leys* is thus
an account of imperial China, from the inside, and also, in a resolutely ironical way, from the outside. As for Bertolucci, he was the first
filmmaker (including the Chinese) to shoot within the bounds of the
imperial city. Still, it is also very much a non-Chinese product, a Hollywoodian rendition of " 'China' served on screen . . . for vicarious
tourists." [62]

The Last Emperor is also an updated *Madama Butterfly* story. Gina
Marchetti has noted the interest of Hollywood since 1915 in the theme
of miscegenation, where stories like that of Madama Butterfly rever-
berate and are its most common expression.[63] Bertolucci's film offers
a more complicated twist to the theme. First, the butterflies are many:
the emperor himself at different stages of his life, the nursemaid, the
ravishingly beautiful Wan Rong devouring orchids. Second, miscegenation occurs in all aspects of the making of the film: on the linguistic
level, where dialogue coaches "tried to find a particular accent, at the
crossroads between Beijing English and Chinatown's, a kind of midroad
tone, undefinable, which would only belong to *The Last Emperor*" (12);
in the costumes, "the general line [of which] had to evoke the esthetic of

Ming as well as Qing dynasty. As if all the heritage of old China could be deployed in front of us . . . the specter of Turandot . . . without Puccini" (28); in the sets, where the imperial scenes were shot inside the Forbidden City but the Shanghai casino scenes in Italy (151); in the music sound track, on which Japanese and British musicians collaborated; and finally with the actors, the most formidable mixture of "Asian types," mixed together: Hong Kong–born but American-raised John Lone, Korean-origin ("best U.S. legs") Maggie Han, Mao look-alike Ric Young from London, and last but not least, Chinese mainlanders such as filmmakers Ning Ying (a very small part), Chen Kaige (as captain of the imperial guard), and the cultural official, Ying Ruocheng (as Pu Yi's detainer).[64]

The very successful film, filled to the hilt with all manner of trompe-l'oeil effects, led, in my opinion, Chinese film people such as Chen Kaige, to pursue the Asian butterfly. Chen's *Bawang bieji (Farewell My Concubine)*, which did win immense international recognition, by being awarded the Palme d'or in Cannes in 1993, is another butterfly story. The very name of the protagonist is Butterfly Attire (Dieyi). Cheng Dieyi is an opera actor who incarnates female 'dan' roles on stage with his life-long opera partner, Duan Xiaolou. Their most famous piece together is used for the title of the film, which is an adaptation of a Hong Kong novel by the popular female writer Lilian Lee (Li Bihua). Dieyi, like Pu Yi—and like all butterfly figures since Puccini's adaptation of Pierre Loti's 1887 novel, *Madame Chrysanthème*—has a tragic fate. Dieyi cannot draw the line between art and life; much like Pu Yi, he becomes a puppet for the Japanese (and the Guomindang). Dressed in his operatic costume, Dieyi (Leslie Cheung) does look like a butterfly: finely embroidered phoenixes and butterflies adorn the silky fabric, similar decorations are attached to hairpieces on his wig, and of course he wears heavy makeup, especially of the eyes. When he performs onstage, his body traces graceful patterns, not unlike a butterfly's flight. As a child, Dieyi (then called Douzi) had become sexually disoriented: he was made to sing the lines, "In reality, I am a girl," and only succeeded after sadistic maltreatment. Dieyi's allure and props are shared with the former prostitute Juxian (Gong Li), the wife of his partner, Xiaolou. The scene where Juxian jumps from a third floor into Xiaolou's arms is, again, highly evocative of the butterfly's flight, the filmy fabric of her robes spreading and swirling in the air. Dieyi and Juxian, competing for Xiaolou's attention, evoke other aspects of the butterfly, with their vampiric, smothering costumes (black capes). At the end of the film, the grotesquely made-up Xiaolou becomes a butterfly figure: under duress during the Cultural Revolution, when he confuses public and private and betrays his wife, Juxian; in the last scene, while Dieyi plays out his dream-life and so dies, Xiaolou play-acts, as if life went on.

Butterflies are most of the time suicidal figures. Juxian hangs herself; Dieyi consumes opium and eventually dies from his own sword—pinned down, one could say. Butterflies are the sign of short-lived good times and of tragic endings. By their transience and ephemerality, they are scapegoats for other living species.[65] In Chen Kaige's *Farewell My Concubine,* the butterfly figure is endowed/bogged down with an amalgam of such European associations as prostitution versus selfless love and homosexuality and exoticism with the specific references of Chinese opera, Chinese makeup, Chinese clothing, and China red (from eye makeup to silk cloth). Chen has created a European-Chinese style of the exotic Asian Butterfly. And superimposed on all this is the indigenous meaning of butterfly as a ghostly, ambivalent state of being. In this sense, his film is not only comparable to Bertolucci's *Last Emperor,* but also to Hongkong productions such as *Yanzhikou (Rouge)* by Stanley Kwan (Guan Jinpeng) and Cheng Xiaodong's *Chinese Ghost Stories (Qiannü youhun, Renjian dao, Qiannü youhun zhi daodaodao).* Ultimately, such films are splendid nostalgia films, proffering redundantly an enigmatic "nevermore."

The riddle to solve has to do with Chinese civilization, with its five-thousand-year history and cultural sophistication. A kite in the form of a butterfly constitutes the visual leitmotiv of another Fifth-Generation filmmaker's work, Tian Zhuangzhuang's *Lan fengzheng (The Blue Kite)* (1993). *The Blue Kite* recounts China's recent history through the perspective of a little boy, Shitou (who is Tian's age), from his birth to the chaotic 1960s. No one ever plays with the kite, which, very early in the film, is caught in a tree branch. As traumatic historical events unfold, the kite becomes more and more weather-beaten. The last shot of the film—when Shitou, who has been trying to defend his mother from the red guard assailants, is beaten up and lying on the ground—is aimed at the tree branch: the blue butterfly's cadaverous shreds hang there limply. It is the sole undiegetic element of the film, which is a chronological, no-fuss account of recent history. Many other things can be seen hanging, but they are all motivated. For example, the numerous portraits and paraphernalia of Mao adorning both public and private spaces; and the paper strips with political slogans that people have to carefully brush aside in order to go by. Shitou's mother is very distraught when the little boy in her arms starts reaching for them and crumpling them up. All the other "decorations," apart from the butterfly, are imposed by the times and not to be tampered with. As in *Farewell My Concubine*, *The Blue Kite* contrasts Chinese "civilization," through its cultural artifact, the butterfly, with Chinese realpolitik, with its climax in the Cultural Revolution. The butterfly becomes a lifeless, inanimate figure, foreclosing projections of a tomorrow.

Anyone, Chinese and non-Chinese, can somehow understand the "meaning" of the butterfly. It constitutes the mediation between cultures and operates in different spaces: it holds the melodramatic potential of these films. The blueness of Tian's kite harks back to romantic European fashionings of nostalgia of the "fleur bleue" type while alluding to past Chinese grandeur. Tian's former films, for example *Daomazei (Horse Thief)* and *Liechang zhasa (On the Hunting Ground)* (1984) also featured nonhuman creatures, but as their titles indicate, they were of the "roots-searching" type: earthy beasts of burden, with which an urban crowd, let alone international viewers, could hardly empathize. Indeed, Tian's first films were shot, like Chen Kaige's and Zhang Yimou's, in faraway, rural lands, in Tian's case in Tibet and Mongolia. In *On the Hunting Ground* the spectator even witnesses an on-screen killing of animals! It is not surprising then, given the "Western" sensitivity to animals, that his first films never obtained any inkling of recognition but that *The Blue Kite* won everyone's heart. A little boy, a young mother, the Chinese people: all beautiful butterflies, constantly pinned down.

More examples could be given to show the multivalent use of aerial motifs (especially that of the butterfly) in 1990s Chinese films, where historical sagas have prevailed. Even Tian and Chen's respective *Da taijian, Li Lianying (The Imperial Eunuch)* and *Bianzou bianchang (Life on a String)* follow this pattern. Eunuchs, much like concubines, are insubstantial, ethereal creatures not bogged down by earthiness (by "world-of-dust" roots) and are eminently identifiable as "Chinese"; similarly, the blind musicians of *Life on a String* are otherworldly thanks to their craft, which stops wars. Note that the younger musician carries on his back a kite, a vividly bright butterfly with huge eyes. The majesty of Chinese culture is presented in riddles, which can now be more or less deciphered anywhere. There are no longer indigenous hieroglyphs such as "ox + urine," decipherable only by native readers. Today, the riddles cross cultural boundaries. Chen Kaige's subsequent film, *Fengyue* (*Temptress Moon*), went far beyond the limits to overstate Chinese butterfly-like qualities: too much opium, too many veils and flowers, too many batpeople, and mummified artifacts. One can say that *Temptress Moon* is a fetishized version of the "China-Asia" fetish build-up.

In this sense, Zhang Yimou's recent works fare better because Zhang is constantly changing genres, and rewriting "the enigma" of China. *Huozhe* (*To Live*) (1994) is a successful full-fledged melodrama that elicits tears, sobs, and belly laughter from the audience. *To Live* is a film on living, on surviving through different political periods, regardless of the time. Two elements contribute to the noble albeit animalistic portrayal of the endurance of the Chinese people: the art of shadow puppets and the telling of animal evolution stories. Again, Zhang has chosen specifically Chinese signifiers to tell the story. The set of puppets is his addition to Yu Hua's novel of the same name,[66] just as the lantern and foot massage rituals in *Raise the Red Lantern* were not in Su Tong's novel. These frail, leather silhouettes that flicker behind a screen, in performances of feudal bandits, courtesans, and heroic historical figures, help the protagonist, Fugui, live through the 1930s right up to the Cultural Revolution. As in his (male) generational peers' films, it is in the Cultural Revolution that the "nevermore" riddle takes on its full force and ambivalence. But Zhang adds a twist that none of his Fifth-Generation peers have thought of: art is magic and art, as both artifice and artifact, can be transformed into yet something else, which is also magical.

In *To Live*, the puppets have been destroyed by fire, but their box is recycled as a nest for little chicks, and therefore also a treasure chest for the grandson who plays with them. The box can be read as many things, depending on its content and on its beholder/viewer.[67] The same is true of the other butterfly strand of the film: the metamorphosis story that Fugui, on and off, tells: "When the chicks grow up, they'll turn into ducks; when the ducks grow up, they'll turn into sheep; when the sheep grow big, they'll turn into oxen." This is much like a fairy tale for children—anything in the animal and human kingdom can happen, as in Alice's Wonderland. Of course it is also a cautionary tale of hope for the adults, who see the use and not the magic in animals. Animal husbandry will eventually bring on larger profit; eating animals and eating off their labor, children will grow up and turn into strong adults; they will ride not only bicycles, but eventually trains, and airplanes. The animal story is also a spoof—or a Chinese version—of the sphinx's riddle about humanity, where both animals and means of transportation are the clues. There are not so many possible readings of the animal story in Yu Hua's novel. It is a zoomorphized tale of the Chinese family, where the end line is the beginning line; that is, the ancestors whose stand-ins are the oxen (11). One ox has a main role. Also called Fugui (Fortunate), it is absolutely Fugui's double or half (41), has the same old, wretched body (20) and is treated by the man as another human. Unlike the film, at the end of the novel, all the relatives have died—by melodramatic coincidences—except for the two Fuguis, the totemic oxen: the wife, children, even the grandchild who (significantly) is not called, as in the film, with a food name Mantou (Steamed Bun) but has an earthy name, Kugen (Bitter Root). Thus, in novelistic form, earthy, indigenous creatures can still be found suturing past and present, country and city. In film form, they have gradually been supplanted by moving, aerial creatures and endowed with polyvalent uses and meanings.

In conclusion, a word about inversions and conversions. Zhang Yimou's *Yaoayao, yao dao waipoqiao (Shanghai Triad)* (1995) closes with an upside-down scene of a countryscape. It is the perspective of a country boy, Shuisheng, who is hanging upside down. The inverted landscape we see happens to be a lonely island where the triad's leader and his gang have escaped and which they are about to leave to return to the big city. This strange shot can of course be read as a visualization of the country versus city life, the latter corrupting and converting the former, the latter being adulthood, the former, youth. But it can also turn both worlds, much like the animal and human world, into connecting rather than opposing modes. In Wong Kar-wai's last film, *Chunguang zhaxie (Happy Together)* (1997), a very similar inversion shot is introduced, also near the end of the film. It is accompanied by the reflection of protagonist Lai Yiu-fai (Tony Leung) on the contiguity of cities/nations.

11. Scene from Zhang Yimou's *Turandot*, 1997.
Photograph courtesy of Gao Guangjian.

After breaking up with his butterfly lover (Leslie Cheung), who has run away with some "white trash," he tries to feel, from his vantage point in Buenos Aires at night, what it's like, right at that moment in Hong Kong, in an opposite time zone and different continent, while the camera shows us inverted highways at the top of the screen. This projection in time and space requires an effort from both actor and viewer, wherever the latter may be, in Hong Kong or Paris, Buenos Aires or New York.

Reading films made by Chinese nationals cannot be strictly nation-oriented. It was perhaps true that the initial Fifth-Generation works were "inconceivable without their relationship to the nation." [68] Even the nation-space of the roots-searching literature unfolds today, as Gang Yue put it, into (at least) "double time": "one immediate, modern and foreign; the other mystical, ancient, and native." [69] Moreover, it is true that Fifth-Generation and roots-searching works are not authentic investigations into Chinese history, an accusation so often heard and read that no footnote could detail all the instances. I have also grown weary of the feminine-versus-masculine axis used to analyze Chinese cultural production. To elaborate on Kaja Silverman's assertion, I would just say that 'male' and 'female' constitute a dominant fiction in Chinese cultural criticism."[70]

I also find that antiorientalist critiques remain within staunch cultural binaries. Hence, I certainly would not agree that the Chinese filmmakers opted for orientalist subjects in the 1990s and that "the 'orientalist' path is not a choice for many Chinese filmmakers, but a step they have to take in order to deal with the reality of their home country in the 1990s."[71] How can such a view encompass Chinese Westerns of the 1990s, such as Zhang Yimou's magnificent documentary-like *Qiuju da guansi (Qiuju, a Chinese Woman)* (1993), or He Ping's hilarious *Shuangqizhen daoke (The Double-Flag Swordsman)* (1991), box-office successes both in China and internationally? Or again how can one account for Fifth-Generation Zhang Jianya's parodies of former Chinese movies, including Zhang Yimou's, in *Wang xiansheng zhi yuhuo fenshen (Mr. Wang's Burning Flame)*?

The message is miscegenation. Some experiments may abort, some not. The most intriguing production lately was realized by Zhang Yimou, who remains the best representative of his generation. It is a staging of an opera, a production of *Turandot* that he directed in 1997 in Italy and staged again in the fall of 1998, in the Forbidden City. No opera is more unsuited for a Chinese national than Puccini's *Turandot*, with its portrayal of China as cannibalistic, sadistic, and incapable of love. The ineptitude, let alone the outrageous inaccuracies, proffered in this lyrical drama set in "Peking, China, in legendary times"[72] are mind-boggling. The three court sages, Ping, Pang, and Pong, sure of their civilization, which has endured "thro' sev'nty thousand centuries" (156) protest "in Sanscrit, in Chinese, and ev'ry lingo" (144) and claim that "Nought [*sic*] exists but Tao!" (112). Turandot herself is the "daughter of heaven" (355) who sends to their death all those suitors unable to decipher her riddle: Hope + Blood + Turandot. She, of course, will surrender, to one man (a prince of course) whose name is . . . Amor! This is certainly a case of inverted and back-and-forth civilizational and cultural relationships, which unfixes fixed representations and sends all the butterflies off for another spin.

5 China's Avant-Garde Art

Differences in the Family

One sees the wagon dragged back,

The oxen halted,

A man's hair and nose cut off.

Not a good beginning, but a good end.

Hexagram 38, "Opposition," *Yijing*

The meaning of avant-garde in China

Since the late 1980s, China has produced what is termed "avant-garde art" 'qianwei yishu.' It was so called after the 1989 Beijing *China/Avant-Garde* exhibition, showing 297 works by 186 artists from all over China. This exhibition was the first and the last large-scale exhibition of its kind in China. This art has more detractors than admirers, and they come from official sources. But there are also critics from within who deny its existence. Indeed, many Chinese critics and artists claim there is no such thing as an avant-garde in China. For example, the conceptual artist and art promoter Ai Weiwei says, "I don't believe there is an avant-garde in China. Well, the real meaning of an avant-garde movement doesn't exist because there is almost no contextual background for it. Any kind of idea, if it has a new, or individual perspective, can be said to be avant-garde." Ai also mentions the lack of an intellectual class, of educated people, but also the concrete living conditions of the Chinese people, including the artists'.[1] His point of view neatly sums up the predicament of avant-garde art in China: China has had no previous avant-garde movements, it has no institutionalized alternative art structures, and the art is intricately mixed with the new emerging consumerist mentality, which makes art works fashion statements. Abstract artist Ding Yi shares some of these views, but he still believes some form of avant-garde is emerging in China. He believes that the Chinese artists "have compressed the West's one-hundred year [art] history into some ten years." He sees avant-garde art in China as allowing "a few individuals to emerge," rather than a school or a movement. Furthermore, "China's contemporary art is precisely in a kind of colonial condition; it relies closely on the West."[2] Conceptual artist Zhou Tiehai not only admits this "dependence" outright but plays on it in his works—which feature himself as a famous person or Chinese sights on faux *Newsweek* or *Artnews* covers—and in his interviews, as for example, in this 1997 conversation:

— Q: It sounds like you are making this work for a Western audience.
— A: Yes, because the cultural power is in the West. So you have to do something here.
— Q: But you would like to show your work in China.
— A: Yes, I want to show my work there, but there's no response, it's not well received. Art is like science. You need knowledge to understand it.[3]

Western conceptions of the avant-garde obviously don't fit the Chinese situation. The Soviet Union's 1920 avant-garde and, closer to today, the American 1960s pop scene with their attacks on bourgeois institutionalized art have no equivalents and cannot be models for China's avant-garde. Hal Foster, revisiting Peter Bürger's conception of the avant-garde, has propounded the need for a redefinition of the avant-garde in terms of critical resistance rather than transgression.[4] He argues that today, everywhere, the utopian and anarchic transgressions of the avant-garde cannot exist; there is no space, time for political idealism, "for there may be no natural limit to transgress in this all-but-global reach of capital" (150). To be efficacious, avant-garde art can only/must resist total recuperation from the institution and from mass culture. It "attempts to de-reify cultural representation" (92), "insists on the here and now, on the spatial and temporal relations" (114), "rests on a critique of representation which questions the truth content of visual representation, whether realist, symbolic or abstract, and explores the regimes of meaning and order that these different codes support" (129), and "investigates the processes and apparatuses which control [representations and generic forms]" (153). Thus, avant-garde art today is not a movement, or a type of representation, or a regional/national phenomenon. Chinese avant-garde art is possible, abstract, and figurative.

In *Recodings*, Foster also delineates a difference between avant-garde art and what he calls "arrière-avant-garde art" (23): skillful recodings, stylish spectacles, ahistorical pastiches, following a logic akin to the dictates of fashion. Such art is " 'provocative' momentarily as a reaction but is precisely reactionary" (75) in its dialectic bind between modernism and mass culture. It is a neoconservative or "dejavunik art" (Harold Rosenberg's term, quoted by Foster, 24), "art that plays upon our desire to be mildly shocked, piqued really, by the already assimilated dressed up as the new" (24). It abides by the apolitical separation of the arts from labor, holds "universal" presumptions (40), believes in the sovereignty of the self in art (75), in its expressive ability, and aestheticizes politics (91). Such art is the overwhelming part of the cultural production today, claims Foster. This Western situation — after all, Foster's focus is Western works — also applies to quite a number of so-called Chinese avant-garde works. I am referring to "political pop," which will be discussed later.

But Foster does admit that "the line between the exploitive and the critical is fine indeed" (29). A few years ago, one could have rather easily differentiated the "avant-garde" from "official" art, simply by noting whose work was exhibited in China and whose never was. Today some artists emerge on the mainland as well as in the international sphere. Portrait artist Shi Chong is such a case. In 1993, his oil painting *A Walking Man (Xingzou de ren),* was a gold-medal winner at the Second Annual Exhibition of Chinese Oil Paintings, a two-week exhibition in Beijing's Chinese Art Museum. And his work was published both in official newspapers, such as *People's Daily,* and unofficial ones, such as the now defunct *Art News (Yishu xinwen).* In 1996, two of his works, also figurative, were included in a German-initiated avant-garde show entitled *CHINA*, which traveled in Europe until February 1998, and in the show's catalogue.[5] Shi Chong's portraits are acceptable in different spheres: the young people (men and women) portrayed may be nude, but their genitals are not fully exposed. More importantly, their poses can be interpreted in many ways. *A Walking Man,* the gold-medal painting, looks like a painted bronze sculpture with a rough texture and gives off some form of pathos, as the young man has a very solemn — or is it resigned? — look. Some kind of existentialist or even allegorical explanation — such as the noble yet difficult walk of life — could be given here. On the other hand, Shi Chong's *The Lucky Young Man* (1995), offers more physicality and surprise. The portrait, done in a perfectly photo-realist style, shows a young man sitting in very white light, cross-legged, with no clothes on, but delicately holding in his hands a red bat (fu), the central focus of the work. The figure looks happy, if not "lucky" (fu). This latter work is decidedly ambivalent and would perhaps not be welcome in any official oil-painting competition.

But then again, the Chinese art scene is unpredictable. Some exhibitions open, only to be closed in a fortnight; some are banned on the eve of their opening (I witnessed such events, still occurring in 1996). Some controversial works are retrospectively redeemed as fine representations of contemporary Chinese art: Luo Zhongli's 1980 *Father (Fu-qin),* for example, which was included in the huge Chinese exhibition at the Guggenheim Museum in 1998. *Father,* first considered an irreverent and ugly portrait of an old peasant, is now an emblem of new Chinese painting. Done in hyperrealist style and in monumental proportions, it now signifies "China": an unkempt and poor man with an "animal"-like expression, who is every(wo)man's father, a noble representative of survival and dignified poverty. But Luo's work is in no way avant-garde. It is a representation of a factual condition, the tough life "out there" in the countryside; it tells a story, defying neither the art-historical past (social realism) nor the political past (the Maoist peasant regime, now over). *Father* is emotionally effective: many viewers have wept in front of it.[6]

Chinese avant-garde works resist any form of direct or indirect commentary of social or political relevance. Most artists refute any ideological interpretation of their work. Because Chinese avant-garde art is mainly seen in international spheres or in joint-venture galleries in

China, the works are unmistakably read as adversarial to the "only big socialist country left," as conceptual artist Xu Bing claims.[7] If, as Foster has noted, "in our system of commodities, fashions, styles, art works . . . it is difference that we consume" (171), China must be different and Chinese art must show a difference. If, as he claims, difference is in fact limited to our expectations that "everyone [should] be different in the same way" (18) or that we should "express [ourselves] . . . but only via the type, only via the commodity" (72), then China should, by this logic, present a recognizably Chinese look. I find that the Chinese avant-garde attempts to resist precisely this unifying portrait of "China." They are, in varying ways, "affirming their resistance to the white, patriarchal order of western culture" (207), and also to their incorporation as "different."

The forty-fifth Venice Biennale in 1993, which for the first time had a China room, was a lesson for the thirteen artists whose works were selected.[8] It was the very first time China had participated in a prestigious international avant-garde show. Before that, Chinese art on the international scene was entirely traditional, even when called modern. Since 1993, as Ding Yi expressed it, "if a country has not done a [contemporary] Chinese art exhibition then it is considered conservative and behind the times."[9] Yet none of the Chinese participants in the 1993 Venice Biennale were very enthused by the "China room." Their impressions can be summed up as culture shock. Many noted the strange homogeneity, the Chineseness of their works, once it was packed into the (small) room. All the works were hanging on the walls; most were paintings, and figurative at that. The overall effect turned them all into "Chinese pop" representatives. What is more, they found that only China had such a national and unified look, in theme (political) and in technique (realist figurative oils). They resented this homogeneity, and their belated arrival on the art scene. Fang Lijun said that the Chinese room looked like a peasant fair 'nongcun jishi' exhibiting its local fare 'tutechan,' and that was probably what attracted the visitors.[10]

Today, although there are still "China" exhibitions, the styles are extremely diversified and there is no one trend. Many artists work in multimedia (Feng Mengbo, Geng Jianyi, Zhang Peili, to name just a few who were in the 1993 Biennale), others deal with conceptual questions (Xu Bing), and even those who have stuck to portraits have distinct orientations (Wang Guangyi, Fang Lijun, Liu Wei). Add to that

12. Untitled, 1995. Oil painting by Fang Lijun. *Photograph donated by artist.*

those artists who have since the 1980s been working against the grain of such Chinese conventions as calligraphy and landscape painting or who have been doing installations or photography, and we see that Chinese avant-garde art is multiform indeed. Having said this, I find that the better works are participating in the global trend toward a deanthropomorphized vision of art and, because they come from China, in a general trend toward a desinicized view of Chinese art.

Bawdy bodies emoting Chineseness

Why would China's avant-garde art still be mainly constituted of figurative oil painting done in a realist (surrealist, photo-realist, hyperrealist) style? After all, official art is also "characterized by a high degree of realism and extreme technical finesse" but "its theoretical foundations may be found in a formalistic nationalism that lays claim to a uniquely

Chinese form of beauty best rendered in a realistic manner."[11] The difference then lies first in the subject matter, in what the avant-garde artists portray, which does not convey "beauty" or a "nationalist" sentiment, nor anything particularly "Chinese." The figures represented are young men with bald heads, pretty women having fun under the sun, foreigners, fleshy nude bodies, the military, all in provocative poses. In this sense, the avant-garde flatly refuses adhesion to the typical, to the every(wo)man on the street with a purpose. The avant-garde either represents its own kind (its own generation) or mocks older generations and plain people with ordinary lives. The style may be realistic, but the scenes are unreal: the danger of the barber's blade on a neck (Geng Jianyi); the kinkiness of an older woman lying down in a sexy pose in front of the television (Liu Wei); the choir all smiles except for the faces left blank for your own (Wang Jinsong).

There are many critical social statements that could be read into the works: the boredom of everyday life in Fang Lijun's yawning look-alikes —or again, as Andrew Solomon, giving a typical postsocialist advocate reading, claims: "howls that could free China";[12] the homogenization of everyone, men and women, in Fang, Wang, Liu, and many others; the lack of communication between members of a family, between couples, such as in Zhang Xiaogang's or Yu Hong's work; the dehumanizing process in Zeng Fanzhi, and so on. Yet, these works do not function according to what Foster has coined romantic "strategies of marginality or nihilism" (147). Actually, they defy representation by not yielding to "the structures of identification typical of the spectacle— scopic, voyeuristic, patriarchal" (92). The people looking so defiant or absent-minded in the works have no diaristic value (autobiographical value), either. The works are clearly fiction; these portraits aim at exposing the artifice of self-representation, instead of a persona and an aura. Indeed, the works dazzle the spectator: strange looks, odd points of view impede identification; reduplicated bodies, mistaken identities, aggressive gestures all question the position of the autobiographical or national subject. They have an attitude, as if they were arrogantly repeating Barbara Kruger's line "I will not become what I mean to you."

Nevertheless, these works—portraits with identifiable Chinese ethnic features—have been unilaterally read as political subversion from China with which the West empathetically identifies. In the first important catalog dedicated to Chinese avant-garde art, *China's New Art, Post-1989*,[13] the critics read the works as products by "Chinese" (dissident) "subjects." Nicholas Jose says that "it is perhaps the first time in China that art has addressed the viewer with such personal directness. 'Here I am! I am You!' The response must vary with the extent to which one identifies."[14] Jeffrey Hantover states that "recent Chinese paintings are collusive, collaborative works of artist and viewer. . . . We see the work filtered through memories of the flickering images of tanks rolling into Tiananmen Square, the Goddess of Democracy tumbling to earth."[15]

Since 1993, that is, since the publication of this catalog and since the forty-fifth Venice Biennale, such readings are definitely no longer tenable. I am not denying that there is a definite dystopian and anarchic efficaciousness in the works, which the Chinese authorities rightly sense and do not wish to exhibit. They can be considered ironic anthropological slideshows or what Foster, in his more recent book, calls "pseudo-primitive" and "pseudo-ethnic artifacts" strategies; they are "a twisting of the paternal law of difference — sexual and generational, ethnic and social."[16] Foster identifies yet another trend today, which is one of "cynical reason, pushed to the extreme, which is a pose of indifference — a simulated imbecilism, infantilism, or autism."[17] This is exactly what I find is happening in Chinese art, at least in Chinese figurative art. Liu Xiaodong makes portraits of himself as a painter, in his bathtub (with a van Gogh–like bandaged ear), in front of a mirror in a peasant's home; he even paints portraits of Westerners, such as Hispanics on some East Coast beach or a gay couple with dog, in their East Village flat (*A Meeting on East Fifth Street — Ren yue dong wu jie*, 1993). They are camera-like portraitures because there is always at least one person looking at the "camera" and because they are so obviously posing. These are anything but stories of the oppressed. As Mark Tansey aptly noted, we must "take [our] temporal blinders off and realize that [we aren't] looking at these paintings — they [are] looking at [us]. Two thousand years of ink painting, about 40 years of Socialist Realism and three years of cultural surge since Tiananmen Square [are] grinning at [our] temporal chauvinism."[18]

In the same vein, Yu Hong makes "self-portraits" in the nude — on a tree, sleepwalking, lying in bed. These works are not erotic because the bodies are bold and impenetrable, not given as "compliant object[s]

13. *A Meeting on East Fifth Street.* Oil painting by Liu Xiaodong, 1993. *Photograph from exhibition catalog.*

of the painting-method's seduction."[19] Her painting *Chinese Princesses (Zhongguo gongzhu)* consists of gleeful little girls all dolled up, fully enjoying themselves while putting on a colourful show for the viewers. Indeed, Yu Hong uses fluorescent tones of warm oranges and pinkish reds for her subjects. All of her (female) groups of friends are oblivious to anyone's gaze on them: they won't notice, as if they didn't care. Alternately, Fang Lijun's people are aggressively looking at the "camera." In the nude self-portrait he gives a peace sign as he leaps—into void?—revealing all of himself; there is no way one could attempt to avoid his body, to feminize it. All of his characters make the viewer feel uneasy because their "unblinking stare" in the blow-ups is piercing and boomerangs the viewer's gaze right back at her/him. The mass-produced, almost identically dressed bald men in the *Second Composition* series

(1992), are actually making faces at the "camera," as if teasingly asking the question, "How do I look?" Fang has commented on the pink faces of his subjects: "I use the commercial readymade flesh color to paint people's skin; if the spectator finds it looks silly, well, shouldn't this signal to us ['tixing women'], that there are ways we consider as established ['jiding'] which are so ridiculous. The reason why the whole world has mixed flesh color in this fashion is because the majority of people in this whole world believe flesh color to be like this."[20] A similar effect is provoked by Geng Jianyi's *Second State (Di er zhuangtai)* (1985), consisting of very yellow faces sardonically grinning at the "camera." Liu Wei's imposture works also command a response to the spectacle. Liu makes "collages" with photogenic Chinese faces, famous ones along with totally unknown ones, political figures alongside Pa and Ma. His portraits—where he often includes himself as a painter or as a political leader (as quasi Mao look-alike in *Two Drunk Painters (Jiugui: liang ge huajia)* or as a painter fraternizing with Hua Guofeng in 1991) are personalized reproductions of all the camera poses that the Chinese repertoire he has experienced can offer: a stern but fatherly Mao, a family portrait in which the male descendants' little genitals are proudly protected by a paternal hand, mock snap-shots of the earnest military, or of the drunken ways of sworn brothers 'gemenr,' or of poor working-class lovers who are oh! so well-off. Liu Wei always hypes up the lustful eyes of men upon women, including ladies on television. All of Liu's people look basically the same: sexless, ageless, yet strangely . . . like himself, but, then, never quite so.

Recently, Chinese art has moved even more clearly onto the international terrain by representing animals and humans without ethnic features (corpses, newborns). Yan Peiming, now residing in France, is a case in point. Yan paints human heads. For a long time, he specialized in two people's heads: Mao Zedong's and his own father's. After his arrival in France, he kept on working on these two figures but also started painting other heads, those of white people as well as black people, eventually erasing all racial features to create generic heads. Yan has moved from any Chinese identifiable source to what one could call "immanent anthropology."[21] His works even adorn the university cafeteria of Maret University, in Dijon, a possible proof of a redefined universal appeal. This is a far cry from Luo Zhongli's highly contextualized, 1980 composition *Father*. Many more examples could be given from all of the above-mentioned artists: now, Liu Wei paints babies and dogs; Fang Lijun, corpses floating in blue water; Wang Guangyi, dogs on visa application forms; Zeng Fanzhi, masked human beings who are accompanied by dogs; Wang Xingwei adds a dog to a *Mao Goes to Anyuan* pastiche.

This blatant politics of ethnic difference (OK, we're Chinese) pushed to its limit of indifference (Shar-pei dogs are Chinese nationals) can be found in all modes of the avant-garde, now including photography. Yang Zhenzhong recently made a computer-processed photograph entitled *A Photograph of the Whole Family: Old/New*. The family is composed of a rooster, a hen, and twenty-six chicks, all facing the camera.[22] Photography, now also a much used art form in China, is very close to avant-garde oil paintings in both subject and effect. The portraits do not allow space for the viewer to investigate their psyche; the space is filled with hard, arrogant bodies of young poseurs. Zhang Hai'er's work in this sense is the most emblematic. His self-portraits are open-mouthed, angry gestures at the camera; his Chinese models tend to be tough youths, both male and female, hooligans who look fearlessly at the camera, while revealing (especially the women) languid, very eroticized bodies that are inaccessible because their gazes are so forbidding (for example, *Guangzhou*, 1989). With photographer Zhang Hai'er and painter Liu Xiaodong, the East/West roles are turned inside out and become meaningless. Now that the Chinese artists travel, they too "catch" Western models with their curious manners, and contradictory environments. Zhang Hai'er shows an unusual transvestite Paris, a violent Switzerland, a Muslim woman next to a sexist advertisement in Germany.[23] Zhang favors theatricality in both Chinese subjects and non-Chinese subjects, and his work is a reflection on humanimal behavior, as spectacle, as display.[24]

In 1996, China's own art auction house, China Guardian, organized a large-scale sale of Chinese art, including a section "Important New Art of China (1949 to 1979)," which comprised Cultural Revolution propaganda works and Mao portraits. For the first time, mainland Chinese buyers showed up en masse and bought works with titles such as *Chairman Mao Is the Red Sun in the Heart of the World's Revolution*. After having first attracted the neighboring Chinese-speaking countries, the Chinese diaspora, and then the West, Maoist art is now hot in China too. Ironically, art of the most anticapitalist period of China is the most

14. *Guangzhou.* Photographic artwork by
Zhang Hai'er, 1989.

valued/valuable today. Political art has been totally aestheticized and
commodified.

That is the case with political pop 'zhengzhi bopu,' an irreverent appropriation of Maoist icons that started in the late 1980s. The first artist to make a portrait of the main model for political pop, that is, the
photogenic Mao Zedong, was Wang Guangyi with his *Mao Zedong Portrait #1, #2* shown at the *China/Avant-Garde* exhibition in 1989.[25] Since
then, Wang has become a celebrity in the international art scene and has
amassed a considerable fortune. In one of numerous interviews, Wang
discusses his mock propaganda posters, specifically a 1990s series entitled *Da pipan (The Great Critique),* which features the resolute revolutionary triad of peasants, soldiers, and workers brandishing their pens

China's Avant-Garde Art   137

against transnational products such as Kodak, Benetton, and Band-Aid. He says: "Of course, I enjoy my own money and fame. I criticize Coke, but drink it every day. These contradictions are not troublesome to Chinese people."[26] Wang's appropriation of political icons and their juxtaposition with consumer goods equates propaganda with publicity, which is after all the double meaning of the Chinese term *xuanchuan*.

This logic of consumption (including its critique) is the drive behind many other avant-garde artists such as Li Shan, Liu Dahong, Yu Youhan, Wang Ziwei, Wang Xingwei, and Zhang Hongtu. For most, Mao remains the favorite icon to play with. Such Mao reworkings are immediately identified as political and as Chinese, and consequently have enjoyed much favor abroad. They are classified as "pop" because the representations are totally lacking in pathos or anxiety; they are comic deviations from the social-realist template. For example, Wang Xingwei rerepresented in 1995 the famous 1968 painting by Liu Chunhua, *Mao Goes to Anyuan* (the sole painterly equivalent of the model operas of the Cultural Revolution), but with a few technical differences. The original traditional Chinese ink-on-paper work representing young Mao with his famous red umbrella is here replaced by a present-day young man in a business suit with a pink umbrella, adopting also a resolute pose but facing in the opposite direction. The revolutionary monk[27] is now a yuppie. Another avid practitioner of the Mao icon is Yu Youhan, who reproduces a plausible social-realist scene, such as *President Mao and Shaoshan Peasants* (1991) where all are smiling — but their flashing smiles are so white that it is all we see at first glance; then the eye notices the floating flowers, then the flowers printed everywhere, on Mao's white shirt as well as on the peasants' outfits, the floor, everywhere. The meeting is thus ridiculed because it is represented as even prettier than a propaganda painting. As Orville Schell put it, Yu's printlike paintings evoke Laura Ashley designs,[28] but slightly off key. In some of his works, flowers even block out Mao's features. Yu therefore represents Chinese Mao stories within an arts-and-crafts idiom, jabbing at the same time at revolutionary peasant art. Liu Dahong, for his part, recontextualizes Mao in a religious setting and within a Chinese traditional painting idiom. In his *Four Seasons: Spring*, 1991, Buddhist and Christian imagery combine in an axonometric perspective: a majestic Mao, with a Christian radiant glow emanating from his head and right hand, addresses a crowd of odd pilgrims who look like Dao-Buddhists meekly seated at his feet, and (following the archaic painting custom) miniaturized. Liu thus offers his skills as a painter versed in indigenous classical conventions as well as in cultural-political cross-cultural jesting.

The youngest to chip into the Maoist voguishness—and also the youngest sent to the 1993 Venice Biennale—is Feng Mengbo, the game artist. His simulations of video games, sometimes paintings on canvases, but most frequently actual computer games, are sheer fun with fantastic archetypes, mixing historical characters and events with *anime*-type heroes. If for Yang Zhenzhong, a family is, as we have seen, Mr. Rooster with wife and offspring, for Feng, a family is his own family album with colorful model opera heroes, revolutionary female militia, and Mao Zedong hailing a taxi, all against a background of Coca-Cola cans on Tiananmen Square. Unlike older practitioners such as Wang Guangyi or Yu Youhan, Feng was not even born in the zealous, chaotic 1960s. Communist heroes and propaganda material are more like curios for him and his generation. It is not a question of profanation of sacred icons, which it seems to be for artists such as Zhang Hongtu, who has said: "If one has never lived under a Communist government, Mao's portrait means nothing: it's just a popular image such as Warhol did, like Marilyn Monroe. But the first time I cut Mao's portrait with a knife and put it back together to make a new Mao image, I felt guilty, sinful."[29] Zhang, who has been living in the United States since 1982, still works with what peopled his childhood, Mao's portrait. In that same interview, Zhang recognizes the religious import of Mao, since his icon replaced the Bodhisattva in the living-room and the stove god in the kitchen in all households (297). To mock that spirit, Zhang created in 1989 a *Last Banquet,* an oil painting in which all thirteen faces, of Jesus and his apostles, are the same one, Mao's face. Interestingly, this painting has been censored in the United States.

Chinese political pop has affinities with both Warhol's pop and with the Soviet Union's political pop of the seventies and eighties. The critic and advocate of political pop in China, Li Xianting, writes that when Rauschenberg was exhibited in 1985 in China, his pop was interpreted as Dadaism, because it turned artists toward Duchampian-style readymades rather than toward political pop, which, in effect, only started in the 1990s.[30] In the mid-1980s, Chinese artists did not incorporate popular culture into their art; this trend also started only in the 1990s. Li dates the advent of pop with the loss of idealism and with the Mao mania that emerged around 1989. The *China/Avant-Garde* exhibition that took place in February of 1989 at the China Museum of Fine Art marks for him the end of idealistic art and the beginning of underground (adversarial) art. This exhibition, where artist Xiao Lu fired a gun at her own installation, sent "all of the eighties art to the guillotine" (61), he claims. Li's influence has been immense in terms of the emergence of an indigenous pop to which his writings have given an ideologically subversive coloration.

Li's vision of pop is modeled on his conception of the Soviet Union's. He states that China's pop and Warholian-style pop yield antipodal effects: China's pop desacralizes, banalizes 'biansu' people, things, and events, while American pop mythifies them. Political pop renders politics absurd. The public looking at Chinese works will laugh derisively at, say, a flowery Mao but faced with a Warholian representation of a Campbell soup, or of Mao, they will be awed by the odd beauty. In other words, Li envisages indigenous pop as more than surface, as deep and serious, and, though linked to consumer society, critical of it.

Pop art always creates estrangement from familiar objects, and at the same time gives a kind of aura to the things or figures depicted. In China, Mao and the hardline socialist era have become "interesting" and have been used in both art and entertainment in the 1990s. Taxi drivers have their Mao good luck charm, karaoke singers their Red Book medley of songs, ordinary people their "East is red" lighter, while artists churn out political pop art. Politics, with Mao as superstar, is a lite topic that rock artists have also taken up, by "singing red [revolutionary] songs in a yellow [unorthodox] fashion" 'hongge huangchang,' and new film directors, by celebrating the freedom of teenagers during the Cultural Revolution. Obviously, this kind of art works much like fashion: as Hal Foster put it, "It answers the need to innovate and the need to change nothing" (24). It looks good, flashy, is almost kitsch, indulging in flattened-out stylistic references, something close to advertising (20).

In the conclusion of his article on political pop, Li claims that political pop is deconstructing politics (63–64). It is not necessarily so. Truly sensitive subjects, such as Deng Xiaoping and other more recent leaders are

15. "Hello, Deng Xiaoping!" Mao Zedong/Deng Xiaoping 1994–95 calendar.

practically untouchable.[31] Superposing, replacing, and mixing politics and popular culture do not, in Foster's opinion, lead to effectiveness. Such techniques can simply be an aestheticization or a dulling of the critical edge. I tend to agree with Foster here, especially when one knows that pop art not only arose in China with consumer culture, but also that it sells well outside of China (especially in Hong Kong, Taiwan, and the Chinese diaspora) and very recently in China too. The year 1993 was the first showing to the world of Chinese political pop; 1993 was also the hundredth anniversary of Mao Zedong's birthdate, which was marked by innumerable Mao memorabilia. Everyone profited from Mao that year. China's pop may not be so far removed from Warhol's cynical attitude toward the market. Lest we forget, Warhol was the first artist to commercialize Mao's looks in the 1970s. As Ellen Johnston Laing notes, Warhol's set of Mao replicas concurred with President Nixon's visit to China and the consequent blooming in the press of photos of Mao.[32] Different historical periods notwithstanding, there is evidence of opportunistic cynicism. But, as with Warhol, a univocal dismissal of any serious or critical intent of the works remains impossible. To a certain extent, political pop, by merely disqualifying the seriousness of Mao and

China's Avant-Garde Art   141

his era, does investigate set political representations and allow space for a questioning of the power of representation.

The invisible, transitory and permanent spaces:
Here, there, anywhere

The Chinese avant-garde is particular, even anomalous, in more than one way; namely, in the spaces it occupies. Avant-garde artists in China do not work within the studio/gallery/museum nexus. Their works are practically hijacked, flown from their studios to foreign collectors' spaces or to international artshows. At the most, five tiny galleries show avant-garde art in Beijing (one in Shanghai, none in Guangdong—to name China's three biggest cities), and they are all tied to foreign enterprises. No museum has yet given them, since the 1989 scandal, much space. (One museum that took a step toward changing this practice was the new Shanghai museum, in spring 1996, which had the good intentions—or was it an effort to coopt a few?—to invest a lot of money in a contemporary art show. But museum officials did not like most of the works, and the curators had to compromise by diluting the threatening works with sweet, commendable ones.)

Avant-garde artists in China live a bohemian life; they are totally unattached: they have no local agent, no gallery, no museum space, no work unit. In Beijing, since 1986, three artists' villages have popped up, all at the periphery of the capital: first, in Yuanmingyuan (beside the ruins of the former Summer Palace), then in Dongcun in the early nineties, and now, further east, in Tongxian County. The Yuanmingyuan village was the most heterogenous, because artists came from all provinces of China and because all forms of art—of varying quality and styles—were being created or contemplated there. A few artists still live there, but it is not an ideal location: the police step in occasionally, property owners raise rents without offering basic services such as running water, and, worse, it has the reputation of being a backwater for wannabe artists. (Actually, many starving ones have gone back to their provincial abodes.) Dongcun was more homogenous because most artists there were graduates from the Central Academy of Fine Arts. But some, such as Ma Liuming, also attracted much attention to the village with his nude performances, which in turn attracted the police to their location. Tongxian County, or more precisely, Xiaobaocun, the latest refuge since its residents started to move there in the summer of 1994, is almost foolproof. The artists are no longer poor tenants but have purchased homes in the village. Several of the new residents are already quite successful (and wealthy), for example, the artists Liu Wei and Fang Lijun and the critic Li Xianting. Although most artists are painters, there are also performance artists, television and film directors, and rock musicians. Foreign buyers are driven to the spacious studios from the airport. Perhaps the next artist village will be "a simulacrum of bohemia . . . recycling poses and styles for media consumption." [33] At the moment, in Tongxian, there are also artists like Chen Guangwu, born in 1968, the self-taught "mad calligrapher" from Liuzhou, Guangxi, who first lived in Yuanmingyuan, then moved to Tongxian; as of 1996, he had not yet sold a single work. Now Chen is contemplating getting into some other form of art, one that might sell: oil painting, perhaps some sort of pop painting?

In the avant-garde field, calligraphic ventures generally don't sell. Calligraphy, both in China and in the West, is a serious indigenous enterprise that one doesn't meddle with. (If a Westerner wants a Chinese calligraphy, he will buy a Tang poem, copied in some famous master's style.) In any case, few artists work solely with the Chinese written code. Artists who do are mostly conceptual artists for whom process rather than end result matter. For example, Xu Bing, Wu Shanzhuan, Gu Wenda, and Huang Yongping use Chinese writing in their works to make (critical) statements on Chinese culture, past and present, and to initiate some form of dialogue between cultures. It is not surprising that these four artists are now living abroad. For example, in 1987, Huang made an installation of a mound of pulped paper, from two art history books, whose title was the result of the process: *"A History of Chinese Art" and "A Concise History of Modern Painting" after Two Minutes in the Washing Machine.* When living in Xiamen, he was a member of the Xiamen Dada group who liked fire; that is to say, they burned their own works. One of Huang's works was the burnt-off beard of a likeness of Leonardo da Vinci, *The Beard Is the Easiest to Set Ablaze (Huzi zui yi ran)* (1985–86). In a manifesto-like text, Huang declared: "If one says that to exhibit works is like keeping watch over a dead body, then setting fire to works is to carry out incineration. Keeping watch over a body is depressing but incinerating is exhilarating. Works of art for the artist are like opium for humans; if one does not destroy art, life cannot be serene, and to be disquieted is more like life. Dada is dead, beware of fire!"[34] This merry wreckage of art recalls the red guards' exploits during the Cultural Revolution. In a similar vein, Wu Shanzhuan recreated in 1986 at the Zhejiang Museum the environment of the Cultural Revolution in an installation entitled *Red Humor (Hongse youmo):* a room was placarded with posters, revolutionary slogans, publicity ads, all in the hierarchized colors of those days—red, white, and black—some hanging, some half-torn, with characters inverted or crossed out. Without really explaining anything, Wu "explains": "Culture is a kind of symbol; writing uses symbols which express symbols. . . . They are the last stronghold of [Chinese] culture. . . . [T]he Chinese language is different from all other languages of the world; it is made up of ideograms. For this isolation, for this construction which can by figures express thought, we will write some Chinese. We will use 70 percent red. We will use 25 percent black. We will use 5 percent white. Black characters are the expression of our feelings; not to have feelings, is the best of all feelings."[35] Wu's sense of humor and artistic projects target accepted conventions, namely popular and official language. His work scoffs at authority of all kinds, including the supposed (economically and politically) disinterested, author/artist. At the 1989 *China/Avant-Garde* show, Wu sold shrimp, and in 1993, at the Ohio Wexner Center for the Arts, he sold battery-operated stuffed pandas in a performance/installation entitled *Missing Bamboo.*[36] Wu also said that the Chinese artist is a panda. Spoken from the context of exile, what do these words mean? That the Chinese artists are taken as exotic (and dumb) creatures, on the brink of extinction? The panda is one of China's more recent symbols, associated with Deng Xiaoping and his regime. It stands alongside Chinese writing as a national cipher, inside and outside of China. Wu therefore sold at the Wexner an idea of China, sold himself, along with the stuffed animals (without the batteries, though).

Artists who have worked with Chinese characters tend to work with more universally recognizable icons when they become expatriates. For example, Gu, who in the 1980s opened up Chinese characters—in a work tellingly entitled *Dislocated Characters (Cuowei de zi)* (1986)—

has been involved, since 1989, in a work in progress delving into sexual taboos. *Oedipus Refound* is an investigation of menstruation, sexual intercourse, sexual difference, (in)fertility, life and death. Gu's use of dried human placenta has been shocking, both in China and in the United States, but more so in the United States. As Gu has confided: "In China, I made exhibitions the authorities would not tolerate. I used made-up characters, and they told me my work had inappropriate political meaning, something about a code for political secrets. In New York, I did exhibitions with Chinese medicine and used a powder made of human placenta. And the authorities told me my work had an offensive religious meaning, talked about abortion and sometimes they didn't let me show."[37] In 1996, Wu Shanzhuan created a work entitled *Terminal,* which included living insects, along with other creatures, in a model of the labyrinthine structures of Amsterdam's Schiphol airport. Xu Bing is best known for his *Book from the Sky (Tianshu),* a four-year project (1987–91) consisting of four thousand invented Chinese characters that he concocted from the Kangxi dictionary, printed in a Song wood-block style and reproduced on rice paper or bound in the traditional fashion; he is now deconstructing the alphabet. He has created a work entitled *Post-Testament,* consisting of 290 identical copies of a "text" made up of bits from the Bible mingled with porn pulp fiction excerpts, that is illegible, like *Book from the Sky.* In another work, aptly titled *Cultural Negotiation* (1993), Xu juxtaposed in a mock library his heavy, leather-bound *Post-Testament* with his delicate *Book from the Sky. Cultural Animals (Wenhua dongwu)* is yet another project, an afternoon performance in Beijing (after months of arduous training) of a couple of copulating pigs on a "bed" of books, the female one tattooed with Chinese script, the male one with alphabet. Now, moving in reverse, he is tackling the alphabet and English words in his *Introduction to English Calligraphy* (1994–96), with signs that are made to look just like Chinese characters. This time they only look illegible: they are plain English words. There's no challenge anymore for earnest sinologists.[38] Xu is now addressing a more global audience, which has to try to read otherwise.

In China, one artist who toys with calligraphy as an art and not with words is Ding Yi. If Ding were not Chinese, perhaps no one would even consider his work as calligraphy; it would be "abstract art." Ding's project is to create plus signs (+) — or tens, for the more sinologically

16. *Van Goghs.* Ink on paper, pasted on soon-to-be-demolished Shanghai tenements, by Hu Jianping, 1996. *Photograph donated by artist.*

minded readers; or simply a technical sign in printing. This has been his ongoing project since 1988: he always makes the same sign, on different surfaces (paper, cloth, canvas, with different media: Chinese ink, oils, charcoal, chalk, etc.). It is obviously anticalligraphic in that he works with ruler and masking tape, anathema to the "natural" flow favored by the noble art. The effect is achieved not only by the great number of repetitions but also by the colors he "automatically" chooses. What also makes his work anticalligraphic — and very contemporary — is his stance against interpretation. "If it's a mountain, I want to see a mountain (and not a face in the landscape, like Ashima's); if it's a painting, then it's a painting [and not a painting-of]."[39] In this sense, his work in progress connects with others like Xu Bing's in their refusal of set associations. However, the difference lies in that Ding avoids visible cultural specificity, China signs.[40]

The Chinese written system, I would say, much more than Mao Zedong himself, is the iconic embodiment of power today. There is and has been such an overwhelming presence of Chinese written ciphers in society—in the recent past, and especially in the Cultural Revolution—that they are anything but innocent signs to use; they ought to be the perfect target and weapon. Yet, images—of bodies, figures—are privileged. And the favored medium is the very Western oil painting, not the traditional "Chinese ink" painting, which, in its emphasis on lines, is akin to calligraphy.[41]

In the West, rebellion against the system for those without access to media has manifested itself in the act of drawing graffiti: lines of words or ciphers on public property. China barely has any graffiti. One person who has been active at leaving his mark on the walls is Zhang Dali, who started this habit in Italy, where, as he confessed, he felt particularly alienated from society.[42] There is also the Shanghai installation artist Hu Jianping, who likes to glue on soon-to-be-demolished buildings his paper paintings of people, from Van Gogh to GI Joe clones. But Hu's work takes on more the allure of a happening, since he does it in the open in front of passers-by, and he does not deface any valuable property.

Perhaps there has indeed been too much scribbling in China during all the various campaigns, culminating but not ending with the Cultural Revolution—one only has to think of the Democracy Wall of 1979. There is real danger in touching public/government property, as we know from the harsh sentences handed down to the three men who threw paint on the portrait of Mao above Tiananmen Gate in 1989: life imprisonment, twenty years, and sixteen years. If, as Hal Foster puts it, graffiti is "a response of people denied response,"[43] then there should also be a lot of graffiti in China. Artists such as Ni Haifeng, Wang Guangyi, Ye Yongqing, Mao Xuhui, Zhang Peili "soiling" their own works—with numbers, ciphers, characters, writing of all sorts—are considered subversive. In December 1993, in Chengdu, an exhibition of works including Ye's and Mao's was closed down precisely because of the "unartistic" state of their works. Mao Xuhui's painted series (thematizing power and authority, such as a bookshelf, a key, a hand poised in a "victory" sign, an official holding his teacup, and caricatured figures of patriarchs) also included a work that was written text. It comprised two legible sentences and some palimpsest-like works: one sentence was by Alvin Toffler ("Man is a product of power") and the other, an offensive one by Madonna ("Power is the most, most powerful of aphrodisiacs")[44] did not go over well with the authorities, who closed down the show. Mao Xuhui, still living in his native Kunming, now channels his critique into objects, his latest (1995–96) weapon being old-fashioned granny scissors, which he paints floating on top of a city, or a sofa, or a living-room. His paintings are touring the world.

Artists who go for terrorist action do it with their bodies most often and never stay in one place. They hold guerrilla-style happenings that leave the cityscape unblemished. Quasi "timeless art" and quasi invisible art are flourishing in all corners of China. Word-of-mouth leads one to such happenings. They are also local performances, which cannot be easily exported. Ai Weiwei published two books with some friends, the *White-Cover Book* and the *Black-Cover Book,* concentrating on such ephemeral art, with the purpose of making visible those who remain invisible. In the *Black-Cover Book,* for example, there is a photograph of a performance by Zhang Huan, *Twelve Meters Square* (1994, Beijing): Zhang himself, nude and coated with honey, is seated in a public latrine infested with flies. The double-standard pricing of the books accentuates the bridge between those who are there and those who are outside of it, namely, foreigners like myself: it is free for the artistic community and Chinese sympathizers, and twenty dollars for the others.

The sculptor Zhang Xin, in Shanghai, works with ice. One such work, entitled *Climate (Qihou)* (1996) was a bust of Madonna and of David who, when melting, yielded fresh (filtered) water for the aquariums placed below. (I can provide no illustration, as the camera and the photo reproduction could not adequately display the work!) In 1993 ceramist Ye Shuanggui served his *Virus Dishes (Bingdu caiyao)* free to the public in a Wuhan restaurant. In Guangzhou the Big-Tailed Elephant group (Daweixiang) has been performing publicly: "only once a year, in order to protect the environment," says Xu Tan, one of the four members, in a tongue-in-cheek manner.[45] In 1993 Xu Tan created *Love Allegories (Ai de yuyan),* consisting of female models made up of torsos of mannequins and mermaid tails in various poses, where love, sex and war are intermingled. He displayed them in the streets of Guangzhou. Xu Bing, as we have seen earlier, in his work *Cultural Animals,* had two tattooed pigs copulating in a Beijing art gallery on a Saturday afternoon in January 1994. Since the *China/Avant-Garde* exhibition in February 1989, with its many installations/performances inside and outside the National Fine

17. *Cultural Animals.* Xu Bing's performance in the Hanmo gallery, Beijing, January 1994. *Photograph donated by artist.*

Arts Museum, ephemeral art is quite frequent all over China but remains largely unknown, precisely because one has to be there then to experience it.

China's avant-garde art has to be discussed in terms of visibility/accessibility. Oil paintings are seen and "possessed" largely by nonmainlanders. Installations and happenings are seen by the art crowd in China, which is made up of artists, foreigners, and accidental onlookers. These performances are rare and hard to get to see, but they are nevertheless more visible in their own country than avant-garde oil paintings. One could say that ephemeral art is the most avant-garde, that it has the greatest potential to be efficacious. It certainly does "insist on the here and now, on the spatial and temporal relations," to quote Foster again (114). When, in 1989, the multimedia artist Zhang Peili sent bits of surgical gloves to the artistic community by mail (to those who were involved in the *China/Avant-Garde* exhibition), he was intersecting many preoccupations: emphasizing art as artifice and not as individualistic creation, commenting on the reality issue of his own paint-

ings, especially a series entitled *X?*—paintings or collages of real surgical gloves; downsizing artists' pretensions to be a cut above ordinary
members of society, since the reception of his gloves terrorized quite a
few addressees; linking art to public discourse, since his mass mailing
coincided with a hepatitis scare in China. Several other artists, including Zhang's friend Geng Jianyi, still perform acts of provocation, as one
can now see in Lyon as well as in Vancouver, and in their home town,
Hangzhou. Geng, for example, has a work entitled *ID Project,* which is a
series of photographs of a single Chinese man from different periods of
his life, ranging from a ballroom class, a hospital entry, a military leave,
next to his various IDs. The person is totally unrecognizable as a single
individual; of course, once one knows it is the same person throughout, one does find a certain family resemblance. The spectator's inquiry
is not of the racial or sexual kind, but moves toward the political and
the strictly anthropological. Such artists, anchoring their work in the
real, do not style themselves as pure, remote artists, nor do they claim
to address Chinese questions for the Chinese only.

Many artists now living outside of mainland China also emphasize
the site-specificity of their art. Gu Xiong, living in Vancouver since 1989,
created for the Vancouver Art Gallery in 1995 an installation entitled
Here, There, Everywhere (Zheli, nali, wulun nali) which thematizes the
artist in shifting cultural environments. The multimedia work consists
of a change of clothes, a silent video of a typical North American bon-
fire set in the middle of an installation of the Chinese hexagrams from
the *Yijing* (*Book of Changes*). There are also two self-portraits (along
with a sketch of his daughter and two Mao posters, one in Chinese, one
in English). The first self-portrait, alluding to his performance at the
1989 *China/Avant-Garde* exhibition in Beijing, shows his body covered
with wires; the second one shows himself dressed in warm clothes with
a picket sign around his neck: it's a reenactment of a protest he took
part in when he worked as a cafeteria busboy at the University of British
Columbia. Gu says, "If [an] artist should move to another culture, he or
she must move just as instinctively to begin to understand the strange
new world in which he or she finds him or herself. It is this dynamic,
this sudden generation of artistic electricity, that fuels change in both
art and life." [46]

Writing in 1993, Ellen Johnston Laing claimed that postmodernism in China is "unlikely" and that China's art lacks criticality. She wrote:

> Chinese artists are still in the throes of trying to win artistic freedom from themselves. Their art cannot engage in the exposé and criticism we in the West have come to expect of post-modern art; nor does art in China really address, or comment on, in any incisive or penetrating way, the contemporary human condition or experience from social, racial, ethnic, gender, sexual, political, environmental, urban or rural stances. Missing is the intellectually stimulating and provocative "collision of images" which permits the viewer to participate in the creative process thereby generating a new and sharper awareness of contemporary life. (215)

Such a position is untenable today. Avant-garde performances do engage the spectator—not only the gallery-going crowd—into questioning the intersections among publicity, politics, mass culture, Western culture, overarching power, and other similar critical terrains. This is art that makes viewers "work," which makes us see the magical manipulation and art grounded in reality. In fact, the range of topics involved may be considered greater than those in Western contemporary postmodern art because Chinese artists also must deal with its imperialistically cultural Other in a very concrete way, by resisting primitivism, "a metonym of imperialism," [47] which the avant-garde painters discussed earlier in this chapter certainly do address in their stance against sinicity and for immanent anthropology. True, China's avant-garde rarely deals with art-historical matters, and so is not, in one sense, "postmodern" or "neoconservatist postmodernist," to use Hal Foster's expressions. In China, unlike in the United States, there are not that many "skillful recodings, stylish spectacles, ahistorical pastiches." [48]

But, as is always the case with a rapidly changing China, even this last criterion is now being satisfied, with works by artists such as Xu Lei from Nanjing. Xu paints in a traditional Chinese way—that is, with Chinese brush, *gongbi* style, on rice paper—exquisite images resembling but not copying traditional Chinese topics. All of Xu's works are framed, curtained like a stage, revealing strange characters: for example, a horse standing in waters, his flank tattooed with blue-and-white designs like those of Ming dynasty porcelain. This is definitely a merry pastiche, a deft reworking of art-historical masterworks. Xu has received mixed reception for his work: he is highly appreciated outside of China, as the beautiful glossy English-Chinese catalog made in Hong Kong by Alisan Fine Arts Gallery in 1995 testifies;[49] within the traditional painters' crowd, Xu himself claims that he is respected for his technique, a sign that he does abide by some of the conventions; in the pop art circle (with Li Xianting as mentor), he is considered a "degenerate" (duoluo),[50] undoubtedly because his work is considered ahistorical, perhaps even seen as a revalidation of the academic, or again as a nostalgic spectacle created for the West. The line "between the exploitive and the critical is fine indeed."[51] Xu Lei's work relaunches the question of the necessity of a visible Chineseness as part and parcel of Chinese art; in his works, not only are the figures obviously Chinese, but so is the style. Is Xu's work a resistance to orientalist readings (by pushing to the limit an obviously bygone China and exaggerating the spectacular)? Or is it simply a fashionable statement, an exploitation of difference, a plundering of Chinese styles and icons, something the West will eagerly consume and something that connects to a certain postmodernism?

In the early seventies, John Berger showed that publicity in the West depends heavily upon the visual language of oil painting.[52] In the 1980s, Foster's analysis of postmodern pastiche furthers this connection: "In the language of painting these vague historical or poetic or moral references are always present. The fact that they are imprecise and ultimately meaningless is an advantage: they should not be understandable, they should merely be reminiscent of cultural lessons half-learnt. Advertising makes all history mythical, but to do so effectively it needs a visual language with historical dimensions."[53] Indeed, some of what is called China's avant-garde art is geared to the (Western) marketplace; it works much like advertising in the West, by its timely strategies. The self-proclaimed new *literatus* 'xin wenren' Xu Lei used to do oil paintings; Zhang Hongtu, at the beginning of the 1980s, created "cheerful canvases"[54] before going political in New York; political pop artist Wang Guangyi first "revisited" Western paintings before doing Mao and other hot Chinese topics and is now problematizing the humanimal world. They may be responding to a demand, something in the air. Undoubtedly, quite a few modern Chinese artworks are more postmodern pastiche or "arrière avant-garde" than avant-garde. The multifocal scenes on which the Chinese works are displayed complexify their reading. But, still, some works do belong to the big, international avant-garde art family. As for their postmodern status, it may not be such a pressing issue after all. As Gayatri Spivak warned, and Hal Foster reminds us, "Whether 'postmodernism' signals a new recognition of cultural differences or is simply 'the last proper name of the west' . . . remains to be debated."[55]

6 Rock Music from Mao to Nirvana

The West Is the Best

He penetrates the left side of the belly.

One gets at the very heart of the darkening of the light,

And leaves gate and courtyard.

Hexagram 36, "Darkening of the light," *Yijing*

"The way the Chinese people have received rock music is a good example [of Mao Zedong's importance]. In the 1960s, Hong Kong and Taiwan started to imitate the West in doing rock music, but up to now they still don't have any real rock music. The mainland only started to do rock music in the mid-1980s with Cui Jian, whose music is true rock. We don't base ourselves on the West's influence, but on the spiritual force Mao Zedong gave us."[1] This is troubadour Zhang Guangtian's assessment of rock music in China in 1995. He is not the only one to have linked China's rock 'n' roll to Mao Zedong. The popular youth writer Wang Shuo and actor-turned-filmmaker Jiang Wen have both compared the effervescence of the Cultural Revolution to a huge rock 'n' roll party, and so has music critic Liang Heping, comparing rock's noise to slogans and other boisterous cries of the Maoist regime at its peak.[2] The *Dictionary of American Pop/Rock* describes rock as emphas[izing] "energy and sensory overload, boldly exploiting various types of distortion . . . to expand the consciousness, liberate the self, and rediscover the world."[3] It is amusing to think that in China, rock's roots (a nice oxymoron) are to be found in Mao's rebellious, permanent-revolution ideology. Of course, contact in the early 1980s with foreign students and the general availability of cassettes, television, and radio transmission is also commonly seen as decisive in the emergence of rock music in China. What matters today is that rock music is now part and parcel of the music industry of China and that it has spun off as many subgenres as rock anywhere in the world. Robert Efird, who played in a Chinese rock band (Mohe) in the mid-1990s, noted that "[Chinese] musicians were extremely fluent in any kind of music; there was no belatedness."[4]

There is indeed a music industry in China and it now caters to all tastes: high-brow, contemporary, and traditional music, folk, rock, pop, Muzak, all both Chinese and non-Chinese, you name it, they got it. There are local and foreign labels vying for the local market: the majors (EMI, RCA/Victor, PolyGram) and small and large domestic recording companies, both state and privately owned, in every province. Music can be seen (on television, from the choirs of the "evening shows" 'wan-hui' and on videoclips, from central television as well as cable) and heard (in public places, from outdoor broadcasting, bars, karaokes, discos; at home or work, on radios, Walkmans, CD players, ghettoblasters). In the midst of all these choices, the newcomer is rock music. In 1993, there was an explosion in the distribution of recorded rock music in China. The first compilations, *Zhongguo huo (China Fire)* and *Beijing yaogun (Beijing Rock)*, date back to 1992 and 1993, the former a local label, the latter a foreign one. In 1995, there were follow-ups to both. Rock is alive and well in China. Most of it has been coopted, following the capitalist edicts of the music culture industry.

The rock critics Simon Frith and John Street both reject the dichotomy between rock and pop.[5] I tend to agree with them, as concerns China's music scene over the past ten years. All forms are somehow political (potentially subversive or submission-inducive) and are inevitably incorporated within the dominant culture. The subversive potential habitually associated with rock music was, in 1980s China, shared with unlikely genres such as film scores and country-and-western tunes. Today, rockers sing of love and croon out Teresa Teng's escapist love songs. A full circuit has been made: Deng Lijun, as the Taiwanese singer was then known, was listened to, hummed to, sung softly to by all generations in the early 1980s.

Popular music is difficult to theorize because it "is by its nature *individualizing*" and "*collective*";[6] because a song's meaning is not reducible to what the lyrics say; because it "depends both on what the listener understands and on what the singer intends."[7] Moreover, given the fact that there are so many varied outlets for music, it is impossible to grasp the overall reception of a "popular music" such as rock. Regardless of the fact that rock in China is given very little air-play, and almost no live performances save for occasional parties in foreign bars and hotels, still it is played and listened to, when not danced to, and it is marketed even in China.

Some work has been written on China's rock music: most noteworthy in English are Andrew Jones, Rey Chow, and Gregory Lee.[8] Although each author has a different agenda when addressing rock music, they all imply that rock music is oppositional. Andrew Jones, whose very informative 1986 book surveys and analyzes different styles of music, concludes that rock and *tongsu* (popular) music have become more and more polarized (147). I don't think this statement is tenable today. The underlying assumption here is the usual one, common also in the West, that rock music is authentic, emancipatory, contestatory, while pop music is mass-numbing. Rock music in the West, especially in the sixties with Bob Dylan and John Lennon, carried the responsibility of challenging dominant culture, of awakening (political) consciousness. Now, rock—a highly generic term—cannot be viewed so simply. China's rock follows the same logic as in the West. It cannot be simply and unilaterally read as a counterdiscourse, as an underground mode for dissident voices. There exists now what is termed "alternative" 'linglei,' but it is, as anywhere, one among many selections that young people can play.

Mellow yellow tunes

My ideal is there, my body is here.

Cui Jian, "The box" ("Hezi")

China has a long tradition of absorbing alternative modes within its mainstream. In the musical sphere, a constant has been to incorporate folksongs by reinterpreting the words or by getting rid of the words and keeping the tune. In 1993, an article on the origin of the once sacrosanct "East is red" (Dongfanghong) was published.[9] The article, an interview with a veteran songwriter, discloses the fact that the revolutionary "East is red" is not, as has been officially stated, the work of the peasant lyricist Li Youyuan but was originally a salacious ditty from northern Shaanxi province, entitled "Zhimayou" (Sesame oil) which, with a few words and interjections, celebrates the pleasures of (male) sexual satisfaction after a hearty meal. Two party members, considering the popular success of the tune, reoriented it toward Mao and the revolution, eventually making it as important (i.e., played constantly) as the "Internationale" during all the years of the Cultural Revolution. The interviewed songwriter also adds that, although in those days his art propaganda team concocted many songs of their own, they never caught on.

This palimpsest quality adds a twist to the complexity of popular music. The recuperation of folk songs has a long history in China, a history of at least three thousand years, if the *Shijing (Book of Songs)* is taken as the first case. In this century, Mao Zedong excelled at recycling old proverbs, sayings from the country people.[10] Mao and his propaganda teams were definitely familiar with Shaanxi music, having spent some ten years in the Yan'an area. Since the Yan'an years, *minge* 'folksongs' from that area have been worked and retuned to suit the contemporary ear, be it in terms of rhythm (ironed out, sped up) or in terms of lyrics (totally changed or reverted to their "original" words). This is China's "western" music, which is everybody's thesaurus, including the rockers'.

Rocker Hou Muren for example, first released an album entitled *Hei yueliang (Black Moon)*, which features a popular Shaanxi song, "Leave the oil lamp on" (Liuxia youdeng guang), as if it were his own composition and delivered it in a slow, romantic fashion. In 1992, with other "rock" friends, he released a CD entitled *Hongse yaogun (Red Rock)*, which also recalls distant Yan'an and more recent Maoist times, but set to a wild, rock 'n' roll rhythm. Hou distorted the tunes of socialist favorites across time, from the "Internationale" itself to such oldies as the pre-1949 "Martial song of the PLA" (Zhongguo jiefangjun junge), the Korean War–era "War song of the volunteer army from the Chinese people" (Zhongguo renmin zhiyuanjun zhange), the Great Leap Forward "Socialism is good" (Shehuizhuyi hao) and "We march on the big road" (Women zou zai dalushang), and last, from the people's communes, "The members of the commune are like sunflowers" (Sheyuan doushi xiangyanghua). The purpose of Hou's album is definitely to offer an irreverent performance of the socialist classics. The mere juxtaposition of all these tunes reduces all of revolutionary China's historical moments to a jumble and implies a lack of respect for history. A young singer, Zhang Chu (who now has at least three rock LPs to his credit) repeatedly yelled out the refrain/slogan: "Socialism is good, / Socialism is good, / In a socialist country, people's status is high." This ear-shattering performance of the simple lines has since been resung in other contexts—by Mou Sen's experimental theater group during training.[11] It serves to release pent-up emotions that are not necessarily if at all linked to the lyrics. Similarly, the heavy metal band, Tang Chao (Tang Dynasty)'s rendering of the "Internationale" was not judged sacreligious; it was even used in 1993 to familiarize high-school students with the otherwise completely unknown universal anthem.[12] Superannuated propaganda songs are always uplifting, and, if accelerated, increased in decibel level, and reused some thirty years later, they are still effective because of their exuberance, excitement—the very "energy and sensory overload" rock is purported to exude. Of course, the pleasure also derives from the thrill of playing with a little bit of danger, with what were once serious socialist songs (but how many of them were first bawdy ditties?). Such appropriation of "red" songs is somewhat akin in their defiant pose, to the political pop art use of political icons in painting. Yet, because rock musicians use the medium of language, it is exclusively geared to Chinese-speaking people. I think such projects would be inscribable in what Frith has called rock's "struggle for fun."[13]

"The politics is in the pleasure"[14] describes many musical ventures of China in the 1990s, especially the redirecting of red songs and tunes.

18. Tang Dynasty rock band. Cover of their album
A Dream Return to the Tang Dynasty, 1992.

From 1991 to 1993, three records came out of the official China Record-ing Company, entitled *Hong taiyang (Red Sun)*. They consist of eulo-gistic songs to Mao Zedong (musically marketing the Mao craze and Mao's 1993 centennial anniversary commemoration). The 1992 album was the bestseller of the year. These songs are also sped up and given a "new rhythm" 'xin jiezou,' actually a disco beat. There followed similar recordings, in slow and swift renderings: Mao Zedong songs for karaoke sing-alongs. Many people, young and old, got into the swinging mood with these revitalized and familiar (for the older generation, all-too-familiar) tunes. Obviously, these productions and the *Red Rock* albums are musically different and aim at different "communities," but merri-ment is the goal of all the releases.

Reappropriation of the socialist past started in the late 1980s in ways that seem incompatible with one another. Su Yue, now a maker of pop stars, composed "Huangtu gaopo" (Hills of yellow earth), which Hu Yue sang in an energetic yet melodious voice. It was heard everywhere in China in 1988. Much like "Leave the oil lamp on," "Hills" is a description of life in cave dwellings (such as those in Shaanxi), where man and animal harmoniously lead a poor yet content life. At the other end of the Yan'an style is Zhao Jiping's music for Fifth-Generation films, especially his "Meimei ni dadande wang qian zou" (Little sister, keep on moving) for Zhang Yimou's celebration of primitive life, *Red Sorghum.* Boisterous renderings of male desire are rendered by hoarse voices and traditional Yan'an instruments. Hu Yue became a television favorite with her "Hills" song, and Zhang Yimou himself made a television appearance to sing "Little sister," the other hit of 1988. Media marketing of Yan'an-type songs were by then inevitable: both "country-and-western" (Hu Yue) and rock (Zhang Yimou) were dislodging sweet Taiwanese songs.

Before them, though, authorities had rejected one rendition, that of Cui Jian who was to become China's rock megastar. In 1987, he sang "Nanniwan"—a canonical communist song celebrating the rural transformation of that desolate Yan'an area, composed in the early 1940s by He Jingzhi (or so it is claimed)—for the annual television gala *One Hundred Stars.* Cui Jian did not change any of the lyrics of this song, which tells how Regiment 359, led by Wang Zhen, went to Nanniwan in 1942, to irrigate the land and make it miraculously fertile. Cui used only the first stanza, thereby omitting the achievements of Wang and his selfless, hardworking troupe. But Wang himself, by then a venerable top-cadre officer, was in the audience that evening and did not appreciate Cui's transformation of the cheerful song into a sad folksong. Cui's "Nanniwan," which has since been recorded, sounds like a funeral hymn, with its slow beat, its sad and raw sounds, a mix of blues and traditional folk instruments. When Cui sung the line "the place is not like it used to be," no one took this to be a positive comment, which it was not, considering that Yan'an is as dirt poor as ever. Cui lost his job as a trumpeter at the Beijing Symphonic Orchestra: he had sung a revolutionary ("red") song in a perverse ("yellow") way 'hongge huangchang.' It would seem that raucousness is fine, but certainly not a slow spelling out of the words, allowing for a critical reexamination of the validity of socialist exuberance and optimism.

The first album of the China Recording Company's *Red Sun* series features another version of "Nanniwan." It is sung by a virile voice, not really preachy, but definitely heroic and enthusiastic, without any reference to the bitter reality of the Nanniwan of both yesterday and today:

Nanniwan, what a nice place.
A nice place, a beautiful vista.
Everywhere, crops growing,
everywhere cows, sheep grazing.
Nanniwan of past times,
deserted mountains, without smoke, without life.
Nanniwan of today,
it is not what it used to be.
It is not at all like before,
northern Shaanxi, what a nice place!

An uncritical, for-profit use of socialist songs is today quite acceptable because it grants some entertainment to the masses (nostalgic release, inoffensive mindless fun) while having the quality of being specifically "Chinese," as well as being tied to official (Party) history.

On the other hand, Cui Jian's execution of the piece rendered a kind of pathos, not a typified folksy treatment but the blues (dejection) of the people within the utopian socialist project. Cui Jian's music is eminently political. His songs insist on the political subtext of apparently naïve peasant folk songs. Thematically, most of his compositions, especially of the first 1989 album, contain political allusions. The title of the first album is telling enough: *I Have Nothing: Rock 'n' Roll on the New Long March (Yiwu suoyou: Xin changzheng lushang de yaogun)*. It coalesces personal grievances and historical events, in this case the Long March of 1934–36, that Mao and his one hundred thousand followers undertook, surrounded on all sides by the Nationalists and under extreme conditions, and which came to a close when the seven thousand or so survivors set up base in the Yan'an region:

One, two, three, four.
Heard about it, never seen it, 25 thousand li.
Some talk about it, none [who] did it,

how [do they] know it wasn't easy.
Buried head, move on, find myself.
Come here, go there, got no base . . .
What can I say, what can I do, to be truly myself?
what can I play, what can I sing, to satisfy my soul?
I walk thinking [of] snowy mountains and plains.
I walk singing [of] leader Chairman Mao.
Oh! One, two, three, four, five, six, seven.[15]

Cui's compositions are plain lyrics loaded with questions and possible interpretations. Until recently, Cui Jian performed in highly coded political gear, another affront to the establishment: a People's Liberation Army vest, old pants with unequal legs, and a little red kerchief suggestive of the red guards, the Young Pioneers, and all of red China (which was said to be "Red all over" 'yipian hong'). While performing his song "Yikuai hongbu" (A piece of red cloth) from the second album *Jiejue (Solution),* he blindfolds himself with the red hankerchief, and some of his musicians gag themselves with the same:

That day you took a piece of red cloth, covered my eyes and covered
the sky.
You asked me what I saw, I said I saw happiness.
This feeling makes me feel good, it makes me forget I've got no place
to live.
You ask what else I want, I say I want to walk your road.[16]

Cui Jian is in many ways China's Bob Dylan. Both have "fulfilled a significant political-cultural role through [their] more detached posture as generational voice."[17] Like Bob Dylan, many of Cui Jian's songs have become anthems for civil rights. During the spring of 1989, Cui's "I have nothing" was continuously heard on Tiananmen Square. Yet, like Dylan, Cui abhors being considered the "spokesman for a generation."[18] Cui has said: "Art has a political responsibility but no political finality."[19] Like Dylan's, Cui's lyrics and imagery can be read innocuously—as love songs, for example—as well as directly oppositional to the establishment. As He Li puts it, "Cui's person, his 'me' ['geren'] is forever glued ['zhanlian'] to history. His lyrics are filled with political innuendos."[20] Gregory Lee goes one step further by qualifying Cui's stance as "within a patriotic discourse": "While he engages in a critique of capitalist consumption and state control and looks to an ideal which is somehow more spiritual, Cui Jian's idealism seems still to be constructed in terms of some sort of overhauled nationalism."[21] Today, it is difficult to maintain this point of view. Again, like Dylan, Cui has, over the years, become more involved with musical experimentation and less so with "saving the country," as a closer study of his later 1995 album, *Hongqi xia de dan (Balls under the Red Flag)* would show.

In the 1990s, other troubadours have emerged, namely Zhang Guangtian, a Shanghaier who also travels the country, singing the blues. But, if Cui Jian used "semiotic guerilla warfare" (Dick Hebdige's expression), then his followers, like Bob Dylan's followers, are "guerillas [who have] simply, without their even realizing it, been incorporated into the regular army of the enemy."[22] At work are both cooptation and perversion. Zhang Guangtian's 1993 album, *Zhang Guangtian xiandai gequ zhuanji (A Collection of Modern Songs by Zhang Guangtian),* includes the ballad titled "Singing along the way" (Yilu zou, yilu chang):

Been through the flatlands,
been through the low hills, been through the grasslands,
been through the towns, been through the big roads,
been through the small lanes, been through the forest,
been through the mines,
been through hunger, found hope,
been through poverty, found [my] ideal. . . . Along the way, I walk
    and think,
along the way I look and sing,
sing of the flowers blooming along the way,
sing of the man who liberates himself along the way.[23]

Such lyrics, reminiscent of Cui Jian's wild transgressions, are, however, of an altogether different sort, a positive humanistic call. "Rebel folksinger preaches his own brand of Maoism" is the *Far Eastern Economic Review*'s description of Zhang Guangtian's venture, one gauge of how the poses that popular musicians take are endorsed by the foreign press.[24] Unlike Cui's songs, Zhang's never provoke uncomfortable, negative feelings. Cui's allegorical use of sexual love is absent from songs by Zhang and other contemporary singers, which sing of love — romantic love—almost literally. Zhang's song "Mao Zedong," for example, from the album of the same name, plays on the listener's nostalgia (whether experienced or not): it tells of the time when life meant having an ideal, and that life's ideal was Mao Zedong. In a clever move, the singer's childhood memories of Mao (via the omnipresent gigantic statues) combine with the memory of his first sweetheart:

> I saw you standing all by yourself,
> your fingers were pointing at the square of my heart.
> Oh! I'll walk with you, Mao Zedong. . . . When this girl came to
>   stand beside me,
> the badge on her breast shone a radiant dream.
> Now that love and struggle have become one,
> give me, oh! give me strength, Mao Zedong.[25]

This adolescent look at the Cultural Revolution feeds into the great nostalgic revival machine of that era, at work now, and into the pop industry's penchant for "puppy love" and/or romantic love. Inoffensive dreams are being manufactured that leave out the tension between official and personal history and turn history into simply personal emotions. Such is the accomplishment of 1993's top-of-the-charts song, "Xiao Fang" (Little Fang), sung by Cantopop Li Chunbo, which pays homage to a nice country girl whom the male singer would have met during his rustication. Of course, he left her behind and now simply wants to thank her for the "good times" during those "hard times" of the Cultural Revolution. Zheng Jun turns Tibet into a love nest in his song "Back to Lhasa" (Huidao Lasa): he is going back to Lhasa, to its pretty temples, where the girls are all giggling, and it feels like he's going "home." The song, in a soft-rock mode, also shot to the top of the charts. Incursions into "innocent" themes are thriving, the most enduring being the campus folk songs, which, accompanied by a simple unplugged guitar, sound like any ballad of the Western world. *Tongzhuo de ni (You Who Shared My Schooldesk)* is the hit of all of these by now endless albums. A male narrator is flipping through his school yearbook and spots the girl who used to sit next to him: "In those days the sky was always blue, the days always long." He recalls her as a cry-baby and now wonders with whom she has married.[26] The songs are full of good intentions, even heartbreaks are sweet, and the lyrics are totally devoid of humor and, of course, of any kind of edge. China's Central Broadcasting Station is now airing these campus folksongs at frequent intervals and sponsored a contest in 1996.[27] Pop music therefore does serve an apolitical political function by marketing, for the times, history as individual history, by serving a proxy democracy. Romantic love, as subject matter and as musical motif has pervaded for good the great symphonic orchestra of all China.[28] If the Taiwanese Deng Lijun's sweet sounds were in the early 1980s secretly adored and endorsed as an escape from the everyday, loud grind, today southern tunes—"Cantopop" (Taiwanese and Cantonese), revamped by northerners—run most of the music mill and top the charts. Indeed, "romantic ideology is central to the organisation of the capitalist record industry."[29]

The range of rock, male and female: No stones unturned

Fortunately, the revolutionary and rebellious spirit of the West is still felt in the north, in Beijing, where there are more than two hundred rock groups.[30] Beijing is still very much the rock capital of China. In the 1996 album titled *Linglei pinpan (Alternative Compilation)*, featuring bands from all over China, the best pieces are all from the Beijing bands: Cangying (The Fly), Ziyue (Confucius Said), and Chen Jin. Other great new Beijing rockers include Xuewei, Zhou Ren, and Luo Qi (A K A Rose). Today, the West is not only Yan'an, but also North America and England. The music critic He Li, even claims that the post–Cui Jian generation is influenced solely by foreign musical genres for the creation of their own brand of hard rock, heavy metal, grunge, and so on.[31] The ultimate model is the Seattle grunge band Nirvana and its lead singer, Kurt Cobain, who committed suicide in 1994. This band is commonly considered sincere and free-spirited. One recalls their strange but not cryptic lyrics ("Polly wants a cracker"), great yet not convoluted musical compositions, but especially their negative attitude toward the rock institution, stardom, and permanence: for example, Cobain's unmacho cross-dressing for interviews or the destruction of their instruments after each show "for pure fun and so as not to have to do encores."[32]

The West has a rock band called Yes, and China has, since 1993, a band called No (the name of the group is in English). To my knowledge, it

19. The rocker Dou Wei. Film still from Zhang Yuan's *Beijing Bastards*,
1993. *Donated by Zhang Yuan.*

is the only underground band with a reputation. Based in Beijing, its
leader (composer and main singer) is Zu Zhou, whose own given name
translates as "Curse." One song, "Wu jie" (No solution), starts with a
long shrill yell, a definite "No!" to many things. His band has only recorded that one song:

> The left leg doesn't know the right leg
> the right leg doesn't know the left leg
> the left hand doesn't know the right hand
> the right hand doesn't know the left hand
> I need to see a doctor, I need an operation
> the left leg has become the right leg
> the right leg has become the left leg
> the left hand has become the right hand
> the right hand has become the left hand
> I need to see a doctor, I need an operation.[33]

This song seems to be an ironic retort to Cui Jian's "Kuai rang wo zai
zhe xuedi shang sadianr ye" (Let me go wild in the snow):

I'm shirtless, I walk into the snowstorm,
running on that road where I escaped from the clinic.
Don't stop me I don't need any clothes
because my disease is that I've got no feeling.

With the crucial difference that Cui's lyrics have more "flesh":

Give me some stimulation old man doctor,
give me some loving my sister nurse.
Quick let me cry, let me laugh.

No's music is dysfunctional music, with off-beat guitar sounds, sloppily slurred repetitious words or phrases such as "Fuck, I'm a dog" ("Gou" — Dog) or the repeated crying out, some thirty times, of the name of the mythic female now adorning a cigarette brand (Ashima).[34]

The No band is antipodal to Cui Jian, the pioneer of Chinese rock, whose second album (of three) and its title song, "Solution," offer a more positive, "youthful" energy than No's despondent performance:

Nowadays there're so many problems, no way to solve them
But always no opportunities, and that's an even bigger problem. . . .
Although my head is filled with problems,
they don't outnumber that unseen infinite happiness. . . .
Me and this world will be solved by you.[35]

No's Zu Zhou has said: "I listen to only two [Chinese rock] groups: Cui Jian and No. Cui Jian, because he can do anything; myself, because I can't do anything."[36] No's songs are of the "no future" type: slasher, schizoid, sadomasochistic, scatological. Their self-representation is mainly as dogs and their imagery tends to privilege crawling creatures, excrement, and very unusual sexual couplings (cross-species, incestuous, necrophiliac). The titles are sufficiently indicative: "Cangying, mayi, qu he pingzi, gangmen, jiu" (Flies, ants, maggots and bottles, anus, alcohol), "Wo shi ni choushui matongli de yitiao she" (I am a snake in your flushing toilet). As He Li notes, there is no transcendence of materiality in their lyrics.[37] Consider this eerie account of evolution:

Maggots are the ancestors of flies
ants are the death knell of maggots

flies are the widowers of ants . . .
alcohol is the pulse of bottles
anuses are made from bottles
bottles, anuses are friends in need.

Rock DJ Sun Mengjin writes: "The No band's music does not come out of China's countryside, it comes from some graveyard, perhaps all of humanity's graveyard." [38]

Sun Mengjin is a rock fan and critic who has run, since June 1993, a radio show devoted to rock that airs twice a week, at night, courtesy of the Shanghai Eastern Broadcasting Corporation. He has an immense following and was the main editor of the internal document 'neibu jiao-liu' *Rock* magazine, which appeared once in 1995.[39] "I don't live well, that is my freedom" (wo huode bu yukuai, zhe shi wo de ziyou) is the type of nihilistic phrase that the intense Sun punctuates his airtime with, along with his own poems, which speak of the bleakness of life, of the wonder and force of authentic rock: "Rock is life, stark-naked." [40] (Youdai is his homologue in Beijing but the differences between them are, precisely like their schedules, day and night. The main difference is that You-dai's three shows, aired on Beijing Music Radio, are thoroughly super-vised; Youdai must translate all songs before they are aired and sub-mit them for approval. Some, of course, don't get aired. Unlike Sun's 1960s rock discourse, Youdai has a "mellow-as-molasses delivery" [41] and much savoir-faire. He has even opened a record store in Beijing. Sun is an unrepentant fan of radical rock figures like Jim Morrison, Jimmy Hendrix, and Kurt Cobain. He recommends only one Chinese band un-conditionally, the No band, which has no access to the media, except perhaps on his show and at an occasional "party."

Sun's review of Cui Jian's album, *Hongqi xia de dan (Balls under the Red Flag),* is highly critical of what he terms Cui's current inauthen-tic ways.[42] While recognizing him as the "father" of China's rock, Sun nevertheless bemoans the fact that Cui Jian, in *Balls,* is no longer an angry young man, no longer revolutionary, an adversary to material wealth and worldly fame. For him, Cui's actual singing of "I having nothing" is empty and false. His new songs are perfect rock composi-tions, but they don't rock anything anymore. Indeed, Sun's views match those of many (Chinese) rock fans and at least one other music critic, He

Li: "Cui Jian as the symbol of rebellion, can no longer be accepted."[43] In the conclusion to his 1995 article on Cui Jian, Sun claims that Cui Jian's era is over but that no new era has yet emerged.

Cui Jian is the only rocker in China who has moved the masses, whose music—in the past at least—has moved with(in) popular culture. The documentary directed by Greg Lanning, *China Rocks: The Long March of Cui Jian* shows Cui Jian in his heyday, following his first album. He was still poor, living with his parents, struggling to find a place to rehearse, but especially aching to perform throughout China, to do his own "long march." This video shows how intimate the link was between Cui Jian's music and the people's aspirations: at Tiananmen Square in 1989, as mentioned earlier, and at his benefit tour in 1989 for the Asian Games, spectators waved, side by side, posters of Cui Jian and Mao Zedong. The raves he received were comparable in intensity to those given to Mao when he appeared on the rostrum during the Cultural Revolution, or (back home) to a Beatles concert. Music critic Liang Heping (interviewed in Lanning's video) compared Mao's charisma to the Beatles, and Cui's appeal to Mao Zedong's. In 1991, Cui was saying things such as "We are not your typical artists who are different from ordinary people—we represent them." Cui Jian's music was indeed the voice of all Chinese people. His ballads, which fed on both Western and traditional Chinese melodies, were adored by all. A most poignant example of this, shown in the Lanning video, is "I have nothing," played by townspeople at a wedding, but using solely traditional instruments (suona, dizi, zheng), while the groom sang the words to his new bride:

> I've asked over and over, when will you come with me,
> but you always laugh at me having nothing.
> I want to give you my dreams, to give you my freedom,
> but you always just laugh at me having nothing. . . .
> Can it be that you're telling me you love me having nothing?

Since, that same song has been performed by pop stars such as Liu Huan, who sings the theme song of the television series *A Beijinger in New York.*

Cui Jian's music reverberates like Bob Dylan's, and like Dylan's, Cui's music has evolved into complex arrangements that do not appeal any longer to all of China. Today, China's rock scene includes very many stars, all in a niche of their own, Cui Jian included. Cui's lyrics continue to play the double-entendre between love and politics. "Beijing gushi" (A Beijing story), a song on his album *Balls under the Red Flag,* turns the love a woman is giving him into a political campaign, into the revolution that changes his life. Throughout his songs, Cui has emphasized personal courage—"Courage belongs to yourself" ("Bu zai yanshi" [No more hiding] from *Rock 'n' roll on the New Long March*)—or guts, if you prefer; he promoted self-empowerment and the expression of one's desires ("Toujifenzi" [Opportunist] from *Solution*). In the song "Balls under the red flag," he states again that "our" courage is still too small (referring to "us," the "bad" eggs born under the red flag), that "we" must not follow in other people's steps, that "we" can trust no one but "ourselves." Cui Jian sung energetically at the beginning of the nineties "Once I'm dead I'll start over again" ("Congtou zailai" [Starting over]), and the crowd joined in. Then and now, in the mid-nineties, he still sings of going forward, against the wind (political and natural). Cui's aura remains exceptionally vibrant because he is active, yet invisible. He is banned from public performances and is promoting emerging bands, such as Ziyue (Confucius Said). He is thus, like it or not, a father figure of the rock scene.

Pluralism in rock music is the order of the day. The selections go from rap, reggae, jazz, World Beat, and heavy metal to punk and even to dance music. The music industry is thriving; tapes and CDs come out in great numbers, from local and foreign labels (still in the forefront are Taiwan's Magic Stone for rock and Hong Kong's Hongxing and Dadi for soft rock or pop, but JVC, RCA/Victor, BMG, EMI, Sony, and Polygram are also recording the more famous rockers). And videoclips give some physicality to what would otherwise remain unrepresented physically, since Chinese authorities continue to prohibit unofficial mass rallies, and therefore large-scale rock concerts. Except for sporadic shows, performances only take place in foreign venues or joint-venture bars and hotels where chic Chinese mingle with the diplomats and foreign students. These events are referred to, in English, as "party."

On the radio, more and more varieties of rock are heard, mixed in with the patriotic and socialist ballads. On local television, although most videoclips are also innocuous odes sung by choirs, most rock bands have made an appearance or two. The few rock bands that were attempting to be authentic at the beginning of the 1990s have since been coopted or are at a standstill. Of these, the Panthers (Heibao) and Tang Dynasty (Tangchao) participated in a nostalgia album entitled *Farewell Rock Album* in 1996, paying homage to the Taiwanese singer of love ballads, Teresa Teng (AKA Deng Lijun), who died in 1995. For the occasion, they all became crooners. The most surprising is of course the heavy metal band, the Panthers, who transformed themselves into purring pussycats: "I gave you my spring and left winter for myself. . . . Love is an eternal melody."[44] They are completely unrecognizable from their haunting débuts where, with raucous voices and pounding rhythm, they flouted convention. The song "Wudi zirong" (Looking for a hole to crawl into), for example, was such a statement of defiance:

> I don't believe anymore, don't believe in any reasoning. . . .
> I don't look back anymore, don't look back at any past.
> I'm not the one I used to be.[45]

Such straightforwardness was, at the beginning of the 1990s, not uncommon in China's rock songs. Another famous song of the early Panthers, "Lianpu" (Masks), stood up against hypocrisy and called out for lucidity:

> Living under pretense. . . . Tear off the hypocritical mask.
> Face this place.
> Choose once more a world of your own.
> Throw out your old shoes, get a brand new face.
> Only then will you find the world you're looking for.[46]

The other group that paid homage to Teng's escapist melodies was Tang Dynasty (Tangchao), a heavy metal band, which has opted for dreamy scenery in which chrysanthemums, ancient swords, mythic tales like that of the herdsman and the weaver, poems by Li Bai (the Tang dynasty's wine-loving poet), deserted ruins, soaring birds, and full moons convey, along with coffee and (always) wine, a sensual utopian atmosphere of nowhere. On the compilation album *Farewell,* Tang Dynasty, somewhat appropriately, sings Teng's "Du shang xilou" (Alone in the western pavilion):

Without words, alone,
I go up to the Western Pavilion,
Moon like a hook,
Lonely wutong tree.

Their famous 1992 song "Menghui Tangchao" (A dream return to the Tang dynasty) is of a similar mood, very distinctively Chinese in its icons, yet with a touch of modernity:

Chrysanthemums, ancient swords and wine, are steeped in coffee in the clamorous pavilion.
A foreign race is worshipping the ancient moon in the altar of the sun.
The heyday of the Kaiyuan era enchants one.
The wind can't disperse eternal regret,
flowers can't dye over a longing for home,
snow can't cast a light on mountain rivers,
the moon won't fulfill the ancient dreams.
[I] Follow my palms' lines where destiny is stamped.
Tonight, [I] waken from wine without dreams.
[I] follow destiny and enter an enchanting thought.
In dreams [I] return to the Tang dynasty.[47]

Tang Dynasty's music is more intellectual than Teng's and its purpose is more diffuse. All these poetic allusions to past glories cannot be mere divertimenti. Tang Dynasty offers the musical connoisseur a refined space to dream China. Its musical arrangements also convey an "oriental" atmosphere, with the use of gongs, while the videos of their songs are set in typically Chinese historic sites, such as the picturesque Ming tombs for "A dream return to the Tang Dynasty," which was voted Best Video in Asia in the 1993 MTV Music Video Awards. These lank, long-haired young men, all dressed in black, are seen performing in a "yellow earth" setting, then running with their hair blowing in the wind, while the high-pitched falsetto voice of the lead singer is heard piercing through clamorous bass guitar sounds. A weird, contrasting effect is successfully created, of an androgynous anyone and a Chinese nowhere. It is "national music" in a way, because of its stress on ethnic cultural symbols. The fact that their music sells well, especially in Hong Kong, confirms the reading of it as a utopian Chinese space for contemporary Chinese youth, no matter where their geopolitical frontiers. It is ironic to note that after their reappropriation of an eternal poetic China comes the reappropriation of the disposable love ballads of Teresa Teng. It is hard to make sense of their musical project because they have also done a very raucous version of the masculinist "Internationale," and because they took the name Tang Dynasty on the suggestion of a foreign student doing research on the Tang dynasty.[48]

One artist to voice a counterdiscourse on China is the bad-boy figure, He Yong, the foremost exponent of punk in China. His pose is definitely contestatory, resolutely contemporary, and definitely urban. He Yong makes blazing antiauthority statements, some of which have sent him to jail.[49] In 1992, He was saying: "My music will remain, as opposed to the Panthers', underground."[50] Of course, one could not have imagined then that the Panthers would one day sing Teresa Teng without the slightest touch of irony. But that has happened, and He Yong himself is certainly not an underground musician any longer. He has emerged in full light in extremely well-made videos, such as the *Zhonggu lou (The Bell and Drum Towers)* clip, in which he is seen sitting in broad daylight on the Beijing city wall, playing a guitar while the whole neighborhood goes about its daily routines. The sounds of the neighborhood chime in with his rhythm: the shoemaker hammering a ladies' high-heel shoe, the blind banjo player, the old ladies playing *majiang*. The lyrics are very down-to-earth, very Chinese, and more specifically, very "Beijing." The lyrics end with

> My home is inside the Second Ring road,
> my home is this side of the Bell and Drum Towers,
> my home it's inside that large courtyard,
> My home my home my home it's right on this earth.[51]

For those who know Beijing, the place could not be more circumscribed. The video was shot in one of the few remaining old quarters of the city's north-east where there are not yet high-rise concrete compounds. The rest of the song talks about the slow provincial life of its inhabitants, of the migrant workers in the restaurants, of the foodstalls, and also of the impending destruction of it all. There is no sweetness in any of He Yong's songs. Actually, most of his songs are aggressive, such as the one which is also the album's title, "Lajichang" (Garbage dump):

The place we live in is like a garbage dump.
The people are like insects.
Everyone's struggling and stealing.
We eat our consciences and shit ideology.[52]

The ecopolitical concerns actually extend to all of the planet: "Some people go on diets, some people die of hunger, die of hunger, die of hunger, die of hunger." Cui Jian said of He Yong that, behind his violence, he has some of the spirit of Greenpeace.[53] He Yong stayed underground until his music, with some altered, internationalized lyrics, was recorded in 1994 by Taiwan's Magic Stone, and accompanying videos were released. The *Garbage Dump* video is a tour de force showing He Yong in a cage, yelling at the top of his lungs, He Yong being shoved around by bad guys (with nylon stockings on their heads), dunked into red dye, and then injected with a syringe containing more red dye. This is a pose, the stylish pose of the sadomasochistic punker who is at the margins of society. Another pose is the bad treatment of women: in "Guniang piaoliang" (Pretty girl), He Yong lines up unlikely images, shocking equations such as: "Should I find myself a girlfriend or raise a pet dog?"[54] He would seem to have a cantankerous stage personality, destroying things on stage, and occasionally speaking out, to the dismay and irritation of the establishment.

He Yong is definitely not mainstream, nor is Tang Dynasty, but they certainly are central in the rock music industry. Many other examples could be given of distinct styles on the rock circuit. One last one that we could take is Dou Wei, who used to be the angry lead singer in the Panthers band and who, since 1993, has been on his own, composing and performing his own songs with an album released in 1994 by Magic Stone. His tunes are introspective, otherworldly. In his videos, Dou poses as a multimedia artist (much like the Canadian artist Robert Lepage). In *Heimeng (Black Dream)* he appears as a scuba diver in the middle of a *hutong* 'lane', only to be immediately transported into a bed full of blood. There are no narratives in his videos, just visual (and of course, auditory) effects. When he sings "Gaoji dongwu" (High-class animals) all kinds of winged creatures float about while Dou Wei sits, nodding slowly and singing: "Where is happiness?" Life, for Dou Wei, now seems to be elsewhere, in a dark, marvelous, self-created world far away from reality. His music, akin to New Wave, has a reggae beat, and his lyrics are delivered in a subdued and detached style. There is no yelling of nihilistic phrases from Dou Wei, but there is an appeal to retire into a self-made spiritual cocoon: The advice "Embrace hope, abandon sorrow" ends his song "Zhu" (Lord).[55]

It would seem, that of all the established rockers, only Cui Jian emphasizes the here and now of Chinese reality. Cui, in a song from his album *Balls* entitled "Feile" (Gone) sings, "But what I want is not out there in the air. / It's definitely not anywhere but here."[56] In "Bi'an" (The other bank), also from that album, Cui attempts to convey musically what Mou Sen's play performed: there is no Nirvana 'bi'an,' nothing but us here "together and facing the same reality."[57] He inserted taped reactions to the 1993 performances of the play as background to the song, which becomes — like so many of his works — a document-like testimony of an era, a fraternizing between young intellectuals and cultural producers who, like him, are tackling Chinese-in-the-world issues. The videoclip for one of his songs, "Gone," made by filmmaker Zhang Yuan, renders very efficaciously Cui Jian's predicament, as political voice and as performing artist. It turns his love-revolution theme into a spectacle, to be read, like a two-story stage, on two levels. On a makeshift stage of large beams, beautiful girls dance alternatively *yangge* (the "bean-sprout" dance of revolutionary days), national minority dances, and enticing strip-tease, each in the appropriate alluring costume. Below them, Cui Jian and his band play; the dancers' scarves or parts of their veils often fall through the cracks, adding more sex appeal to the scene. But what makes the show complete is the audience, represented as sitting in a bleak, anonymous auditorium and composed of elderly, Party-like members applauding away. The video makes visible the invisible, the impossible: Cui performing today in front of the authorities, who are enjoying his antiauthority songs, while the girls suture the scene, appealing to performers and audiences, on- and offstage. Guerrilla action is never public; it can only be simulated as such.

Although everyone agrees that rock is a male bastion linked to higher levels of testosterone, still, in China, as elsewhere, there are women performers, and they come in a full range of poses and genres.[58] For Ai Jing, the look is almost that of the girl next door; her songs exude the light-heartedness of an ordinary girl. No other woman, except for big-time formula stars who top the charts like Mao Amin and Wei Wei, has become a star so fast, and she has done it with a simple "autobiographical" rhetoric and an excellent video clip by filmmaker Zhang Yuan. Ai Jing's tunes are like her poses: plain, a little understated, with a touch of humor on political issues. Her best song, with accompanying videoclip, is "Wo de 1997" (My 1997). She starts off by telling us about her musical family background, then moves on to her departure at the age of seventeen from northern China (Shenyang) for Beijing, where she studied music:

> Because of my voice my life has not been so filled with anguish.
> From Beijing I sang on the Bund in Shanghai.
> and then from Shanghai I finally sang in the South.
> I stayed quite a while in Guangzhou because my boyfriend is in
>   Hong Kong.

The message of the song is clear enough:

> Since when does Hong Kong exist?
> How are the people out there?
> He can come to Shenyang
> I can't go to Hong Kong. . . . Let 1997 come a little bit faster
> I wonder just how the clothes are in Babaiban?
> Let 1997 come a little bit faster
> so I can go to Hong Kong.
> Let 1997 come a little bit faster
> so I can go to the midnight movies with him.[59]

Ai Jing's video shows her right in the middle of a Beijing street, playing her guitar with an irresistible, coy smile. She is one of the first of a series of "rock" star packagings. Her first record in 1993 was produced by Hong Kong's Dadi in collaboration with Shanghai's Yingxiang and was promoted by CIM, a Beijing-based Hong Kong cultural enterprise. Regardless of talent—which Ai Jing definitely has—would not any musician with such support have also become a star overnight? Ai Jing's songs continue to be ballads, about "personal" memories; in her second album, she, the Asian jetsetter, recalls her grandfather picking garbage off the streets.[60]

China's only all-women rock band, Cobra (Yanjingshe, often called Nüzidui, the Girls' Band) strikes a more marginal posture. They emerged with the swarm of rock bands in 1993. One song, "Ziji de tiantang" (My own paradise) was included in the first rock compilation *Beijing Rock*. Cobra makes jazzy, danceable music with lyrics that are on the verge of being cynical. A better qualifier would be "offbeat," as, for example, in the song "My own paradise":

Like an idiot
I have my own paradise.
Can't remember what roaming is.
I'm satisfied, I'm in good health,
don't need to be like you.
I eat and dress, don't need money or food,
don't need to be like them,
don't need a bed to sleep in.
What does abnormal mean?
What's happiness and sorrow?
Don't tell me what to do,
I haven't worried about it in a while.
Don't ask me about the future,
you can't help anyways.
Like an idiot I have my own paradise.[61]

Since then, Cobra has managed to record here and there a song or two and has even toured Europe and the United States, backing up megastar Cui Jian's concerts. Cobra regularly plays in Beijing bars and clubs and "parties." Its drummer and lead singer Wang Xiaofang even played a small (musical) part in the television series *Haima gewuting* (*Seahorse Karaoke*) in 1994. Their first solo release, with the English title *Hypocrisy,* under the World Beat Records label, was produced in 1996 in Beijing by rock veteran Wang Di and launched in a downtown New York HMV store. So much for marginality. Despite positive foreign press reviews,[62] even their fans find they are in a rut, repeating the same tunes over and over again, the same depressing statements, in songs on the impossibility of heterosexual relations — "Yishan men, yidu qiang, yizuo fen" (A door, a wall, a tomb) — or on the bleakness of life — "Bushi youxi de nianji" (It's not a time for games). The impact of their grim lyrics is strangely diluted by their jazzy pop tunes, delivered onstage by hip-hoppers.

One young woman who has the fiery rock spirit is Luo Qi (AKA Rose). Luo Qi released two consecutive albums, in 1995 and 1996. One song was included in the *Beijing Rock* compilation, "Qing zou renxing dao" (Please take the sidewalk). Her idiom is of the 1960s Western rock appeal: sex, drugs, and rock 'n' roll. Her song "Kuaile jiqi" (Pleasure machine) is a turn-on to serious fun:

> Let's turn ourselves into pleasure machines:
> give me a night of carnival, I'll give you a Valentine's Day.
> Turn this lonely city into a pleasure machine.[63]

Luo Qi's voice, a cry from the gutter and the guts, is perhaps the most powerful rock voice in China. Unfortunately, she is ill-served by her mediocre band, Zhinanzhen (Compass), and recordings of rather poor quality.

And then there is Wei Hua, the former English-channel anchor-woman who had, with Huxi (Breathing Band), taken quite strong positions on the usual rock themes — freedom, self, truth — but who then came out with another album, totally divergent in ideology. It is a full acceptance of life's new pleasures and commodities. Somewhat in the light tone of Ai Jing, Wei Hua now celebrates in her album *Xiandai-hua/Modernization* the modernization of her desires and the lifestyle of a consumerist society. In "Sunday," her pleasure is to go to Pizza Hut, Kentucky Fried Chicken, or to stay at home, without makeup; in "Visa" — which is sung completely in English — she lists what she wants to do, now that she has her visa:

> I just wanna hang around with my honey in hand;
> It's OK, I just wanna learn to be cool,
> walk the streets of Rome and L.A.
> I just wanna buy a few things, coffee, cheese, books, clothes,
>   perfume.[64]

ISRC CN-E01-95-377-00/A·J6

BORN IN CHINA
Shanghai Performance Doll

广灵音合字第96 (001) 号

A: 1. 少女的梦　　B: 1. 都市浪漫曲
　　2. 青春　　　　　2. 想、想、想
　　3. 舞之魅　　　　3. RAP-青春活力
　　4. 蓝天使　　　　4. 你知道不知道
　　5. 每個早上　　　5. 青春路上

20. Shanghai Performance Dolls. Cover of their album *Born in China,* 1995.

The whole album revolves around glamour, a desire for glamour, while Wei Hua herself is already its personification and her album is very slick indeed. Now that's transformation for a rocker.

A group of very young girls, much like the Spice Girls, are adding zest to the pop rock scene without any allusion whatsoever to even mildly troubling subjects. They are the Shanghai Performance Dolls, who unabashedly sing that they can't knit, can't cook, don't read, but listen to their Walkman, fix new hairdos, go to karaoke, and say sayonara to fresh new boyfriends. Their album is a sampled mix of rap, funk, dance music, enka, you name it. "Memories are for old people" [65] says one song. Wei

Hua's lyrics, although slightly cleverer, are nevertheless in keeping with this pop girlie stuff. Wei reaching the yuppie crowd; Shanghai Performance Dolls, the prepubescent and adolescent.

It would seem that rock music in China has followed, in the past ten years, so many roads that no single point of view can account for them all. Performers, too, follow multiple trends. In 1995, for example, a veteran rock singer, Zang Tianshuo, was the bestselling rocker in China. In his soft rock album titled *Wo zhe shi nian (My Last Ten Years)*, Zhang has incorporated many trends of the 1986–96 period. It is a medley of feel-good music. All forms of nativist sounds are incorporated into the basic (seventies) Western rock beat: Chinese traditional instruments blend in with Buddhist and Tibetan chants, Beijing opera, and folk songs from the Yan'an region; in turn, to these are added rap beats (some rap is delivered in English) some jazz runs, even a little bepop.

With his throaty macho voice, Zang sings in mostly slow rhythms. In the background—to enhance his masculinist stance—a female choir is heard. The everywhere/nowhere context is rather confusing, both musically and thematically. In his song "Shuo shuo" (Just say it), the whole world is covered. Zang starts from the "middle of the world," namely, China, with Cultural Revolution heroes such as Lei Feng, mentioning of course Mao's quotations but harking back to Chinese classical books such as *The Romance of the Three Kingdoms (Sanguo yanyi)* and *The Water Margin*. This epic saga is recited in a rap beat, with suona (reed flute) emphasis here and there. Then, the discourse moves on to the rest of the world (aid to Kuwait and Iraq, the dismemberment of the Soviet Union) and ends with "If there's a problem, let's sit down and talk about it."[66] With his populist philosophy and optimistic common-sense Zhang attempts to make sense of life and of the world, using an eclectic approach that irons out all differences, musical and political. Fortunately, his pop rock digest is just an extreme example of unequivocal commodification.

Some musical styles, though, could not have fit within Zang's lite agenda: for example, the nihilistic, counterculture, punkish "death" rock. At the moment of writing, such radical, disruptive rock is done by bands who have not yet released albums. Earlier in this chapter, I mentioned the No band, which puts human beings at the lowest ladder of the animal hierarchy. So does the band Xuewei, with its piece "Weibuzudao" (Insignificant), which is sung in a muffled voice that enacts the insignificance of their condition. The song opens with the bleating of sheep and the whole piece drones and blurs. Another group whose style would not suit Zang's agenda is Cangying (Fly). Fly's song "Shi qiang haishi zidan?" (Gun or Bullet?) asks whether sex is a means (gun) or an end (bullet) and coolly claims that the only thing worth having is sex. Their "theme song" is called, like them, "Flies," and it tells of flies on a shit pile that "say": "We shout out love ya-ya, / we sing human life, yeah-yeah."[67] The Flies also have a song on what it's like to defecate in a country outhouse called "Niepan," which means . . . Nirvana.

Conclusion

A World Wide Web of Words

Nothing transforms things so much as the ting. A ting with legs
   upturned
Furthers removal of stagnating stuff.
Hexagram 50, "The Caldron" (Ting), *Yijing*

Since 1992 many books on China's new idioms, on unofficial and street
language, have appeared, attesting to the disappearance of a uniform
all-China discourse. Most of these "new" expressions are anything but
new: some are revivals of pre-1949 Chinese; some are takes on socialist
jargon; and some are pirated (mainly via film and television) from Hong
Kong and Taiwan and from English and international signs. These novel
ways of using Mandarin Chinese indicate the vibrancy of contemporary
mass culture, but especially the diversification of Chinese culture as it
"moves toward the world."

The fast-forward motion of post–Mao era slogans has made for a fluid
semantics: 'zouxiang shijie' (*to advance* toward the world), 'gaige kai-
fang' (*to open* to reform), 'dakai guomen' (*to open* the country's door),
'guoji jiegui' (*to link up* internationally). Words are used in idiosyncratic ways, they are manipulated in all directions; some surface, only
to quickly disappear, others resurface to be resemanticized. Words are
on the move, too (as if there was no looking back).

Takes on socialist rhetoric

Perry Link has written a book on informal talk that stresses the importance of unofficial speech in China since the 1980s.[1] He offers the following doggerel attesting to the popularity of expressing oneself, of chatting away:

> One billion people, nine hundred million tongues churning,
> The other hundred million are in the process of learning.[2]

Popular sayings, now as in the past, tend to reach out widely and to encompass large entities, whole classes, even a whole nation, often through satirical epigrams. Many of today's new sayings deal with inequality between the ruling classes and the people. The following example shows the hierarchy of types in the so-called classless society, where the last type designates the masses still plodding away:

> The first type is a dignitary. When trouble comes there's sanctuary.
> The second type is public servant. Travels about in search of merriment.
> The third type rents a business. Eating, drinking, whoring, gambling—all in the expenses.
> The fourth type is a landlord. Cheating, duping, queering, frauding—and on the side a bawd.
> The fifth type is a famous singer. Ticket sales & wealth beyond measure.
> The sixth type is an entrepreneur. All earnings and losses his to endure.
> The seventh type is a propagandist. Gluts his maw at all the banquets.
> The eighth type is a famous painter. Draws crabs and shrimps and grows the richer.
> The ninth type wears a police helmet. Eats from the plaintiff and from the defendant.
> The tenth type is the rest of the population. We study Lei Feng and make revolution.[3]

These sayings, spreading through the "national grapevine,"[4] are retouched over and over again by various groups for their own critical purposes. Another statement on all China is "One billion people, eight hundred million are gambling, two hundred million are dancing," which decries the Chinese people's present craze for entertainment. Most of the sayings that have sprung up deal with rampant corruption, the privilege of the few, and the resulting poverty of the rest: the people, the intellectuals, and the young. " 'The scalpel of the brain surgeon earns you less than the razor of the barber' was repeated, in fall 1988, by elderly engineers in Beijing as well as by young painters in Guangzhou" (Link, 22). The television series *Heshang (Deathsong of the river)* quoted it, with its equivalent, "Better to move pianos than to play them," probably making it even more widespread, thanks to the medium. Another saying was put in entrepreneur Yu Deli's mouth, the "moving-toward-the-world" character of the popular television series *Stories of an Editorial Board* in 1991: "Money isn't everything, but without money you just can't do anything." In 1991, there was this pithy song:

> While the grandads in their 70s lead the nation,
> Uncles in their 60s take care of modernisation.
> Those in their 50s retire and take it easy;
> Our brothers in their 40s are with money-making busy.
> They say only once you're 30 do you really understand.
> But where in all this do we 20-year-olds stand?[5]

Most likely, the song derives from street sayings, jingles that pop up anonymously with their main target being ruling authority. All these are from "the people" 'minjian,' a highly valorized term in the 1990s.

Almost all popular expressions disrupt official ways of speaking. For example, the expression "eight hundred million people gambling" is a version of an official slogan: "Eight hundred million people: eight hundred million soldiers."[6] The new designation for business people is "neither three nor four" 'bu san bu si,' an old saying equivalent to "neither fish nor fowl," but which also undoes the neat official ordering of the people into workers (one), peasants (two), soldiers (three).[7] Socialist statements are always so confident, leaving room for neither hesitation nor exceptions. What is more, China's particular brand of socialist rhetoric is not only euphemistic but also highly dramatic both in its lexicon ("spiritual pollution," "poisonous weeds") and its repetitions of superlatives. The Cultural Revolution was of course the high point of such hyperbolic prose. One fine example is Lin Biao's creations: "The Cultural Revolution's damages will be the very, very, very smallest, while the gains will be the very, very, very biggest."[8] The thrice-repeated "very" 'zui' became the characteristic style of the Cultural Revolution. Praise to Mao Zedong and insults to the enemies were all draped in colorful — albeit fixed — disguises, Mao being the "red, red, reddest sun" and the enemies, all manners of animals, from cattle to flies. The metaphorical red language, as well as its assertive syntax, are now bandied about by almost everyone in China.

Two striking examples come from popular culture: the first from a popular genre, crosstalk (comic dialogue); the other from the most popular writer of the early 1990s, Wang Shuo. Both parody the absurd formulaic quality of that paroxystic prose and its ubiquitousness in people's fixed linguistic patterns. The following crosstalk of 1978, takes place between the revolutionary shopkeeper of a revolutionary photography shop and a customer:

A (customer): "Serve the People!" May I ask a question?
B (clerk): "Oppose Selfishness and Revisionism!" Go ahead.
A: "Annihilate Capitalism and Uphold the Proletariat!" Could I take a photo?"
B: "Destroy the Private and Establish the Public!" What size?
A: "The Revolution is Faultless." Three-inch size.
B: "The Revolution Is Justified." Okay, pay up.
A: "Stress Politics." How much?
B: "Criticize Reactionary Authorities." Sixty-three cents.[9]

Wang Shuo's mockery goes one step further by mixing with the endless glorious formulas, discordant epithets: "Beloved, wise, dear teacher leader helmsman guide pioneer developer architect beacon torch dogcudgel father mother grandpa grandma old ancestor old ape overlord sovereign Jade Emperor Guan Yin bodhisattva commander-in-chief... We little people, rustic people, common people, lowly people, children, grandchildren, little sprouts, little dogs, little cats, vulgar herd, ignorant masses, broad masses, and ordinary folk feel entirely blessed, entirely excited, entirely unworthy. . . ."[10]

Not all ordinary people have Wang's verbosity, but they have all (especially the young) taken to this humorous irreverent style of shooting the breeze, called *tiaokan* or *kan (da) shan* by distorting official language, past and present.[11] If a person goes against one's own will, he or she will be labeled as *fandong* 'reactionary'; a buddy will have "good roots" 'gen zheng'; oaths between friends will be taken on "President Mao's head" 'xiang Mao zhuxi baozheng'; poker players "study" the "number 54 document"; those leaving the country are said to "join an overseas brigade" 'cha yang dui'; those having two jobs, their assigned one and another that pays more money, follow the "one entity, two systems" policy 'yiren liangzhi' (an inversion of "two entities, one system" 'yiguo liangzhi,' which is the official slogan for China's policy for Hong Kong, Macao, and eventually, the government hopes, for Taiwan); those who can't enjoy a festive atmosphere are said to have an "old-society face" 'yilian jiu shehui.' The list of retouched slogans is endless and is being constantly updated, all over China, and spiced up with regional flavor. For example, in Shandong province, "political transparency" 'zhengzhi toumingdu' (a definite oxymoron anywhere) is used to refer to daring women's fashions and in Hebei, the communal pot 'daguofan' now refers to a "loose" woman.[12]

We are the world

China as one culture is very much a willed myth. If one looks at unofficial language as a whole, one can see that not only do people not care to listen to, let alone speak the official "cultural" language, they go against its very grain by mimicking it. One can also note the many particular local ways of saying and the great number of dialects, thriving more than ever in Chinese popular culture today; for example, and naming only the most obvious, Hong Kong and the Cantonese area, which, by their sheer existence, deflate the pomposity of majestic Mandarin authority. Gregory Lee sees a subversive potential in Hong Kong's "vulgar" Cantonese, a happy mix of Cantonese and broken English with a rather poor written Chinese.[13] In fact, most of the new expressions that Beijing, Shanghai, and other regions embrace today come from the south, from Hong Kong, that linguistic and political hybrid of a city. As Lee notes, Hong Kong is largely a mass culture, a visual and aural culture, that has, as one can detect in its cinematography, a great capacity for self-mocking, cynicism, and biting irony.

Beijing is now happily contaminated, as is Shanghai, which has always kept its close link to Hong Kong (sharing a dialect, an international or colonialist look, numerous family connections, and such colloquialisms as *Afei*). One of the more widespread new expressions is "to jump into the sea (of business)" 'xia hai,' which alludes to the harbours of both Shanghai and Hong Kong. Mandarin spoken by the young is now interspersed with English ("Miss," "love," "party") and ubiquitous expressions like "bye," "OK," "CD," "DJ," which were first adopted by the Hongkongese. Another favorite expression, to "stir-fry" 'chao,' that is, to speculate, to resell for a higher price, to hype the marketability of events or products, so that you can make even greater profit, comes from the culinarily-talented Cantonese. Actually, *chao* has many meanings, especially when linked to other words, such as "to stir-fry squid" 'chao youyu': to get fired, therefore to roll up your bedding just as squid rolls up when cooked; there are even "stir-fry buddies" 'chao you,' those who resell stock shares for you.[14] Trendy ways of talking about transportation are also Cantonese, in this case, Cantonese pidgin English: "ba" 'bus' and "di" 'taxi,' replacing the heavy and lengthy *gonggong qiche* 'public transportation vehicle' and *chuzu qiche* 'leasing vehicle.'

Some terms have traveled to China by way of Taiwan, especially words dealing with entertainment. Taiwan, which also speaks Mandarin and is therefore readily connected to mainlanders, first caught on to words such as "MTV," "show" 'xiu,' "karaoke" 'kalaok,' "microphone, mike" 'maike,' probably via Japan, though the terms are now current in all Asian regions. The sweet nothings one can whisper in a lover's ear are most likely to emanate from a Taiwanese ballad (*mi* for "honey"; *sa* for seductive, sexy); the return of Chinese feudal galantry, with *junzi* 'master' for "my man" and classical poetic expressions like *yunyu* 'clouds and rain' for lovemaking. Some expressions come either from Taiwan or from Hong Kong, which got into the world of fast-paced business, communication, and general commodification before the mainland. For example, the Chinese don't "exchange sex" 'xingjiao' anymore but "make love" 'zuo ai'; they also "kiss" 'keisi.' They buy gold with a lot of *K* 'karats' and ask for their restaurant checks, as if they were in Taipei or Kowloon, with the Cantonese expression "Maidan!" instead of *jiezhang*. The most traceable new term, *dageda* 'cellular phone,' literally "big brother big," comes from 1980s Hong Kong gangster flicks where the main gangster, called a "big brother," would inevitably hold what then was inaccessible to the mainlanders, the by now ever-so-present portable phone. (If you are undermonied, then you just have a "bibiji" 'BBJ,' 'beeper.')

There is however no homogeneity or constancy in the use of new words. Today, highbrow Chinese urbanites—yuppies, DINKs (double-income, no kids), all terms now current in China—don't use the vulgar term *dageda* to designate their phone. They have created a word, following the conventional logic of word creation, that is, by paraphrasing the object, 'shouji' (a portable instrument). It is the same fate for *maidan* (cheque, please) amongst hip Beijingers whose fad for all things Cantonese, perhaps because of Hong Kong's present lack-luster state, is almost passé. Now, Beijingers tend to revert to the mandarin *jiezhang*. Elegance, for some, matters. Many obsolete 1920s expressions, such as *modeng* 'modern' are making a comeback. And advertising is targeting precisely those with its seductive vocabulary of naturalness freedom and harmony, a paradigm available anywhere in the world. One of the more striking frequent words is the term *wenxin* 'warm and fragrant,' which can be applied to anything from villas, to coffee, to condoms, to beauty parlors.

A journalist has questioned this strange use of the term *wenxin*.[15] Zhou Guoping notes that it originally referred to adolescent girls' romantic reveries. Now, it includes adults' daydreams, perhaps of the American dream? Zhou criticizes this materialistic rage for Simmons beds, XO Cognac, Ray-Ban glasses, and the like and blames it on popular music. I'd say television with its dual marketing certainly contributes as a vital instrument in this force of persuasion. In its 1997 survey in China, Gallup shows that the Chinese are increasingly "brand aware" 'mingpai,' not only of the domestic but also of Japanese, American, and German wares.[16] In linguistic terms, this translates as a preference to name things by the brand, rather than by the generic term: people now eat Kentucky 'Kendeji,' not chicken 'ji' and Christies 'Kelijia,' rather than plain biscuits 'binggan.' The advertising world vies to supply elegant or quaint words to seduce the consumer; those who don't, don't survive. For ex-

21. East Health Soap. Design by Xiao Song, 1993. *Photograph from catalog.*

ample, Maxwell House instant coffee lost to its rival Nescafé because it used a simple transliteration, "Mai-si-wei-er," while its competitor translated the meaning of its brand into *Quechao* (sparrow 'que' and nest 'chao'), which evokes the coziness of one's nest: Nescafé also sweetened its ad, on television and radio, by using a highly popular Taiwanese song, "Genzhe ganjue zou" (Follow your feeling).

Gentrified words side with a liberal use of the Roman alphabet and imagistic designs. In 1994 newspapers, one advertisement often seen was for women's makeup. It read "WOMAN de zhen" (OUR real [self]), the word in capital letters left in the Roman alphabet, allowing for a linguistic double entendre. Such flaunting of foreign words flatters upwardly mobile consumers in their partaking of things "Western." Other linguistic flatteries can be found worldwide, namely, in the euphemistic designations of ordinary things, elevated by words such as "mansion" for low-cost housing projects or "palace" for food joints. Words allow people to dream on.

China-as-state, with its will to move in the fast-forward mode, has also created its own terms, for example, *xiaokang* 'comfortable living standard,' and has had to make allowances for new words designating new realities, even when they are highly frowned upon. A new official Chinese dictionary, published in 1996, the *Xiandai hanyu cidian (Modern Chinese Dictionary)*, includes 9,000 new entries. The vulgar *ba* for "bus" may be absent, but *bashi* (its longer transliteration) is included; so are many terms from computer science and other scientific fields, as well as new social phenomena (*anlesi* 'euthanasia'; *kala-OK* 'karaoke') and wares (*T-xu(shan)* 'T-shirt').[17] The word for AIDS, a reality long dismissed in China, is now, in the official neologism, *aizibing*, a transliteration of the sounds "aizi" with the suffix for "disease." However, the initial official invention, its homophone, meant the love 'ai' capitalism 'zi' disease, a rather low blow to foreign devils.[18] In Taiwan, it is officially coined "love's disease," also homophonic, *aizhibing*. As for homosexuality, the Chinese officially call it "same-sex love" 'tongxinglian,' but in the gay communities all around China, the word *tongxue* 'schoolmate' is often heard. In Taiwan and in Hong Kong, gays and lesbians, perhaps with an in-your-face intent akin to the English "queer," call themselves "comrades" 'tongzhi.' Considering the round-trip trajectory of so many terms, the appellation *tongzhi* may well boomerang back to mainland China any day, with that connotation.[19] "Comrade," the ubiquitous form of address to all during the Mao era, already makes everyone giggle when used today. Obviously, there is an impulse to turn words upside down, to lighten them, to shake off set associations.

Words are often used as codes, which is nothing new for China, which harbored in the past numerous secret societies and alternative associations, from theater guilds to esoteric sects. One such association today is constituted of profiteers 'daoye,' literally the "lords of resale." They and other "lords" (*foye* 'thieves,' *kanye* 'ravers'), in this self-mocking designation—which nevertheless has bite, for they are kings of the road, in a way—have resurfaced in the era of reform with their idiosyncratic talk. It seems each region in China has now its "secret" terms for banknotes and its money dealing. Much of the trendy, urban slang for transactions come from the black market.[20] Amusing ones are "worker-soldier-peasant" 'gong-nong-bing' for banknotes, alluding to the depiction of this triad on the fifty-yuan note; "to drive a tractor" is to be loaded with money. Other new groups include the *pizi* 'bums,' 'hoodlums,' who share, with the racketeers, a host of curse words, unearthed from "feudal" China where the words for female genitals and all manner of animals are tossed in for a shocking effect. High-school students, like any other social group, have also caught on to codes for their activities, some of which are rather funny: they refer to a textbook as "the Red Lantern" 'Hongdengji,' the antiquated Cultural Revolution model play; music class is *kala yongyuan OK* (karaoke is always okay); history is *zai hui shou* (let's do it again).[21] The world of popular music (including rock) has had, more than any other artistic field, to deal with foreign specialized terms. "Rap" was translated by some as *raoshe* (literally, to let your tongue go), a pretty adequate description of that style of delivery; and by others as *pizi shuochang,* that is, "hoodlums" 'pizi' doing *shuochang,* a traditional intoned singing, also a clever translation. Similarly, "blues" is either romanized into *bu-lu-si* or its meaning is translated into *landiao* 'blue melody.' Ingeniosity is at work here; still, most "in" musicians just use the English word: "rap," "blues," "rock," and so on.

In journalistic articles appearing in the People's Republic of China over the past few years, one often encounters a highly connotative term: *zu* 'group.' Before its new fashionings, it referred to the extended family 'jiazu,' to the people as a nation 'minzu'; national minorities, for example, are *shaoshu minzu,* 'minority groups.' Today, it still refers to clans, but to clans with no ethnic or blood ties. They are "special interest groups" like groupies, literally "star seekers" 'zhuixingzu,' video game fans 'dianwanzu,' majiang players 'majiangzu,' TOEFL candidates 'tuofuzu,' DINKS 'DNKzu,' the "new wave crowd" 'xinchaozu,' the bowling fans 'baolingzu,' and even the "9-to-5 group" 'shangbanzu' because they are rarer than ever.[22] This partitioning signals a true diversification of activities, but it especially emphasizes the fact that all these groups or cliques are related by personal inclination. Advertising targets some of these groups. Sony, for example, advertises to the "new wave" crowd 'xinchaozu' to sell its hi-fi equipment and thus validates that group's mode of speech, where words such as "alternative" 'linglei,' "avant-garde" 'xianfeng' pop up, along with some English words ("party," "guitar," "happy").

As for the emerging critics of China's mass culture, namely Chen Xiaoming, Dai Jinhua, and Zhang Yiwu, they opt for the term *quan* 'clique' to describe particular phenomena within the cultural field. They juggle incessantly with concepts to be translated, images to be created to analyze these changes and discuss mass culture, alternately designated as *dazhong wenhua* or *daliang wenhua,* to discern to what extent it differs from "elitist" 'jingying,' "official" 'zhuliu' culture, and what is "counterculture" 'fanwenhua,' "underground" 'dixia,' "local culture" 'diyuwenhua,' "indigenous" 'bentuwenhua,' and "acculturation" 'wenhua yiru.' Media is referred to as *meiti* or else as an even closer transliteration, *meidiya.* Fluent in English and in postmodern cultural critique, the new critics' texts abound with the prefix *hou* 'post' which tempers the omnipresent "new" 'xin,' and the suffixes *xing* 'quality,' 'nature,' *hua* 'transformation,' *zhuyi* '-isms.' Much like anywhere, they discuss the "public sphere" 'gongyong kongjian' and the "PC" (politically correct, 'zhengzhi zhengquexing') global era. One example of a string of modifiers, for the critique of a beauty contest, should suffice: "a one-time, legitimized, libidinized, spectacular mass event" (yici hefaxing de gongzhong yuwanghua guanshang huodong).[23]

All of China is searching for words, finding and replacing expressions to suit the times. One computer world term I find particularly euphonic is "Wan Wei Wang" 'Ten-thousand-link net' for "World Wide Web."[24]

My concluding words go however in a much less prominent field than that of technology: poetry. One poet has stirred people in China and worldwide with his words. He is Yu Jian, occasional collaborator to Mou Sen and a militant on the subject of words, which he believes must be vigorously cleansed. Yu believes words can do things and that poetry is not an obsolete activity. Poems should not be conveyors of an idea, but of the dynamic of words themselves 'liudong de yugan.'[25] Poetry as he sees it, is for the public arena, to be spoken out; its words are to be taken from the everyday and turned inside out. Allegories, recondite symbols and images, narrative traps are to be dissected, exposed. What he calls "ready-mades" 'xianchengpin,' is all the language that has fallen to you, that you have not lived with or moved with. Words should be, by

22. Recreation of a calligraphy created for the series *"Word": Introduction to English Calligraphy.* Ink on paper, by Xu Bing, 1998.

poetic operation, opened up. That, for Yu Jian, is a very serious affair, for which current cynicism is out of place.

Yu Jian believes that poetry is not a cry of the heart 'nahan.' Surveying twentieth-century Chinese poetry, he claims that poets have always had a sense of mission, wanting to shake up their compatriots, to yell out the inequalities, and that it has been the main mode of expression right up to the end of the 1970s with Misty poets like Bei Dao. Looking farther back, into classical times, Yu finds no poet speaking from his or her own personal position. He conceives today's poetry as that written by one person speaking from his or her situation, a poetry that will be most familiar 'zui shuxi' to a contemporary audience, because it uses the everyday words of the time and appeals to each reader's own experience. That reader will be Chinese, but not exclusively so, since the world is becoming the same, while each linguistic community maintains its language's specificity. Even an antipatriotic, anticolonialist poet like Yu Jian may write about roses, although his hometown, southwestern Kunming, is better known for camelias.[26] The layers of language as used by him comprise his own experience of rose-petal candies, roses growing outside his office window, and the "women are roses" of English romantic poetry. This antitranscendental position is what I call, rather than "archeological" (which uses a depth/surface metaphor and assumes an inanimate object), a vivisection of language.

Such an endeavor is essential for any human culture, since language is, after all, part and parcel of human animals. The Chinese have their own special task to perform, which is to make evident the amnesia at work in the current discourse of novelty. Many articles report that the new generation of those born after 1976, sometimes called the "petty group" 'xixiaozu,'[27] do not even know who Mao Zedong is, or when the People's Republic of China was founded.[28] But lived-in, living poetry can link subtexts, unearth the living dead, and generate wondrous hypertexts for us all.

Glossary of Chinese Terms

'93 *xiju kalaOK zhiye*	'93戏剧卡拉OK之夜
"100 *ge dongci*"	100个动词
A Can	阿灿
A Cheng	阿城
Afei	阿飞
AhQ tongzhi	阿Q同志
AhQ zhengzhuan	阿Q正传
ai	爱
Ai de yuyan	爱的寓言
Ai Jing	艾敬
Ai Weiwei	艾未未
aizhibing	爱之病
aizibing	艾滋病
aizibing	爱资病
anlesi	安乐死
Ashima	阿诗玛
ba	巴
Ba Jin	巴金
ba wan ba	八万八
ba wo shaohui	把我烧毁
"Bababa"	爸爸爸
baolingzu	保龄族
"Baoying"	报应
baozhuang	包装
baozi	包子
bashi	巴士

Bawang bieji	霸王别姬
Bei Dao	北岛
"Beijing gushi"	北京故事
Beijing yaogun	北京摇滚
Beijing zazhong	北京杂种
Beijingren zai Niuyue	北京人在纽约
ben	本
ben benr	本本儿
bentu wenhua	本土文化
Bi'an	彼岸
Bianjibu de gushi	编辑部的故事
biansu	变俗
Bianzou bianchang	边走边唱
Bingdu caiyao	病毒菜肴
binggan	饼干
Bingzai	丙崽
bu san bu si	不三不四
"Bu zai yanshi"	不再掩饰
"Bushi youxi de nianji"	不是游戏的年纪
buxiang de yugan	不详的预感
Can Xue	残雪
"Canglao de fuyun"	苍老的浮云
Cangying	苍蝇
"Cangying, mayi, qu he pingzi, gangmen, jiu"	苍蝇，蚂蚁，蛆和瓶子，肛门，酒
canku xiju	残酷戏剧
Cao Guilin	曹桂林
cha yang dui	插洋队
chadui	插队
Chaguan	茶馆
chao	炒
chao you	炒友
chao youyu	炒鱿鱼
chen gen	尘根
Chen Guangwu	陈光武
Chen Jin	陈劲
Chen Kaige	陈凯歌
Chen Ran	陈染
Chen Xiaoming	陈晓明
Cheng Dieyi	程蝶衣

Cheng Xiaodong	程小东
chongxian	重现
chuan zai yiqi	串在一起
chudian	触电
Chunguang zhaxie	春光乍泄
chuzu qiche	出租汽车
ciji	刺激
"Congtou zailai"	从头再来
Cui Jian	崔健
"Cunzai"	存在
Cuowei de zi	错位的字
"Cuowu"	错误
Da pipan	大批判
Da taijian Li Lianying	大太监李莲英
dageda	大哥大
daguofan	大锅饭
Dahong denglong gaogao gua	大红灯笼高高挂
Dai Jinhua	戴锦华
Dai'er	黛二
dakai guomen	打开国门
daliang wenhua	大量文化
dan	旦
dao	刀
Daomazei	盗马贼
daoye	倒爷
Dasaba	大撒把
dawan	大腕
Daweixiang	大尾象
dazhong wenhua	大众文化
Deng Lijun	邓丽君
di	的
Di er zhuangtai	第二状态
dianwanzu	电玩族
didishi de meimei	弟弟式的妹妹
"Die zhiyao de san zhong fangfa"	叠纸鹞的三种方法
Ding Yi	丁乙
Diwudai	第五代
dixia	地下
diyu wenhua	地域文化

dizi	笛子
DNKzu	DNK族
dong	动
Dong gong xi gong	东宫西宫
dongci	动词
"Dongfanghong"	东方红
"Dongwu xiongmeng"	动物凶猛
Dou Wei	窦唯
"Du shang xilou"	独上西楼
duandai xingshi	断代形式
duiwu	队伍
duli	独立
duoluo	堕落
Erzi	儿子
fandong	反动
Fang Lijun	方力钧
fanshen	翻身
fanwenhua	反文化
fasheng	发生
fei	废
Feidu	废都
"Feile"	飞了
Fen Ma Liuming	芬马六明
Feng Mengbo	冯梦波
Feng Xiaogang	冯小刚
Fengyue	风月
foye	佛爷
fu	蝠
fu	福
fugai	覆盖
Fugui	福贵
Fuqin	父亲
Furongzhen	芙蓉镇
"Fuxi Fuxi"	伏羲伏羲
gaige kaifang	改革开放
Gao Bo	高波
Gao Xingjian	高行健
"Gaoji dongwu"	高级动物
Ge Fei	格非
Ge You	葛优

gemenr	哥们儿
gen	根
gen zheng	根正
Geng Jianyi	耿建翌
"Genzhe ganjue zou"	跟着感觉走
geren	个人
Gong Li	巩俐
gongbi	工笔
gonggong qiche	公共汽车
gong-nong-bing	工–农–兵
gongyong kongjian	共用空间
"Gou"	狗
"Goudao"	狗道
gouniang	狗娘
Gu Changwei	顾长卫
Gu Wenda	谷文达
Gu Xiong	顾雄
Guan Jinpeng	关锦鹏
guangchang	广场
Guangchang	广场
Guanjianci: youxing, youdang, yousi	关健词：游行，游荡，游思
Guangzhou	广州
Gufeng	股疯
"Guniang piaoliang"	姑娘漂亮
Guo Shixing	过士行
guoji jiegui	国际接轨
guoxiang	果香
Haima gewuting	海马歌舞厅
Haiziwang	孩子王
"Haiziwang—Shuwang—Qiwang"	孩子王–树王–棋王
Han Shaogong	韩少功
Haomeng	好梦
He Jingzhi	贺敬之
He Li	何鲤
He Ping	何平
He Yi	贺奕
He Yong	何勇
Hei yueliang	黑月亮

Heibao	黑豹
Heimeng	黑梦
"Hese niaoqun"	褐色鸟群
Heshang	河殇
"Hezi"	盒子
Hong gaoliang	红高粱
Hong gaoliang jiazu	红高粱家族
Hong taiyang	红太阳
Hongdengji	红灯记
"Hongfen"	红粉
hongge huangchang	红歌黄唱
Hongloumeng	红楼梦
Hongqi xia de dan	红旗下的蛋
Hongse niangzijun	红色娘子军
Hongse yaogun	红色摇滚
Hongse youmo	红色幽默
hou	后
Hou Muren	侯牧人
Hou San'er	猴三儿
houwei	后卫
Hu Jianping	胡健平
Huzi zui yi ran	胡子最易燃
Hu Yue	胡月
hua	化
huaju	话剧
Huang Haha	黄哈哈
Huang tudi	黄土地
Huang Yongping	黄永砯
Huang Zongluo	黄宗洛
"Huangtu gaopo"	黄土高坡
"Huidao Lasa"	回到拉萨
Hundun jia ligeleng	浑沌加哩咯嘚
"Huozhe"	活着
Huozhe	活着
"Hushao"	嗯哨
hushenfu	护身符
hutong	胡同
Huxi	呼吸
ji	鸡
Jia Pingwa	贾平凹

Jia Zhangke	贾樟柯
jiandao	剪刀
Jiang Wen	姜文
Jiang Yue	蒋樾
jianzhi	监制
jiazu	家族
jiba	鸡巴
jiba wanyi	鸡巴玩意
jiding	既定
jiegui	接轨
Jiejue	解决
jiezhang	结帐
Jin Ping Mei	金瓶梅
Jin Xing	金星
jingying	精英
Jinlian	金莲
Jinshan	金山
Jiugui: liang ge huajia	酒鬼：两个画家
juben	剧本
juben	具本
juben, juben, yi ju zhi ben	剧本，剧本，一剧之本
Judou	菊豆
junzi	君子
kala yongyuan OK	卡拉永远OK
kalaOK	卡拉OK
kan (da) shan	侃（大）山
kanye	侃爷
keguan de zhenshi	客观的真实
keisi	剋斯
Kelijia	克力加
Kendeji	肯德鸡
keneng	可能
"Kuai rang wo zai zhe xuedishang sadianr ye"	快让我在这雪地上撒点儿野
"Kuaile jiqi"	快乐机器
Kugen	苦根
Lajichang	垃圾场
Lan fengzheng	蓝风筝
landiao	蓝调
Landiao zai dongfang	蓝调在东方

laoshi	老实
laoyin	烙印
lazhu	蜡烛
Lei Feng	雷锋
Leiyu	雷雨
Li Bihua	李碧华
Li Chunbo	李春波
Li Jianming	李健鸣
Li Shan	李山
Li Shaohong	李少红
Li Wei	李委
Li Xianting	栗宪庭
Li Youyuan	李有源
Liang Heping	梁和平
"Lianpu"	脸谱
Liechang zhasa	猎场札撒
liegenxing	劣根性
Lin Daiyu	林黛玉
Lin Zhaohua	林兆华
Ling Dang'an	0档案
Linghun chuqiao	灵魂出窍
linglei	另类
Linglei pinpan	另类拼盘
Liu Chunhua	刘春华
Liu Dahong	刘大鸿
Liu Heng	刘恒
Liu Huan	刘欢
Liu (Shuyou)	刘（书友）
Liu Sola	刘索拉
Liu Wei	刘炜
Liu Xiaodong	刘晓东
Liu Xiaoqing	刘晓庆
Liu Xinwu	刘心武
Liu Yue	柳月
liudong de yugan	流动的语感
Liulang Beijing: zuihou de mengxiangzhe	流浪北京：最后的梦想者
liumang	流氓
Liushou nüshi	留守女士
"Liuxia youdeng guang"	留下油灯光

Louding	楼顶
Lu Xun	鲁迅
Luo Qi	罗琦
Luo Zhongli	罗中立
Ma Liuming	马六明
Ma Xiaoqing	马晓晴
Ma Yuan	马原
maidan	买单 （埋单）
maike	麦克
maitian shouwangzhe	麦田守望者
majiangzu	麻将族
Mama	妈妈
Manhadun de Zhongguo nüren	曼哈顿的中国女人
Mantou	馒头
Mao Amin	毛阿敏
Mao Xuhui	毛旭辉
"Mao Zedong"	毛泽东
meidiya	美迪亚
Meiguo lai de qizi	美国来的妻子
"Meimei ni dadande wang qian zou"	妹妹你大胆地往前走
meimeishi de didi	妹妹式的弟弟
meiti	媒体
Meng Jinghui	孟京辉
"Menghui Tangchao"	梦回唐朝
mi	迷
mi	谜
mi	蜜
mian	面
ming fu qi shi de guanggunr	名符其实的光棍儿
minge	民歌
mingong	民工
mingpai	名牌
"Mingren zhi si—Can Xue tan yishu"	名人之死—残雪谈艺术
minjian	民间
Minjing de gushi	民警的故事
minzu	民族
"Mizhou"	迷舟
Mo Yan	莫言

modeng	摩登
mofang	模仿
Mohe	磨合
Mou Sen	牟森
mu	母
Mulan	木兰
Na Ying	那英
nahan	呐喊
nalai zhuyi	拿来主义
nangen	男根
"Nanniwan"	南泥湾
nanqiang beidiao	南腔北调
neibu	内部
neibu jiaoliu	内部交流
neixin shenchu	内心深处
niandai	年代
Niang, niang, shang xitang	娘，娘，上西堂
Niao ren	鸟人
Ni Haifeng	倪海峰
Niepan	涅槃
Ning Ying	宁瀛
Niu	牛
niu	牛
Niu Yueqing	牛月清
nongcun jishi	农村集市
niu + shui	牛 + 水
"Nününü"	女女女
Nüwa	女娲
Nüzidui	女子队
OK, gupiao	OK, 股票
pizi	痞子
pizi shuochang	痞子说唱
"Pokai"	破开
Qi	棋
qi	妻，其，奇，欺
"Qi qie cheng qun"	妻妾成群
Qi ren	棋人
qianfeng	前锋
Qiannü youhun zhi daodaodao	倩女幽魂之道道道
"Qianwanci de wen"	千万次的问

qianwei yishu	前卫艺术
qi'er	弃儿
Qihou	气候
"Qing zou renxing dao"	请走人行道
Qinggan caolian	情感操练
"Qinghuang"	青黄
"Qingnian shiyan dianying xiaozu"	青年实验电影小组
"Qingshu"	倾述
qingyi	情谊
Qiuju da guansi	秋菊打官司
quan	圈
Quechao	鹊巢
rancheng	染成
raoshe	饶舌
"Regou"	热狗
Ren yue dong wu jie	人约东五街
Renjian dao	人间道
Renjian zhinan	人间指南
ruan guanggao	软广告
sa	飒
Sadan	撒旦
Sange nüren	三个女人
Sanguo yanyi	三国演义
Shadan	傻蛋
shagua	傻瓜
shangbanzu	上班族
shangxue	上学
Shangyidang	上一当
"Shanshang de xiaowu"	山上的小屋
shaoshu minzu	少数民族
"Shehuizhuyi hao"	社会主义好
"Sheyuan doushi xiangyanghua"	社员都是向阳花
Shi Chong	石冲
"Shi qiang haishi zidan"	是枪还是子弹
Shi Tiesheng	史铁生
shidai	时代
shijian yishu	实践艺术
Shijing	诗经

"Shishi ru yan"	世事如烟
shiyan	试验
shouchaoben	手抄本
shouji	手机
Shuangqizhen daoke	双旗镇刀客
"Shui bi shui sha duoshao"	谁比谁傻多少
Shuihuzhuan	水浒传
"Shuo shuo"	说说
Si	四
si	死
Sifan	思凡
Sihai weijia	四海为家
siheyuan	四合院
sijuan	四卷
Siren shenghuo	私人生活
sixiang gongzuozhe	思想工作者
Songlian	颂莲
Sunüjing	素女经
Su Tong	苏童
Su Xiaokang	苏晓康
Su Yue	苏越
Sun Mengjin	孙孟晋
suona	唢呐
Tang Chao	唐朝
Tang Wan'er (wan'er)	唐宛儿（玩儿）
tansuo	探索
taode	淘的
ti	替
Tian Zhuangzhuang	田壮壮
Tianbai	天白
"Tianchuang"	天窗
Tianhuang	天黄
Tianqing	天青
Tianshu	天书
tiaokan	调侃
tixing women	提醒我们
tongsu	通俗
tongxinglian	同性恋
tongxue	同学
tongzhi	同志

Tongzhuo de ni	同桌的你
"Touji fenzi"	投机份子
tuhua	图画
tuofuzu	托福族
tutechan	土特产
tuteng	图腾
tuxiang	图像
T-xushan	T-恤衫
Wa jutuan	蛙剧团
Wan Wei Wang	万维网
Wande jiu shi xintiao	玩的就是心跳
Wang Fu	王福
Wang Guangyi	王广义
Wang Jinsong	王劲松
(Wang) Judou	王菊豆
Wang Shuo	王朔
Wang Xiansheng zhi yu huo fen shen	王先生之欲火焚身
Wang Xiaofang	王晓芳
Wang Xingwei	王兴伟
Wang Ziwei	王子卫
"Wangshi yu xingfa"	往事与刑罚
wanhui	晚会
"Wanzhu"	顽主
wei	伪
Wei Hua	蔚华
Wei Wei	韦唯
"Weibuzudao"	微不足道
weiji	危机
"Weilanse"	蔚蓝色
weilanse wenming	蔚蓝色文明
Wen Hui	文慧
Wenhua dongwu	文化动物
wenhua gongsi	文化公司
wenhua yiru	文化移入
wenxin	温馨
Wo ai cha-cha-cha	我爱 x x x
"Wo de 1997"	我的1997
wo huode bu yukuai, zhe shi wo de ziyou	我活得不愉快，这是我的自由

"Wo shi ni choushui matongli de yitiao she"	我是你抽水马桶里的一条蛇
Wo zhe shi nian	我这十年
WOMAN de zhen	WOMAN 的真
"Women zou zai dalushang"	我们走在大路上
wotou	窝头
Wong Kar-wai	王家卫
"Wu jie"	无解
Wu Liang	吴亮
Wu Shanzhuan	吴山专
Wu Wenguang	吴文光
Wu Youwu	吴友吾（无有无）
Wu Yuzhong	吴玉中
"Wudi zirong"	无地自容
"Wuguan yulu sanze: daiba jian dui yige mingci de kaozheng"	无关语录三则：代跋兼对一个名词的考证
xia hai	下海
xianchengpin	现成品
Xiandai hanyu cidian	现代汉语词典
Xiandaihua	现代化
"Xianfeng"	先锋
xianfeng	先锋
xiang Mao zhuxi baozheng	向毛主席保证
xiangsheng	相声
"Xiangyu"	相遇
xiangzheng	象征
xianshi	现实
"Xianshi yi zhong"	现实一种
"Xiao Fang"	小芳
Xiao Lu	萧鲁
Xiao Shan hui jia	小山回家
xiaokang	小康
xiaotiao	萧条
Xie Jin	谢晋
"Ximalaya guge"	喜马拉雅古歌
xin	新
Xin changzheng lushang de yaogun	新长征路上的摇滚
Xin dalu	新大陆

xin jiezou	新节奏
xin wenren	新文人
xinchaozu	新潮族
Xing	杏
xing	性
xingbie yaoqiu	性别要求
xingjiao	性交
xingwei yishu	行为艺术
Xingzou de ren	行走的人
Xinhua	新华
xinshang	欣赏
Xinwen lianbo	新闻联播
xiong you cheng zhu	胸有成竹
xiu	秀
xixiaozu	细小族
X-Ma-Ma	X妈妈
Xu Bing	徐冰
Xu Kun	徐坤
Xu Lei	徐累
Xu Tan	徐坦
xuanchuan	宣传
"Xuduo zhong shengyin— Zhongguo wenxuemeng"	许多种声音—中国文学梦
Xuewei	穴位
"Xugou"	虚构
xun	埙
xungen	寻根
Yan Peiming	颜培明
yang	阳
Yang Tianqing	杨天青
Yang Zhenzhong	杨振忠
yangchadui	洋插队
yangge	秧歌
Yangguang canlan de rizi	阳光灿烂的日子
Yangniu zai Beijing	洋妞在北京
yang—yin	阳—阴
Yanjingshe	眼镜蛇
Yanzhikou	胭脂口
Yaoayao, yao dao waipoqiao	摇阿摇，摇到外婆桥
yaogai jiu gai ba	要改就改吧

"Yaogun "Gu' er" "	摇滚 "孤儿"
Yaogun mengxun	摇滚梦寻
Yaogun: Jinianban	摇滚：纪念版
Ye Shuanggui	叶双贵
Ye Yongqing	叶永青
Yijing	易经
"Yiwu suoyou"	一无所有
yi zhong fuhao	一种符号
yicixing de gongzhong yuwanghua guanshang huodong	一次性的公众欲望化观赏活动
yiguo liangzhi	一国两制
"Yikuai hongbu"	一块红布
yilian jiu shehui	一脸旧社会
"Yilu zou, yilu chang"	一路走一路唱
Ying Ruocheng	英若诚
yipian hong	一片红
yiren liangzhi	一人两制
"Yishan men, yidu qiang, yizuo fen"	一扇门，一堵墙，一座坟
Yishu xinwen	艺术新闻
you	有
Youdai	有带
"Youshen"	游神
"Youxing"	游行
Yu aizibing you guande	与艾滋病有关的
Yu Hong	喻红
Yu Hua	余华
Yu Jian	于坚
"Yu wangshi ganbei"	与往事干杯
Yu Youhan	余友涵
Yunnan (nan)	殒楠（男）
Yunnan	云南
yunyu	云雨
yuyan	语言
zai hui shou	再回首
zancheng	赞成
Zang Tianshuo	臧天朔
Zeng Fanzhi	曾凡志
"Zenme huishi"	怎么回事

Zhang Chu	张楚
Zhang Dali	张大力
Zhang Guangtian	张广天
Zhang Guangtian xiandai gequ zhuanji	张广天现代歌曲专辑
Zhang Hai'er	张海儿
Zhang Hongtu	张洪图
Zhang Huan	张洹
Zhang Jianya	张建亚
Zhang Peili	张培力
Zhang Xian	张献
Zhang Xiaogang	张晓刚
Zhang Xin	张欣
Zhang Yimou	张艺谋
Zhang Yiwu	张颐武
Zhang Yuan	张元
zhanlian	粘连
Zhao Jiping	赵季平
Zhaole	找乐
Zheli, nali, wulun nali	这里，那里，无论哪里
zheng	筝
Zheng Jun	郑钧
zheng ming	正名
zhengzhi bopu	政治波普
zhengzhi toumingdu	政治透明度
zhengzhi zhengquexing	政治正确性
zhenli	真理
Zhi Qing	智清
"Zhimayou"	芝麻油
zhiming	致命
Zhinanzhen	指南针
zhiqing	知青
Zhonggu lou	钟鼓楼
Zhongguo gongzhu	中国公主
Zhongguo huo	中国火
"Zhongguo jiefangjun junge"	中国解放军军歌
Zhongguo keyi shuo bu	中国可以说不
"Zhongguo renmin zhiyuanjun zhange"	中国人民志愿军战歌
Zhou Li	周励

Zhou Min	周敏
Zhou Ren	周韧
Zhou Tiehai	周铁海
"Zhu"	主
Zhuang Zhidie	庄之蝶
Zhuang Zhou	庄周
Zhuangzi	庄子
zhuixingzu	追星族
zhuliu	主流
zhuyi	主义
"Ziji de tiantang"	自己的天堂
ziji shi zenme hui shi	自己是怎么回事
ziyou zuojia	自由作家
Ziyue	子曰
zong you yitian ke bu shi xianzai	总有一天可不是现在
zongxing	综性
zouxiang shijie	走向世界
zu	族
Zu Zhou	诅咒
zui	最
zui shuxi	最熟悉
Zuihou de guizu	最后的贵族
zuo ai	作爱
zuopin zai jinxing zhong	作品在进行中

Notes

Introduction

1 Marie Claire Huot, *La petite révolution culturelle* (Arles: Philippe Pic-quier, 1994).
2 *The I Ching, or Book of Changes,* trans. Cary F. Baynes, from Richard Wilhelm's German trans. (Princeton: Princeton University Press, 1950). The chapter epigraphs come from this book.

1 *Literary Experiments*

1 Fredric Jameson, "Third-World Literature in the Era of Multinational Capitalism," *Social Text* 15 (fall 1986): 65–88. Jameson is too often quoted as saying that all third-world texts are national allegories, which is out-right misreading. He said that often, "we" (Americans) read texts from other cultures (here, I'm expanding on his "third-world") as national allegories, because we are not within that culture and can only see the different national/cultural references.
2 Ma Yuan, "Xugou," in *Jiegouzhuyi xiaoshuo (Structuralist Novels),* ed. Wu Liang et al. (Changshun: Shidai wenyi, 1989), 54–105. Trans. J. Q. Sun, as "Fabrication," in *The Lost Boat,* ed. Henry Zhao (London: Wellsweep, 1993), 101–44. The quoted passages in the text are from this published translation, with modifications. (All quotations in this book will refer to the translation when available and are cited in the body of the text. Un-less specified, the translations are mine.) The term *xugou* translates as "fabrication," as well as "fiction," and Ma Yuan obviously plays with this double meaning. I often prefer the latter, as is the case here.
3 Wu Liang—who says he found an adequate match in Ma Yuan (Wu also

dropped out of the "lit crit business") — notes that the same friends who pop up in Ma's different stories, especially his earlier ones, are Ma's real friends (251). Wu claims that the stories were indeed written for them. Wu Liang, "Ma Yuan de xushu quantao" (Ma Yuan's narrative snare), in *Xunzhao de shidai—xinchao piping xuancui (An Inquisitive Period—New Wave Criticism)*, ed. Li Jiefei et al. (Beijing: Beijing shifan daxue, 1992), 248–60.

4 Ma Yuan, "Die zhiyao de san zhong fangfa," *Xizang wenxue (Tibet Literature)* 3 (1985): 333–48. I thank Jing Wang for having sent me this text. Trans. Zhu Hong as "More Ways Than One to Make a Kite," in *China's Avant-Garde Fiction: An Anthology*, ed. Jing Wang (Durham: Duke University Press, 1998), 246–63.

5 Wu Liang, "Ma Yuan de xushu quantao," 249.

6 "Deities tend to be blindly self-confident. This is how they acquire their overweening sense of mastery. Each thinks he or she is unique, but in fact they are remarkably similar, as the various genesis myths demonstrate. The gods' method is fundamentally one and the same—repeated fabrication" ("Fabrication" ["Xugou"], p. 6). The epigraph is an imitation of a Buddhist sutra that is, according to Wu Liang, an invention of Ma Yuan (259). Ma tried his hand at sutra "copying" throughout the 1980s, and it can be found, as an "authorial citation," opening other short stories by Ma, such as "Tuman guguai tu'an de qiangbi" (A wall covered with weird motifs).

7 Henry Y. H. Zhao, "Ma Yuan the Chinese Fabricator," *World Literature Today* (spring 1995): 315–16. Zhao's reading, however, emphasizes formal (narrative) aspects as the "meaning," whereas mine interconnects writing, telling, and expressing another culture (Tibet).

8 Ma Yuan, "Cuowu," in *Zhongguo xinshiqi wenxue zuopin xuan 2 (A Selection of Chinese New Era Literature 2)*, ed. Yang Yang (Hong Kong: Dadi, 1988), 75–80. Trans. Helen Wang, as "Mistakes," in Zhao, *The Lost Boat*, 29–42.

9 Strangely, this passage is not translated in the English version, yet it is essential for the impact of the story. I therefore refer exclusively to the Chinese version here.

10 Ma Yuan, "Qingshu," in *Xugou (Fiction)*, ed. Chen Juntao (Wuhan: Changjiang wenyi, 1992), 323–63.

11 Ma Yuan, "Ximalaya guge," in Wu, *Jiegouzhuyi xiaoshuo*, 106–21.

12 Ma Yuan, "Youshen," in *Bayue jiaoyang: Bashi niandai Zhongguo dalu xiaoshuoxuan 5 (August's Scorching Sun: A Selection of Mainland China's Novels of the Eighties 5)*, ed. Zheng Shusen (Taipei: Hongfan shudian, 1988), 125–54. Trans. Caroline Mason as "A wandering spirit," in Wang, *China's Avant-Garde Fiction*, 264–83.

13 Wu Liang has noted the liberal borrowings and circulation of characters and events in Ma's stories. Wu, "Ma Yuan de xushu quantao," 254–55.

14 This is Jing Wang's term for Ge Fei in *High Culture Fever: Politics, Aesthetics, and Ideology in Deng's China* (Berkeley: University of California Press, 1996), 242.

15 Namely, by Tan Yunchang in a roundtable on Ge Fei's "Hese niaoqun" (A flock of brown birds) published in the same issue as the story itself, " 'Hese niaoqun' zuotan bilu" (Notes from the roundtable on "A flock of brown birds"), *Zhongshan (Purple Mountain)* 2 (1988): 101–2. Also, more recently, by Zhang Xudong in *Chinese Modernism in the Era of Reforms: Cultural Fever, Avant-Garde Fiction, and the New Chinese Cinema* (Durham: Duke University Press, 1997), 173, 183, 193.

16 Ge Fei wrote an article on Robbe-Grillet indirectly claiming him as his master: "Shuo 'Xiangpi'—jieru yu youdao zhiyi" (About 'The erasers' —involvement and enticement), *Jinri xianfeng (Today's Avant-garde)* 1 (1994): 21–23.

17 Ge Fei, "Hese niaoqun," in *Hushao (Whistling)* (Wuhan: Changjiang wenyi, 1992), 125–53.

18 Ge Fei, "Mizhou," in *Yidianyuan de caodong: Xing'ai xiaoshuo xuancui (Restlessness in the Garden of Eden: Collection of Sexual Love Novels)*, ed. Lan Dizhi et al. (Beijing: Beijing shifan daxue, 1989), 293–315. Trans. Caroline Mason as "The lost boat," in Zhao, *The Lost Boat*, 77–100.

19 Here again, I use the Chinese version, since I am referring to Chinese expressions.

20 Ge Fei, "Xiangyu," in *Xiangyu* (Taipei: Yuanliu, 1993), 163–214. Trans. Deborah Mills as "Meetings" in *Abandoned Wine: Chinese Writing Today* 2, ed. Henry Zhao (London: Wellsweep, 1996), 15–49.

21 Ge Fei, "Qing huang," in *Hushao*, 58–79. Trans. Eva Shan Chou as "Green yellow," in Wang, *China's Avant-Garde Fiction*, 23–42.

22 Ge Fei, "Hushao," in *Hushao*, 219–41. Trans. Victor H. Mair as "Whistling," in Wang, *China's Avant-Garde Fiction*, 43–68.

23 Zhang Xudong, *Chinese Modernism in the Era of Reforms: Cultural Fever, Avant-Garde Fiction, and the New Chinese Cinema* (Durham: Duke University Press, 1997), 180.

24 "The characters are props," are "objectified," says Ge Fei of Robbe-Grillet's novel, *Les Gommes (The Erasers)*. Ge Fei also adds: "The reader is totally free," "has nothing to rely on," "the author having disappeared." See Ge Fei, "Shuo 'Xiangpi'—jieru yu youdao zhiyi."

25 In *High Culture Fever*, 245.

26 Gilles Deleuze and Félix Guattari, "What Is a Minor Literature?" in *Out There: Marginalization and Contemporary Cultures* (New York: New Museum of Contemporary Art, 1990), 60–61. To my mind, Yu's texts reso-

nate with several of Kafka's works. Deleuze and Guattari's study of Kafka's "machine" casts some light in understanding Yu Hua's enterprise. Traces of Deleuze and Guattari's reading can therefore be found in this section.

27 Andrew F. Jones, "The Violence of the Text: Reading Yu Hua and Shi Zhecun," *positions* 2, no. 3 (1994): 596.

28 Yu Hua, "Xianshi yizhong," in *Hebian de cuowu (Mistake by the Riverside)* (Wuhan: Changjiang wenyi, 1992), 50–95. Trans. Jeanne Tai as "One kind of reality," in *Running Wild: New Chinese Writers* (New York: Columbia University Press, 1994), 21–68.

29 Yu Hua, "Shishi ru yan," in *Hebian de cuowu*, 96–140. Trans. Andrew F. Jones as "World like mist," in *The Past and the Punishments* (Honolulu: University of Hawai'i Press, 1996), 62–113.

30 Yu Hua, "1986," in *Yu Hua zuopinji* 1 (*Yu Hua's Collected Works*) (Beijing: Zhongguo shehui kexueyuan, 1994), 142–80. Trans. Andrew F. Jones as "1986," in *The Past and the Punishments*, 132–80.

31 Instead of quoting this very gory passage at length, I refer readers to Jones's translation of "1986," especially 157–60.

32 Add to this that horror is enmeshed with beauty: "Fresh blood oozed like sunshine" ("1986," 165, with modifications). The same applies to many stories where gruesome details are set in an enchanting scenery of peach blossoms, as in "World like mist" and *Hebian de cuowu*.

33 Yu Hua, "Wangshi yu xingfa," in *Hebian de cuowu*, 177–91. Trans. Andrew F. Jones as "The past and the punishments," in *The Past and the Punishments*, 114–31.

34 Yu Hua, "Xuwei de zuopin" (Hypocritical writings), in *Yu Hua zuopinji* 2 (*Yu Hua's Collected Works: 2*) (Beijing: Zhongguo shehui kexueyuan, 1994), 278.

35 Deleuze and Guattari, "What Is a Minor Literature"? 64.

36 Yu Hua, "Xuwei de zuopin," 277.

37 Yu Hua, "Wo. Xiaoshuo. Xianshi" (Myself. Novels. Reality), *Jinri xianfeng* 1 (1994): 19.

38 What interests Yu in Robbe-Grillet is the French writer's view that literature changes constantly because reality is forever changing. Yu Hua, "Xuwei de zuopin," 278.

39 Yu Hua, personal communication, April 6, 1994, Beijing.

40 Can Xue, letter to her French translator, Françoise Naour, quoted in Can Xue, *Dialogues en paradis* (Dialogues in Paradise), trans. Françoise Naour (Paris: Gallimard, 1992), 170.

41 Visual games, with insects and other crawling creatures, abound in her texts. They proliferate as radicals, which can even prompt images. For example, a husband's nose is described as hard and bright, like a "candle." This weird image, although explainable—*à la limite*—in realistic terms,

does not conform with the depiction just given of the husband, which is in terms of the vegetal. It can, however, be justified, as a carrying over of the two radicals that make up the word "candle" 'lazhu' in Chinese, i.e., "insect" and "fire." These two have been in the background of the tale of a marriage since the beginning of the story (earthworms are dug out in the yard, caterpillars swarm inside the house), while firecrackers are their aural counterpart. This example is taken from Can Xue, "Amei zai yige taiyang tianli de chousi" (A Mei's black thoughts on a sunny day), in *Huangdanpai xiaoshuo (Absurd School Novels)*, ed. Wu Liang et al. (Beijing: Shidai wenyi, 1988), 301–3.

42 Can Xue, "Shanshang de xiaowu," in *Hese niaoqun: Huangdan xiaoshuo xuancui (A Flock of Brown Birds: A Selection of Absurdist Novels)*, ed. Lan Dizhi et al. (Beijing: Beijing shifan daxue, 1989), 94–98. Trans. Robert R. Janssen and Jian Zhang as "The hut on the mountain," in *China's Avant-Garde Fiction*, 212–16. A collection of her stories has appeared as *Dialogues in Paradise*, trans. R. R. Janssen and Jian Zhang (Evanston: Northwestern University Press, 1989). However, for the purpose of my demonstration I will in most cases use my own more literal translations and refer to the Chinese version for all of Can Xue's works.

43 In "Tianchuang" (Skylight), for example, the word "mushroom" appears frequently out of the blue: there are "mushroom clouds" (311); she goes looking for "mushrooms" (314); there is "mushroom smoke" (317); with the old man she used to go picking "mushrooms" (317). "Tianchuang," in Wu et al., *Huangdanpai xiaoshuo*, 306–18.

44 Samuel Beckett, *Molloy* (New York: Grove Press, 1955), 51, 21.

45 Can Xue, "Tianchuang," 306–18.

46 See Lü Tonglin's chapter on Can Xue, where she studies the political (Maoist) subversion in Can Xue's work. Lü Tonglin, "Can Xue: What Is So Paranoid in Her Writings?" in *Misogyny, Cultural Nihilism, and Oppositional Politics: Contemporary Chinese Avant-Garde Fiction* (Stanford: Stanford University Press, 1995), 75–103. Also see Françoise Naour's introduction to *Dialogues en Paradis*, which explains Can Xue's images as outgrowths of her youth when cared for by a nice witch, her grandmother, and also as reflective of the political environment. Françoise Naour, "Clefs pour Can Xue" (Keys to Can Xue), in *Dialogues en paradis*, 7–41.

47 In her speech at the Shanghai roundtable on her novel *Tuwei biaoyan*. Can Xue, *Tuwei biaoyan (An Out-of-the-Encirclement Performance)* (Shanghai: Shanghai wenyi, 1990), 332. I thank Lü Tonglin for having given me a photocopy of this bravura speech by Can Xue and especially for having introduced me to Can Xue's "world."

48 "Mingren zhi si" (Death of a famous person), in *Huangnijie (Yellow Mud Road)* (Wuhan: Changjiang wenyi, 1996), 359–63.

49 This example was brought up (for other purposes—the blurring of the boundary between reason and madness) by Susanne Posborg in "Can Xue: Tracing Madness," in *Inside Out: Modernism and Postmodernism in Chinese Literary Culture* (Aarhus: Aarhus University Press, 1993), 94. The translation is Posborg's. Can Xue, "Canglao de fuyun" (Aging clouds), in Wu et al., *Huangdanpai xiaoshuo,* 219–300.

50 In her correspondence with her French translator, Françoise Naour. Can Xue, *Dialogues en paradis,* 171.

51 "Pokai" (Breakthrough), in *Zhanzai wuren de fengkou (Standing in a Draft Where There Is No One)* (Kunming: Yunnan renmin, 1995), 93–128.

52 During a roundtable on Chen Ran's novel *Siren shenghuo (Private Life),* organized by the National Writers' Association (Beijing, April 10, 1996). I thank Dai Jinhua for having invited me to the event and, a few years earlier, for having introduced me to Chen's work.

53 In "Yu wangshi ganbei" (A toast to the past), in *Zuichunli de yangguang (Sunshine between the Lips)* (Wuhan: Changjiang wenyi chubanshe, 1991), 3.

54 Jane Gallop's title and thesis fit the general picture for Chen Ran. *The Daughter's Seduction: Feminism and Psychoanalysis* (Ithaca: Cornell University Press, 1982).

55 Judith Butler's term comes from her work *Gender Trouble: Feminism and the Subversion of Identity* (New York: Routledge, 1990).

56 In the roundtable on *Private Life,* already mentioned, critic Zhang Yiwu rightly emphasized the importance of the city in Chen Ran's work.

57 Wendy Larson, "Women and the discourse of desire in postrevolutionary China: The Awkward Postmodernism of Chen Ran," *boundary* 2 (fall 1997): 201–24. Quote on pp. 215–16. Wendy Larson kindly gave me a copy of her paper before it was published. I thank her here.

58 In "Yu wangshi ganbei," 7–10; in *Siren shenghuo (Private Life)* (Beijing: Zuojia chubanshe, 1996), 151–54.

59 See Chen Ran's interview with Xiao Gang, "Ling yishan kaiqi de men" (Another opened door), in Chen Ran *Siren shenghuo,* 262.

60 In the sense in which Judith Butler in *Gender Trouble* describes drag, cross-dressing, and other subversive acts of gender: you can no longer believe anything—the "originals" are as "natural" and as unbelievable as their copies (141).

61 Xu Kun, "Regou" (Hotdog), in *Regou (Hotdog)* (Beijing: Zhongguo huaqiao, 1996), 169–232.

62 Xu Kun, "Xianfeng" (Avant-garde), in *Regou,* 276–334.

63 In "Youxing" (Parading), the "catcher in the rye" reemerges, this time applied to amateur rockers who play their gigs at subway entrances (20). Xu Kun, "Youxing," *Zhongshan* 6 (*Purple Mountain*) (1995): 4–27.

64 Ron Gluckman, "The Americanization of China," in *Asiaweek,* July 4, 1997, 38–44.

65 Xu Kun, "Youxing."

66 In English in the text, 10.

2 *Away from Literature I*

1 This was writer Wang Meng's answer to my question whether there are any women writing somewhat like Wang Shuo. At a roundtable, at the University of Montreal, April 28, 1996.

2 Xu Kun works in the Chinese Literature Section of the Academy of Social Sciences in Beijing.

3 Wang Shuo was, in the spring of 1997, "somewhere" in the United States and thinking of possibly staying there. See Jamie James, "Bad boy: Why China's most popular novelist won't go home," in the *New Yorker,* April 21, 1997, 50–53. His English translator, Howard Goldblatt, confirmed to me that Wang has since returned to Beijing (August 1, 1997).

4 Geremie R. Barmé, *Shades of Mao: The Posthumous Cult of the Great Leader* (Armonk, N.Y.: M. E. Sharpe, 1996), 6.

5 Wang Shuo, "Wanzhu" (Troublemakers), *Shouhuo (Harvest)* 6 (1987): 24–52. The following references are to this edition. There is also a film by the same title by Mi Jiashan (1988).

6 *Bianjibu de gushi (Stories of an Editorial Board),* twenty-five-part series, dir. Zhao Baogang and Jin Yan, Beijing Television Arts Center, 1991.

7 This clever translation is Jing Wang's in *High Culture Fever: Politics, Aesthetics, and Ideology in Deng's China* (Berkeley: University of California Press, 1996), 274.

8 Wang Shuo said this when told that the ending of his novella "Fuchu haimian" (Surfacing), 1985, had to be changed. Quoted by Zuo Shula, "Wang Shuo: yige ganyu miaoshi changgui de 'suren'" (Wang Shuo: A "vulgar person" who dares to despise convention), *Dazhong dianying (Popular Film)* 433 (July 1989): 10. Wang said the same thing when his film *Baba (Daddy)* needed revision (personal communication, Beijing, March 27, 1996).

9 Liu Xinwu and Zhang Yiwu, *Duihua lu: "Houshiji" de wenhua liaowang (Recorded Dialogues: Cultural observations at the "post-century")* (Guilin: Lijiang, 1996), 202–3.

10 In 1991, James Lull was noting the absence of sitcoms in Chinese television: "In order of overall popularity, these [categories] are drama, sports, information, and light entertainment programs. Situation comedies, by far the most popular American prime-time genre, do not appear

on Chinese TV." Lull, *China Turned On: Television, Reform, and Resistance* (Routledge: London, 1991), 155. At the time of Lull's research, not only were there no sitcoms but even the first Chinese soap opera, *Kewang (Yearnings)*, 1990 — to which Wang Shuo's name is also attached — had not yet aired.

11 Another high-quality and intelligent sitcom is *Yidi jimao (Trivia all Around)*, 1994. Adapted from Liu Zhenyun's novella of the same name (1991) and his "Danwei" (Work unit) (1989), it was made by Feng Xiaogang, with Wang Shuo at the helm as general supervisor. The editorial room has been replaced by the civil servants' office: not much work seems to be accomplished there either. It is a biting critique of bureaucratic ways, and of the poverty of its employees. Understandably, its airing was severely controlled, with the result that very few people got to see the series.

12 Feng Xiaogang, Wang Shuo, et al., "Zhe deng hao xiju wei shenme dansheng" (Why this good comedy was born), in *Bianjibu de gushi: jingcai duibai xinshang (Stories of an Editorial Board: The Best Dialogues)* (Beijing: Zhongguo guangbo dianshi, 1992), 5. Feng Xiaogang said this to me almost verbatim when I met him in April 19, 1996. Both Wang and himself, he said, deal with only two topics, social questions and "matters of the heart" 'yanqing.'

13 Not all of the scripts have been published. Professor Zhou Yimin of the Beijing Normal University kindly lent me his copy of the unpublished manuscripts, which includes the two quotations, respectively "Pangzi de fannao" (A fat man's vexations) and "Shuang shuang" (Doubly Double).

14 Wang Shuo, "Shui bi shui sha duoshao" (Who's dumbest), in *Bianjibu de gushi* (Hong Kong: Tiandi tushu, 1993), 49.

15 Both quotations are from "Shui shi shui fei" (Who's right), unpublished.

16 The three quotations are taken from Wang Shuo, "Qu ge shenme hao" (Who'd be a perfect wife), in *Qingchun wuhui: Wang Shuo yingshi zuopin (No Regrets for Youth: Wang Shuo's Television and Film Works)* (Beijing: Zhongguo shehui kexue, 1993), 297, 300, 305.

17 "Qu ge shenme hao," 307.

18 "Shui bi shui sha duoshao," 19.

19 "Shui bi shui sha duoshao," 18.

20 Wang Shuo, "Xiugai hou fabiao" (Publication after revision), in *Bianjibu de gushi*, 102.

21 Wang Shuo, "Mengran wuzhi" (Muddled ignoramus), in *Bianjibu de gushi*, 130.

22 Geremie Barmé, "Wang Shuo and *liumang* ('hooligan') culture," *Australian Journal of Chinese Affairs* 28 (July 1992): 58.

23 Wang Shuo, *Playing for Thrills*, trans. Howard Goldblatt (New York: William Morrow, 1997), 186. The original is *Wande jiushi xintiao*, in Wang

Shuo, *Wang Shuo quanji, 2: Zhiqing juan (Complete Works of Wang Shuo, 2: Friendship Volume)* (Beijing: Huayi, 1992), 345.

24 Quoted by Jamie James, "Bad boy: Why China's most popular novelist won't go home," 50–53.

25 Wang Shuo, "Dongwu xiongmeng" (Wild beasts), in *Wang Shuo quanji, 1: Chunqing juan (Complete Works of Wang Shuo, 1: Sentimental Volume)* (Beijing: Huayi, 1992), 406–93.

26 A frequent call of young male rockers is to the mythical figure of youthful beauty, Ashima. For example, at one end of the spectrum, Mongolian rock singer Teng Ge'er languidly cries out to her, while at the other end, the No group yells out her name in mockery of love as salvation, because "Ashima" is now a brand of cigarettes.

27 Just as *In the Heat of the Sun* uses the music of Mascani's nineteenth-century *Rustic Cavalier* to create a highly romantic atmosphere, *A Beijinger in New York* starts each show with a tune highly reminiscent of another nineteenth-century classical composition, the finale of Dvorak's New World Symphony.

28 In an interview with A. Solomon, "Not just a yawn but the howl that could free China," *New York Times Magazine,* December 19, 1993, 44+.

29 In an interview with Sandrine Chenivesse, "La Grande Révolution culturelle: Un goût de fête" (The great cultural revolution: A big party), *Perspectives chinoises* 25 (Sept.–Oct. 1994): 55.

30 I was granted a visit to the Sun Film company and an interview with Jiang Wen on April 3, 1996. Jiang's office has a collection of military hats; in the meeting room are portraits of Mao, Stalin, Marx, Engels, and Lenin, much like the Cultural Revolution relics in the film.

31 For example, in 1994, for television alone, and mentioning only the best known names, twenty-eight writers (including Wang Shuo, Liu Yiran, Shi Tiesheng, Liu Zhenyun, and Su Lei) collaborated in the writing of the series *Haima gewuting (Seahorse Karaoke).* In the same year, Liu Yiran, Mo Yan, and Yu Hua wrote a thirty-two-part series *Ai shui shi shui (Love the One You're With)* for filmmaker Huang Jianzhong. Both series were comedies. In 1996, in a "serious," "literary" vein, Liu Yiran turned television director to make a series with writer Yu Hua and musician Zhang Guangtian, based on a Mao Dun story. The painter Zhao Bandi has also been devising his own television series.

32 Feng Xiaogang was also one of the scriptwriters, along with Wang Shuo, for *Stories of an Editorial Board.* He has written many other scripts, including *Dasaba (Freewheeling)* for filmmaker Xia Gang; since *A Beijinger in New York,* he has directed another television series, *Yidi jimao (Trivia All Around)* (1994), and acted in Wang Shuo's directorial debut in the film *Baba (Daddy)* (1996).

33 Luo Yulan and Ding Renren have written a detailed account of the shoot-

ing of *A Beijinger in New York*. It is perhaps China's first "making of" book, and definitely the first book on a television production. Luo Yulan and Ding Renren, *Feiyue Taipingyang: "Beijingren zai Niuyue" de muhou jingtou (Crossing the Pacific: Behind the Scenes of "A Beijinger in New York")* (Beijing: Zuojia, 1993).

34 *Feiyue Taipingyang*, 193.

35 According to Luo and Renren, Feng used this phrase to encourage his team. *Feiyue Taipingyang*, 193.

36 This is the epigraph of the adapted novel, the lyrics of a Western song the hero listens to on the radio. Glen Cao (Cao Guilin), *Beijingren zai Niuyue (A Beijinger in New York)* (Beijing: Zhongguo wenlian, 1991).

37 Song Qiang, Zhang Cangcang, and Qiao Bian, *Zhongguo keyi shuo bu (China Can Say No)* (Beijing: Zhonghua gongshang lianhe, 1996).

38 Jiang Wen, "Beijingren ruhe kan Beijingren zai Niuyue—*Beijingren zai Niuyue* zuotanhui fayan zhaiyao" (How Beijingers perceived *A Beijinger in New York*—Summary of the roundtable on *A Beijinger in New York*), *Beijing wanbao (Beijing Evening News)*, October 15, 1993, 5.

39 Or so claims the *China Daily*, January 3, 1994.

40 Cao Guilin (Glen Cao), "Qianyan" (Preface), *Beijingren zai Niuyue*, 1–5. Following the television adaptation, the novel was published in serial form in various evening papers throughout the country. In 1992, perhaps in the hope of yet another success story, someone by the name of Fan Xiangda wrote *Shanghai ren zai Dongjing (A Shanghaier in Tokyo)* (Beijing: Zuojia 1992).

41 Zhou Li Fochler, *Manhadun de Zhongguo nüren (Manhattan's China Lady)* (Beijing: Beijing, 1992).

42 It is customary in Chinese works to insert photos of the author. These overseas Chinese did the same, pointing, however, to their respective new American environments.

43 Erica Marcus, *A Child's Eye View of China's Cultural Revolution*, press kit for *The Monkey Kid*, a film by the Beijing-San Francisco Film Group, 1995.

44 Liu Sola, *Hundun jia ligeleng* (Beijing: Zhongguo huaqiao, 1994). I refer here to the excellent English translation by Richard King: *Chaos and All That* (Honolulu: University of Hawaii Press, 1995).

45 Artist Mao Xuhui also told me all about what kind of running shoes you had to wear, how to tie them, how teenagers dyed their clothes black, how their caps were held on with elastic, how pants had to be baggy, oversized, and worn out to a certain degree, how the vest had to have two pockets and not the usual four (March 13, 1996). It was just as complex and hermetic as styles among today's teenagers.

46 In the same line see (male writer) Wang Xiaobo's extremely popular novel *Huangjin shidai (Golden Years)* (Beijing: Huaxia, 1994). See, in par-

ticular, part 1, which is predominantly about sexual prowess during the Cultural Revolution.

47 Liu Sola, *Blues in the East/Landiao zai Dongfang*, Island Records, 1994.

48 Liu Sola, "Liu Sola zai Meiguo" (Liu Sola in the United States), *Qingnian zhoumo (Youth weekender)* [Beijing], February 21, 1997, 12.

49 See *Liu Sola zai Meiguo* for her diatribe against pop music's attempts to "package" her.

50 But not in China, where there is no particular interest for such residual stuff. Also, as Xiao Ding points out, some details seem to be geared to the international (i.e., nondomestic) viewers: in *On the Beat*, when the old lady in charge of contraceptives enumerates in detail all the various types of contraception, it seems a rather unlikely thing to say. Xiao Ding, *Mingjing gushi* suixianglu (Random Notes on *On the Beat*), *Zhongguo yinmu (China Screen)* 9 (November 1996): 37. Non-Chinese, however, read her film as "equal parts satire and ethnography." Jerry White, "The Films of Ning Ying: Unfolding in Miniature," *Cineaction* 42: 2–9.

51 In an interview with Jean-Michel Frodon, "Les Tribulations d'une chinoise en Chine . . . et ailleurs (The adventures of a Chinese woman in China . . . and elsewhere), *Le Monde*, March 10, 1994, 5. This is strikingly similar to the position of female fashion mogul Rei Kawabuko of Comme des Garçons. Although her styles are seen as derived from kabuki and other traditional Japanese art, Kawabuko claims to have no interest whatsoever in such things and to have been to kabuki only once, when she was in primary school. Quoted in Dorrine Kondo, *About Face: Performing Race in Fashion and Theater* (New York: Routledge), 67.

52 For an interesting study of two most frequent uses or meanings of the city in Chinese film, that is, refusal and disengagement versus cultural and political participation, see Tang Xiaobing's article "Configuring the modern space: Cinematic representation of Beijing and its politics," *East-West Film Journal* 2 (July 1994): 48–69.

53 Quoted in an article by Arjuna Ranawana, "Pride and prejudice: Many Asian women directors still face typecasting," *Asiaweek*, February 9, 1996, 36–37.

3 *Away from Literature II*

1 Arjuna Ranawana, "Pride and prejudice: Many Asian women directors still face typecasting," *Asiaweek*, February 9, 1996, 36–37.

2 See for example *Xiju dianying bao (Theater and Film Journal)* 790 (March 1996).

3 As reported in the *China Daily*, November 1, 1993.

4 Antonin Artaud, "En finir avec les chefs-d'oeuvre" (To be done with

masterpieces), in *Le théâtre et son double (Theater and Its Double)* (Paris: Gallimard, 1964), 115.

5 Zhang Xian also says that he writes what he calls "closet" 'chouti' plays, that is, serious, avant-garde works that won't find either funders or audience and therefore stay in the closet. See Xu Hailing, "Zhang Xian *Loushang de majin* hen jianrui" (Zhang Xian's *The Margin Upstairs* is incisive), *Zhongshi zhoukan (China Times Weekly)* [Taipei], July 10-16, 1994, 54–55; and Lincoln Kaye, "Shanghai Fables," *Far Eastern Economic Review,* April 14, 1994, 50–51. Zhang has now six film scripts to his credit, the last being the very upbeat *Tan qing shuo ai (A Crazy Little Thing Called Love),* made by his Shanghai partner, Li Xin.

6 Produced by Lin Zhaohua, who seems to give many young "experimenters" a helping hand these days.

7 As written in the 1994 program notes of *Linghun chuqiao (When Conscience Speaks),* a production of the Fire Fox Independent Theatre Group. That group seems to relish inventive program notes. For the 1996 production of *Louding (Rooftop),* the program notes consisted of a one-page vocabulary, including words such as *majiang:* "a thick sesame sauce which Beijingers use as a spice for Mongolian hotpot or with noodles"; or again "HAPPY" (in English): "a fashionable word to describe a certain kind of happiness." Considering that some funds came from Hong Kong, could those notes have been directed at that public? One thing is sure: the pop theater likes to use the irreverent 'tiaokan' expressions of streetwise slang.

8 See Chen Xiaomei, *Occidentalism: A Theory of Counter-Discourse in Post-Mao China* (New York: Oxford University Press, 1995). Her book's examples are taken mainly from theater.

9 Program for the annual *Festival d'automne* [Paris] (1995), 38.

10 Meng Jinghui, "Guangyu *Wo ai XXX* xiju de chanshi" (About the play *I Love XXX*), [*Bai pishu*] *(White-Cover Book)* (Hong Kong: Dadi, 1995), 73. The book is untitled and referred to by the color of its cover.

11 See Matt Froney, "Final Curtain," *Far Eastern Economic Review,* January 30, 1997, 34–35.

12 "The dumplings [*baozi*] were a little salty" was Meng's sardonic reaction to Mou Sen's play, *Yu aizibing you guande (Things Related to AIDS),* performed in 1995. I would rather not mention my informant here. Meng's play, *Sifan (The Tale of the Nun and the Monk),* was performed again in the same year as Mou's and, not surprisingly, was far more of a success. Meng was part of the company that Mou Sen founded in 1987, the Frog/Wa Theater Group (Wa jutuan); they produced Ionesco's *Rhinoceros,* possibly the first "experimental" production in China.

13 Mou's work is also antipodal to his teacher Lin Zhaohua's concerted efforts to make theater "fun," like karaoke. Of course, it is also at odds with any idea of entertainment.

14 Gao Xingjian, *Bi'an (The Other Bank)*, in *Gao Xingjian xiju liuzhong (Six Plays by Gao Xingjian)* (Taipei: Guoli zhongyang tushuguan, 1995), 1–69. I thank Annie Curien for kindly sending me a copy of this play. In his afterword (68), Gao writes that Lin Zhaohua was supposed to stage his play around 1986, but it never worked out. Lin's production would probably have kept the "profound" meaning of the play, the (sexist) difference between men and women's roles, the symbolic use of rope, and so on. An uncut version of the play was finally performed in 1995, in Hong Kong, where audiences must have relished the allegory.

15 Gao Xingjian himself talks about his own play in terms of abstraction and of a search for one's subjectivity! See "*Bi'an* yanchu de shuoming yu jianyi" (Explanations and suggestions for the production of *The Other Bank*), in *Dui yizhong xiandai xiju de zhuiqiu (In Search of a Certain Kind of Contemporary Theater)* (Beijing: Zhongguo xiju, 1988), 144–47. William Tay has described Gao's 1980s theater as "a kind of revived 'critical realism.'" William Tay, "Avant-garde theater in post-Mao China: *The Bus-Stop* by Gao Xingjian," in *Worlds Apart: Recent Chinese Writing and Its Audiences,* ed. Howard Goldblatt (Armonk, N.Y.: M. E. Sharpe, 1990), 111–18. Now living in France, Gao liberally uses Beijing opera masks in his plays, which he sometimes writes directly in French. For him, theater transcends nationality. See Gao Xingjian, *Dialoguer interloquer: Pièce en deux actes (Conversations and Rebuttals),* trans. Annie Curien (Sainte-Nazaire, [France]: M.E.E.T., 1993), 135. The original title is *Duihua fanji.*

16 Yu Jian, "Guanyu *Bi'an* de yihui hanyu cixing taolun" (A Chinese grammatical discussion on *The Other Bank*), *Jinri xianfeng (Today's Avant-Garde)* 1 (1994): 65–83.

17 In a personal interview, March 1996.

18 In Yu's afterword to "'Bi'an' de yihui hanyu cixing taolun," 83.

19 Ding Fang and He Yi, "Cong *Bi'an* zhuiwen bi'an" (Questioning the other bank by way of *The Other Bank*), *Yishu chaoliu/Art Currents* 4 (1994): 67–73.

20 Antonin Artaud, "En finir avec les chefs-d'œuvre," 130.

21 Here is the original. "[Estragon:] What do we do now? [Vladimir:] Wait for Godot. . . . Thinking is not the worst. [Estragon:] Perhaps not, but at least there's that. [Vladimir:] That what? [Estragon:] That's the idea, let's ask each other questions. [Vladimir:] What do you mean, At least there's that?" Samuel Beckett, *Waiting for Godot* (New York: Grove Press, 1954), 41–42.

22 Jerzy Grotowski, *Towards a Poor Theatre,* ed. Eugenio Barba (London: Methuen, 1975), 58. Actually, Mou Sen studied Grotowski's techniques and put them in practice with his young actors. He trained them for six months, and made them do exercises from Sirshana and Hatha yoga. As seen in Jiang Yue's documentary *The Other Bank* and in many photo-

graphs, the actors tearfully embrace Mou Sen and even touch his head with religious fervor at the end of the show. More on this later on in this chapter.

23 See above, note 12, for a peer response. Another disenchanted spectator was the well-known woman novelist Lin Bai. See Lin Bai, "Kan Mou Sen de huaju" (Watching Mou Sen's plays), in *Deerwo de yueguang (Delvaux's Moonlight)* (Kunming: Yunnan renmin, 1995), 71–85. Undoubtedly, the performance was meant to have people ask themselves (after having wondered what the play had to do with AIDS), "What does AIDS have to do with me?" Mou Sen had then just returned from collecting video materials on AIDS-stricken people on China's southwestern frontier.

24 And commissioned by Brussel's Kunsten Festival des Arts.

25 Milan Kundera, *The Book of Laughter and Forgetting* (New York: Harper Perennial, 1996), 120.

26 Yu Jian, "Ling Dang'an" (File 0), *Da Jia* (*Great Masters*) 1 (1994): 48.

27 He Yi, "Jiushi niandai de shige shigu: ping changshi 'Ling dang'an'" (An accident in 1990s poetry: A critique of the poem "File 0"), *Da jia* 1 (1994): 61.

28 Quoted in Wu Wenguang, " 'Ling dang'an': Cong shi dao xiju" ("File 0": From poem to play), *Jinri xianfeng* 2 (1994): 65.

29 Mou Sen, at a roundtable during Montreal's Festival de théâtre des Amériques, 1995. Similar statements can be found, for example, in Wu Wenguang, " 'Ling dang'an': cong shi dao xiju."

30 The term is José Munoz's in "The autoethnographic performance: Reading Richard Fung's queer hybridity," *Screen* 36, no. 2 (1995): 83–99. It refers to Fung's presentation of himself in terms of race, nation, and sexual orientation. Mou is the least likely person to talk of himself. Of all the artists I have met in China in the past years, he is one of the few to have been more interested in learning about what's happening outside, namely in Canada (my country) rather than promoting or simply talking about himself.

31 Again, this can be found in many articles on Mou. It is quoted verbatim, and in English, in the publicity material for *File 0*.

32 Of course, there was simultaneous translation, but the "alienation effect" (a Brechtian one?) was very much in operation, even when the interpretation was superb, as was the case in Montreal.

33 Alain Robbe-Grillet, quoted in Geneviève Serreau, *Histoire du "nouveau théâtre" (A History of "New Theater")* (Paris: Gallimard, 1966), 10–11.

34 Jean Genet, quoted in Geneviève Serreau, *Histoire du "nouveau théâtre,"* 126.

35 Hanif Kureishi, *The Buddha of Suburbia* (London: Penguin Books, 1990).

36 I thank Wen Hui for having lent me a video of her performance. For the background and an analysis of "100 verbs/words of action," see Su

Hei, "Shenti de jinxingshi: Wen Hui he tade 100 ge dongci" (The body's in-progress: Wen Hui and her 100 verbs), *Jinri xianfeng* 4 (1996): 58–65.

37 I only saw the performance on video, and it was a very poor quality copy.

38 See "The Flight of the Butterfly," *Asiaweek: Eyewitness,* February 9, 1996, 39. A very informative interview with her is Xu Xiaoyu's "Wudao pinghengle wo" (Dance straightened me out), in "Tanhua ji shi daolu" (Speaking one's way through), unpublished manuscript, Beijing, October 1995 and April 1996.

39 Ma Liuming, "Ma Liuming suibi" (Random notes of Ma Liuming), *Jinri xianfeng* 4 (1996): 118. The other quotations are also from this text.

40 Some of these films are, however, shown in international film festivals.

41 One hundred thousand yuan maximum.

42 "Successful" here means succeeding in making more than one film, in being shown, in finding funding. Other independent filmmakers include He Yi who has two films to date, *Xuanlian (Red Beads)* (1993) and *Youchai (Postman)* (1995). His second film is the most antitouristic film on Beijing I have ever seen: the ugliest quarters of the city are shot in dreary winter weather. He has succeeded in showing, in a fictional film, the malaise young men feel when they are around women. His films are surveys of strange behaviors, aiming to show psychological profundity (through a frequent use of long shots and repetition). As for Wang Xiaoshuai, his latest film, *So Close to Paradise (Biandan guniang)* was three years in the making due to financial and political difficulties. His first film, *Dong Chun de rizi (The Days)* (1993) relates art and love by telling the story of two painters' life together and their break-up; it is played by the couple Liu Xiaodong and Yu Hong, who are painters in real life. Mao Ye (Keno), a Japanese critic, upon seeing *The Days,* wrote that these artists' lives are pretty much like "ours," except that their everyday life is not. For example, they have no hot water in the house. See Mao Ye (Keno), "Wo kan Zhongguo shiyan dianying" (Watching Chinese experimental film), *Yishu xinwen (Art News)* [Beijing], August 18, 1993. The film opens with a steamy love scene that would not be acceptable to Chinese censors. Both He and Wang have been at times assistants to Fifth-Generation filmmakers: He for Chen Kaige, Tian Zhuangzhuang, and Zhang Yimou, and Wang for Wu Ziniu. For a general account of the underground filmmakers, see Zheng Xianghong, "Duli yingren zai xingdong: Suowei Beijing 'dixia dianying' zhenxiang" (Independent filmmakers are on the go: A true picture of Beijing's so-called underground cinema), *Dianying gushi (Film Stories)* (May 1993): 4–7.

43 Lao Lin, "Liulang Beijing zazhong" (Bastards bumming in Beijing), *Zhongguo Daobao (China Guide)* 3 (1993): 4–11, quote on p. 8.

44 As befits the situation of underground cinema, Zhang's films are very difficult to get to see. I would like to thank Zhang Yuan who let me view

his films on video at his home on two occasions (in 1994 and in 1996) and who discussed them with me.

45 This film, shot by Zhang and an assistant, Duan Jinchuan, was filmed on the sly. It is interesting to me that *The Place* was shot the same year as Zhang Yimou's *Qiuju Da Guansi (Qiuju, a Chinese Woman)*, which also uses hidden cameras and is Zhang Yimou's first documentary-like film, an exception in his filmography. This is, however, where the similarity between the two Zhangs ends.

46 To my mind, such unbearable scenes only have one equivalent and that is in the films *Vive l'amour, The River, The Hole*, by the Malaysian-Taiwanese filmmaker, Tsai Ming-liang.

47 He Yi, "Liulang, duli, taowang" (Roaming, independence, escape), in Wu Wenguang, *Liulang Beijing: Zuihou de mengxiangzhe (Bumming in Beijing: The Last Dreamers)* (Taipei: Wanquan tushu, 1995), 291.

48 *Liulang Beijing*, 307.

49 Wu's other documentary, *1966: Wo de hongweibing shidai (1966: My Red Guard Period)* (1993), as the title announces, interviews middle-aged people about their experiences as red guards. Like his other documentaries, it shows the homogeneity of thought (or rather of memory) because the five interviewed (all of different professional backgrounds) say somewhat the same things. So Spivak's contention that Americans presume they are all individuals though they all think and utter the same might also be applied to China, or even be universally valid. See Gayatri Chakravorty Spivak, "Reading the world: Literary studies in the eighties," in *In Other Worlds: Essays in Cultural Politics* (New York: Routledge, 1988), 95–102.

50 For many years now, Jiang Yue has been trying to find funding to finish a film on another sensitive topic, mine workers who have been laid off. An offer has come from Japan to fund a film on the Tiananmen hunger strikers, which he might take up in order to finish his project on the miners. Personal communication, April 16, 1996.

51 Jia Zhangke, "Wo de jiaodian" (My standpoint), *Jinri xianfeng* 5 (1997): 197.

52 Jia Zhangke, "Women shi yiqun dianying mingong" (We are migrant workers in film), *Xiju dianying zhou bao (Theater and Television Weekly)* 790 (March 1996).

53 Not only is this reminiscent of the young ill-fated actors in Mou's play; but it also reminds me of the Iranian film *Salam Cinema* by Mohsen Makhmalbaf, where the whole country, it seems (i.e., five thousand applicants for one hundred small roles), is dying to be in the movies.

1   The first two generations of filmmakers worked before the founding of the People's Republic of China, the first from 1900s to 1920s, the second during the golden years of the 1930s and 1940s. At present, there are four living generations: the third through the sixth. The Third Generation is comprised of the "revolutionary workers" of the 1940s and 1950s who served to adapt cinema to the new country's needs. Their emblem is Xie Jin, as, for example, in his latest film, *Yapian zhanzheng (The Opium War)* (1997), on the return of Hong Kong to the motherland. The Fourth Generation is made up of filmmakers who came to film late, the 1980s, because they came of age during the Cultural Revolution and were not able to film in that period. Their films followed those of the famous Fifth Generation, not those of the Third. The Fifth Generation is the first class of graduates of what was then the only film school in China, the Beijing Film Institute, at the onset of the era of the reform of 1982. The Sixth Generation consists technically of those who graduated from the same school after 1989, but it is a contested designation. For a fuller account of the first five generations, see Zhang Xudong, *Chinese Modernism in the Era of Reforms: Cultural Fever, Avant-Garde Fiction, and the New Chinese Cinema* (Durham, N.C.: Duke University Press, 1997), 217–25. For the Sixth Generation, see Lin Xudong, "Diwudai"zhi hou, "diliudai"? (After the "Fifth Generation," the "Sixth Generation"?), *Jinri xianfeng (Today's Avant-Garde)* 3 (1995): 79–90.

2   See Lu Xun, "Nalai zhuyi" (Grabbism), in *Lu Xun quanji (The Complete Works of Lu Xun)*, vol. 6 (Beijing: Renmin wenxue, 1995), 38–41.

3   Teshome H. Gabriel, "Towards a critical theory of third world films," in *Questions of Third Cinema* (London: British Film Institute, 1989), 50, 39.

4   For a Daoist reading of *Yellow Earth*, see Esther C. M. Yau, "*Yellow Earth*: Western analysis and a non-Western text," in *Perspectives on Chinese Cinema*, ed. Chris Berry (London: British Film Institute, 1991), 62–79. And in the same volume, for an esthetic reading, see Catherine Yi-Yu Cho Woo, "The Chinese montage: From poetry and painting to the silver screen," 21–29. For a critique of such readings, and a discussion of Chinese cinema within the "third cinema" framework, see Rey Chow, "Silent is the ancient plain: Music, film-making, and the conception of reform in China's new cinema," *Discourse* 12, no. 2 (spring–summer 1990): 82–109.

5   Main contributors were Su himself and Wang Luxiang. For the Chinese version, see *Heshang* (Beijing: Xiandai, 1988). For the English translation of the text, which also includes the script (text and images) and notes and various articles, see Richard W. Bodman and Pin P. Wan, *Deathsong of the River: A Reader's Guide to the Chinese TV Series "Heshang,"* Cor-

nell East Asia Series (Ithaca, N.Y.: Cornell University East Asia Program, 1991). Unless otherwise noted, the quotations are from this translation.

6　Alfonso M. Iacono, *Le Fétichisme: Histoire d'un concept (Fetishism: The History of a Concept)* (Paris: Presses Universitaires de France, 1992), 5.

7　Iacono dates the term "fetishism" and its exotic currency to 1760, *Le Fétichisme*, 5.

8　Following the Tiananmen events, a global denunciation of the series was initiated by the government. Newspapers nationwide published the "silly errors" 'miuwu' which Chinese scholars of various disciplines were made to search for and denounce.

9　Richard Bodman, "From history to allegory to art: A personal search for interpretation," in *Deathsong of the River*, 18. The most telling example — which is also the easiest to attack — is the comparison between Chinese classical scholars (Wang Yangming, Gu Yanwu) and heterogeneous Western figures (da Vinci, Magellan, Copernicus, Galileo): "While Westerners were researching the planets and stars, the human body, levers, and chemical substances, Chinese were studying books, Chinese characters, and old piles of paper" (149).

10　James Lull, *China Turned On: Television, Reform, and Resistance* (London: Routledge, 1991), 136. Since *Deathsong*, there have been similar other documentary incursions into the roots of Chinese culture, but none has had the same timely impact. That includes a production by the same director, Xia Jun, *Dongfang (The East)* in 1994.

11　"Qiwang" (King of chess), *Shanghai wenxue (Shanghai Literature)* 7 (1984): 15–35; "Shuwang" (King of trees), *Zhongguo zuojia (Chinese Writers)* 1 (1985): 85–102; "Haiziwang" (King of children), *Renmin wenxue (People's Literature)* 2 (1985): 4–19 (my version: *Qiwang Shuwang Haiziwang* (Taibei: Xindi wenxue, 1990), 119–175. "Qiwang" is perhaps the most famous. It was also adapted for the screen, by a Fourth-Generation director, Teng Wenji. His film was never distributed internationally.

12　The trilogy has been translated into English, French, and many other languages, and a spate of critical articles have been written about them. For an English translation, see *Three Kings: Three Stories from Today's China*, trans. Bonnie S. McDougall (London: Collins Harvill, 1990). For a recent review of the critical work on A Cheng, see Gang Yue, "Surviving (in) 'The Chess King,'" in *positions* 3, no. 2 (fall 1995): 564–94. Yue criticizes the prevalent readings of A Cheng's work as traditional national culture outside of time. His own position is to prove (by the concreteness of things such as food and chess) that A Cheng's work is not about some Chinese essence, but very much inscribed in a postrevolutionary consciousness redefining local history.

13　Gang Yue, in "Surviving (in) 'The Chess King,'" recounts A Cheng's acceptance speech when his literary work was awarded a prize. "In a public occasion designed to evoke the three-thousand-year-old grandeur of the Written Word, the prize-winning writer emphatically talks about the 'exchange value' of his writing in balancing his family budget. In this sense A Cheng's words must be read as food" (583). The same practical attitude is taught to the children: writing is a useful tool.

14 Laura Mulvey, "Some thoughts on theories of fetishism in the context of contemporary culture," *October* 65 (summer 1993): 7.

15 Sigmund Freud, "Fetishism," in *Standard Edition of the Complete Psychological Works,* trans. James Strachey, vol. 21 (London: Hogarth Press, 1961), 157.

16 Well, almost of the same name. Mo Yan's five-part novel is entitled *Hong gaoliang jiazu (The Red Sorghum Clan)* (Beijing: Jiefang jun wenyi, 1987; Taipei: Hongfan Book Co., 1988). From the latter unexpurgated edition comes the translation by Howard Goldblatt, *Red Sorghum: A Novel of China* (New York: Viking Penguin, 1993).

17 More than thirty suona flutes were used for the climactic scene, the roll in the sorghum fields, says the music composer of most of Zhang Yimou's films, Zhao Jiping. "They sound like a human cry." Reported in the documentary made by Allan Miller, *Zhao Jiping* (Alternate Current, 1996).

18 Chiao Hsiung-ping, "Ti 'wo yeye' zheng kouqi — Xiangjiang zhuanfang Zhang Yimou" (On behalf of 'my grandpa' — An exclusive interview with Zhang Yimou), *Wenxing (Literary Stars)* 1 (May 1988): 50. On the other hand, in *Yellow Earth,* even the singer at the opening wedding banquet is a real-life singer from that area of Shaanxi province. In the documentary *Zhao Jiping,* both Zhao and Chen Kaige insist upon the authenticity of the regional music for *Yellow Earth.*

19 Chiao "Ti 'wo yeye' zheng kouqi," 50.

20 The novella is entitled "Fuxi Fuxi," the reduplicated name of the legendary creator of writing and, with his sister, Nüwa, of humanity. Liu Heng, "Fuxi Fuxi," in *Zhongguo xiaoshuo 1988 (Chinese Novels, 1988),* ed. Huang Ziping and Li Tuo (Hong Kong: Sanlian, 1989), 80–171. The novel was translated, after the film, and given the same title as the film, *Judou, or The Obsession* (Beijing: Panda, 1991). The translation has been completely expurgated of all its irony (and graphic passages), so the translations are mine.

21 In the novel, she outlives both of her men and prays on their tombs, not knowing who is who. The narrator adds this wisecrack: "Were the guy [Tianqing] alive today, he would probably be deeply hurt to see that his little dove [Judou] is no longer a little dove, nor an eagle, but an old hen that has lost its feathers. There's nothing wrong with an old hen. The old hen is taking care of her chicks, and of her chicks' chicks. A hen is after all a hen; hens will forever have something that cocks can't replace or imitate. Tianqing can rest in peace" (169).

22 Rey Chow, "The force of surfaces: Defiance in Zhang Yimou's films," in *Primitive Passions: Visuality, Sexuality, Ethnography, and Contemporary Chinese Cinema* (New York: Columbia University Press, 1995), 169.

23 Anthony Tatlow, a professor at the University of Hong Kong, found a link between this film and Racinian tragedy. See Lynn Pan, "A Chinese Master," in the *New York Times Magazine,* March 1, 1992, 38.

24 Su Tong, "Qi qie cheng qun" (Wives and concubines), in *Hunyin ji jing* (*Scenes of the Married Life*) (Nanjing: Jiangsu wenyi, 1993), 107–61. The English translation uses the title of the film adaptation: *Raise the Red Lantern,* trans. Michael Duke (New York: William Morrow, 1993), 11–99.

25 One could make another reading of the film by including the servant as the fifth candidate. She would then be the fire element (passion); and perhaps feel love (passion) for the man. Such a melodramatic reading could be pursued, following that servant's fate: both as a twisted social realist fable and as a modern-day Cinderella-Galatea fairy tale gone awry.

26 Jean Rohou, *L'Évolution du tragique racinien (The Evolution of Racinian Tragedy)* (Paris: Sedes, 1991), 207.

27 Instead, ghostly music heightens the eerie, glacial atmosphere. The operatic choral music of "ligeleng" — in lieu of tragedy's chorus — springs up at two sacrificial moments: the servant's slow death in the snow and the third wife's hanging, which also occurs in winter. Zhao Jiping notes that *ligeleng,* in Beijing opera, means "insignificant": furies here spell out the nothingness of women. A more detailed study of this film's music with that of Zhang's former films would also prove the fundamental difference in effects and affects. For example, *Judou*'s leitmotiv is an ocarina flute, a *xun,* which sounds like a human wail.

28 Unlike Judou (or Jiu'er in *Red Sorghum*), who reaches out visually to both her lover and us.

29 Philip Wheelwright, "The Guilt of Oedipus," in Sophocles, *Oedipus Tyrannus: A Norton Critical Edition* (New York: Norton, 1970), 257. Songlian has excessive confidence that her wit and science will make her change her own destiny (for example, feigning pregnancy means the man will favor her, often sleep with her, and thus eventually impregnate her).

30 Rey Chow, one of the few feminist critics to give some credit to Zhang Yimou, nevertheless, syllogistically reduces his use of the fetish to an artistic expression: "What Zhang 'fetishizes' is primarily cinematography itself," in "The force of surfaces," 149.

31 Chow, "The force of surfaces," 146.

32 A student in my orientalism class (fall 1997), Olga Duhamel said that colonial discourse thrives on taxidermy.

33 Since Kafka at least, literature has been decentering Homo sapiens. Recent works include Andrzej Zaniewski's *Rat: A Novel*, trans. Ewa Hryniewicz-Yarbrough (New York: Arcade, 1994), which is about the life of a

rat, as radical departure from the human oedipal model; Marie Darrieus-secq's *Truismes* (Paris: P.O.L., 1996), which retells and deconstructs the Circean myth with a story, told from a physiological point of view, of a woman who turns into a sow.

34 Zhang Yimou chose, in *Judou,* to dramatize Liu's ironic illustration of this Chinese custom of naming and equivalences. The most vivid visualization is when Judou and Tianqing bar a funeral procession forty-nine times (they throw themselves down on the road in front of the procession) while the little boy, Tianbai, sits impassively on a donkey, with the ancestor's tombstone between his legs.

35 The etymological investigation of male semes (from Fuxi to the ancestor's stele to the sun and all "yang" words) is fully developed and detailed in my "Liu Heng's *Fuxi Fuxi:* What about Nüwa?" in *Gender and Sexuality in Twentieth-Century Chinese Literature and Society,* ed. Lü Tonglin (Albany: State University of New York Press, 1993), 85–105.

36 Han Shaogong, "Wenxue de 'gen' " (The "roots" of literature), *Zhongguo zuojia (Chinese Writers)* 4, no. 2 (1985): 2–5.

37 Sigmund Freud, "Totem and taboo," in *The Standard Edition of the Complete Psychological Works of Sigmund Freud,* trans. James Strachey et al., vol. 13 (London: Hogarth Press, 1986), 56.

38 Han Shaogong, "Bababa" (Dadadad), in *Xiangzhengzhuyi xiaoshuo (Symbolist Novels),* ed. Wu Liang et al. (Changchun: Shidai wenyi, 1988), 1–40.

39 In a personal interview, Hainan, December 10, 1993.

40 In *Zhongguo dangdai zuojia xuanji congshu (Collection of Selected Contemporary Chinese Writers)* (Beijing: Renmin wenxue, 1994), 175–225.

41 In an interview with Helmut Martin, published in Helmut Martin and Jeffrey Kinkley, *Modern Chinese Writers: Self Portrayals,* trans. Linette Lee (Armond, N.Y.: M. E. Sharpe, 1992), 111.

42 Shi Tiesheng's "Mingruo qinxian" (Like a banjo string) was adapted into a film by Chen Kaige as *Bianzou bian chang (Life on a String).* Chen must have felt more affinity with the urban "roots-searchers," while Zhang Yimou was allied with the peasant background writers, Mo Yan and Liu Heng.

43 Zhang Yimou understandably chose to adapt the more people-centered part 1 (with incursions into part 2, where the sorghum takes the lead).

44 With slight alterations of H. Goldblatt's translation (359) (following the Chinese version published by Hongfan).

45 Robert J. Stoller, quoted by Valerie Steele, in *Fetish: Fashion, Sex, and Power* (New York: Oxford University Press, 1996), 219, note 13.

46 I have changed the past tense of H. Goldblatt's translation to the present.

47 As used by Hal Foster speaking of the perfect composition and gloss of Dutch still-life, in "The art of fetishism: Notes on Dutch still life," in *Fe-*

tishism as Cultural Discourse, ed. Emily Apter and William Pietz (Ithaca, N.Y.: Cornell University Press, 1993), 251–65.

48 Mo Yan, "Tianma xing kong" (The celestial horse roams the sky), in *Hong gaoliang (Red Sorghum),* ed. Xi Xi (Taibei: Hongfan Shudian, 1988), 251–53.

49 Su Tong, "Qi qie cheng qun" (Wives and concubines), 107–61. References are to Michael Duke's translation, except that I have not translated the women's names, as Duke has, and have kept to a literal translation of the original title in order to distinguish the novella from its film adaptation (*Raise the Red Lantern*).

50 Su Tong, "Hongfen," in *Hongfen* (Wuhan: Changjiang wenyi, 1992), 1–44.

51 *Hongfen,* 307.

52 Lü Tonglin in her chapter on Su Tong, "Femininity and masculinity" (129–54) in *Misogyny, Cultural Nihilism, and Oppositional Politics: Contemporary Chinese Experimental Fiction* (Stanford: Stanford University Press, 1995), 133, 154. However, Lü Tonglin concludes in her chapter on Su Tong that the debasement of women raises the status of men. I cannot read any signs of male superiority in Su Tong's "women's novels."

53 Wittgenstein's concept, as discussed by Karatani Kojin in *Architecture as Metaphor,* trans. Sabu Kohso (Cambridge, Mass.: MIT Press, 1995), 138 and passim.

54 See Kam Louie's paper on one of Jia's stories, "Renji" (Human extremities), "The politics of masculinity in Jia Pingwa's 'Human Extremities,'" in *Modern China* 17, no. 2 (April 1991): 163–87.

55 In the afterword. See Jia Pingwa, *Feidu (Wasted Capital)* (Beijing: Beijing, 1993), 526.

56 A marketing ploy that was wholly successful: no book in the People's Republic of China has fared so well, its price, already high (12.50 yuan in 1993), being doubled if not tripled on the black market of the night stalls.

57 The author self-censored, or played on the attraction of the idea of censorship, by replacing words in sex scenes with little black boxes and inserting the note "The writer deleted *x* words." The variable number would titillate the reader into imagining the scene.

58 The *Sunü Classic (Classic of the Essential Woman),* an ars erotica dating from the Han dynasty.

59 The promise of lewd scenes worked: the figures given range from 1 to 5 million yuan for the profit made in the six months following the publication of the novel.

60 Jiang Xin, "*Feidu* chuangzuo zhi mi" (Behind the creation of *Wasted Capital*), in "*Feidu* zhi mi" (The Enigma around *Wasted Capital*) (Beijing: Tuanjie, 1993), 15.

61 Fabien S. Gérard, *Ombres jaunes: Journal de tournage* Le Dernier Empe-

reur *de Bernardo Bertolucci (Yellow Shadows: Diary on the Making of* The Last Emperor *by Bernardo Bertolucci)* (Paris: Seuil, 1987). The examples that follow are also taken from this diary.

62 Rey Chow, "Seeing modern China: Toward a theory of ethnic spectatorship," in *Woman and Chinese Modernity: The Politics of Reading between West and East* (Minnesota: University of Minnesota Press, 1991), 11.

63 Gina Marchetti, *Romance and the "Yellow Peril": Race, Sex, and Discursive Strategies in Hollywood Fiction* (Berkeley: University of California Press, 1993), 78.

64 Ying Ruocheng, a Chinese Han gentleman, plays an even more unlikely role in another Bertolucci film, *Little Buddha:* in it he is a Tibetan lama searching for the reincarnation of the Dalai Lama!

65 "If I were to define the writer," Kafka wrote in 1922, "I would say: he is a scapegoat for humanity, he enables people to enjoy sin without — or almost without — a sense of guilt." From *I Am a Memory Come Alive,* quoted in Peter Stine, "Franz Kafka and Animals," *Comparative Literature* 22, no. 1 (1981): 79, note 49. Butterfly protagonists fill the same role.

66 Yu Hua, "Huozhe" (To live), *Shouhuo (Harvest)* 6 (1992): 4–42.

67 In Rey Chow's as always fascinating reading, this time of *To Live,* she writes of the puppet box, "tradition, now an empty box." "We endure, therefore we are: Survival, governance, and Zhang Yimou's *To Live,*" *South Atlantic Quarterly* 95, no. 4 (fall 1996): 1057. I thank Rey Chow for sending me her papers on Chinese cinema, even before I knew they were published.

68 Zhang Xudong, *Chinese Modernism in the Era of Reforms,* 205.

69 Gang Yue, "Surviving (in) 'The Chess King,'" 568.

70 " 'Male' and 'female' constitute our dominant fiction's most fundamental binary opposition." Kaja Silverman, *Male Subjectivity at the Margins* (New York: Routledge, 1992), 568.

71 Sheldon Hsiao-peng Lu, "National cinema, cultural critique, transnational capital: The films of Zhang Yimou," in *Transnational Chinese Cinemas: Identity, Nationhood, Gender,* ed. Sheldon Hsiao-peng Lu (Honolulu: University of Hawai'i Press, 1997), 130.

72 Giacomo Puccini, *Turandot* (bilingual edition) (Milan: Ricordi, 1978), 30.

5 *China's Avant-Garde Art*

1 In an interview by Zhuang Hui, "Interview 1995 September 5th," trans. Tang Di and Karen Smith, appendix to [*Baipi shu*] (*White-Cover Book*) (Hong Kong: Dadi, 1995), 12.

2 In an interview by Xu Xiaoyu (July 16, 1996), "Meiyou Zhongguo tedian

de yishu: Ding Yi" (Art without Chinese characteristics: Ding Yi), in an unpublished manuscript "Tanhua jishi daolu" (Talking one's way through), no page numbers.

3 "A conversation between Jiangnan Artist Zhou Tiehai, project Organizers Xia Wei and Hank Bull, and front editor Kerri Embrey," in *Flash Art*, Press kit for Zhou Tiehai's exhibition at the Presentation House Gallery, North Vancouver, March–April 1997, no page numbers.

4 Hal Foster, *Recodings: Art, Spectacle, Cultural Politics* (Seattle: Bay Press, 1985), 7. The quotations from Foster that follow, are from this work unless otherwise noted.

5 *Zeitgenössische Malerei (CHINA: Contemporary Painters)* (Bonn: Kunstmuseum/Dumont, 1996), 120–23. Many of the artworks mentioned in this chapter have been published in non-Chinese catalogs, like this one, and so I do not have a Chinese title for them.

6 Wang Yuejin, "Anxiety of portraiture: Quest for/questioning ancestral icons in post-Mao China," in *Politics, Ideology, and Literary Discourse in Modern China*, ed. Liu Kang and Xiaobing Tang (Durham: Duke University Press, 1993), 243.

7 Li Xianting et al., "Shenhua—Xifang yu Zhongguo: Di 45 jie Weinisi shuangnianzhan canzhan yishujia guilai tan ganxiang" (Myth: The West and China: Impressions from the participating artists upon their return from the 45th Venice Biennale), *Jinri xianfeng* (*Today's Avant-Garde*) 2 (1994): 10.

8 The works were selected mainly by the influential Beijing critic Li Xianting, who is also responsible for the naming of "schools" within the contemporary art scene, that is, those he favors: cynical realism 'popi xieshizhuyi' and political/cultural pop 'zhengzhi wenhua bopu.'

9 Xu Xiaoyu, "Art without Chinese characteristics."

10 These impressions are taken from "Shenhua—Xifang yu Zhongguo," 6–28.

11 Julia F. Andrews and Gao Minglu, "The avant-garde's challenge to official art," in *Urban Spaces in Contemporary China: The Potential for Autonomy and Community in Post-Mao China*, ed. Deborah S. Davis (New York: Cambridge University Press, 1995), 221.

12 Andrew Solomon, "Not just a yawn but the howl that could free China," *New York Times Magazine*, December 19, 1993, 44+.

13 *China's New Art, Post-1989 (Hou bajiu Zhongguo xin yishu)* (Hong Kong: Hanart/TZ Gallery, 1993). The English version contains all the material (articles and plates); the Chinese version contains only the articles. Marlborough Fine Art Gallery published the artworks in a bilingual catalogue of the same name, also in 1993.

14 Nicholas Jose, "Towards the world: China's new art, 1989–1993," in *China's New Art, Post-1989*, xxxix.

15 Jeffrey Hantover, "What you see is not what you get: Chinese painting after June 4," in *China's New Art, Post-1989*, lxiv.

16 Hal Foster, *The Return of the Real: The Avant-Garde at the End of the Century* (Cambridge, Mass.: MIT Press, 1996): 199, 161.

17 Foster, *The Return of the Real*, 124.

18 Mark Tansey, *Transformations*, leaflet catalogs of Liu Xiaodong, Chen Danqing, Yu Hong, and Ni Jun's New York exhibition, 1994.

19 John Berger, *Ways of Seeing* (London, Penguin, 1972), 92.

20 Fang Lijun, *China Avant-Garde (Qianwei yishu)* (Berlin: Haus der Kultur der Welt, 1993). The Chinese version was published by Oxford University Press, 1994, see p. 135.

21 A beautiful and comprehensive catalogue of Yan's work is *Yan Pei-ming* (Issoire: Centre Culturel Pomel, 1996).

22 Seen on New York curator Barbara London's web site *Stir-Fry, http:// www.adaweb.com/context/stir-fry/9-19.html*. This site is a visual and textual diary of London's 1997 visit to artists in China. Another wonderful website to visit is www.shanghart.com which is regularly updated. It is produced by Shanghai's ShanghART gallery, directed by Lorenz Helbling.

23 Zhang Hai'er, *Guangzhou (Photo Album)*, printed by Libreria Borges, 1996, as postcards.

24 Most art photography I have seen in China is however of another type, of the more classical anthropological type, questioning its own culture. Han Lei's 1995 exhibition in Beijing, tellingly entitled *Alienation (Shuli)*, is such an example. It is representative of urbanites' "stealing pictures" from China's strange peoples, from faraway Tibet to the countryside right outside of Beijing, in Hebei province. Han Lei's work reminds one not only of similar Western images (e.g., those of the American Diane Arbus or the Canadian Raymonde April) but also of pictures taken in China by foreigners: a father holding two bicycles on which his twin infants are seated, old women with bound feet on typical Beijing streets, and so on.

25 Leng Lin and Zhao Li, *Zhongguo dangdai youhua xianzhuang (The State of Contemporary Chinese Oil Painting)* (Beijing: Jinri Zhongguo, 1993), 49.

26 Solomon, "Not just a yawn," 47.

27 This is Mao's famous description of himself as a lone monk wandering the world with a leaky umbrella 'heshang da san, wu fa wu tian,' given to Edgar Snow in the 1930s.

28 Orville Schell, *Mandate of Heaven: A New Generation of Entrepreneurs, Bohemians, and Technocrats Lays Claim to China's Future* (New York: Simon and Schuster, 1994), 289.

29 "Zhang Hongtu/Hongtu Zhang: An interview," interview with Jonathan

Hay, in *Boundaries in China,* ed. John Hay (London: Reaktion Books, 1994), 294.

30 Li Xianting, "Zhengzhi bopu: yishi xingtai de jishixing 'xiaofei' " (Political pop: Immediate "consumption" of ideology), *Jinri xianfeng* 1 (1994): 58–64.

31 One memorably audacious work is the 1994–95 calendar, which features, for 1994, Mao and his mates (Jiang Qing, Lenin, and so on) and, for 1995, Deng Xiaoping with his grandson playing pool or doubled up at the crossroads. Designed in Shenzhen but printed in Hong Kong (Xianggang chuanbo yinwu gongsi), it was distributed strictly among friends.

32 Ellen Johnston Laing, "Is there post-modern art in the People's Republic of China?" in *Modernity in Asian Art,* ed. John Clark (Broadway: Wild Peony, 1993), 220.

33 Craig Owens, quoted by Hal Foster in *Recodings,* 35.

34 Huang Yongping, quoted in Gao Minglu et al., *Zhongguo dangdai meishushi 1985–1986 (A History of China's Contemporary Art, 1985–1986)* (Shanghai: Shanghai renmin, 1991), 346–47.

35 Wu Shanzhuan, quoted in Gao Minglu, et al., *Zhongguo dangdai meishushi,* 191–92.

36 See the catalog by Gao Minglu and J. Andrews, *Fragmented Memory: The Chinese Avant-Garde in Exile* (Columbus: Wexner Center for the Arts, Ohio State University, 1993).

37 Gu Wenda, interviewed in Solomon, "Not just a yawn," 71.

38 I refer here to the challenge many Chinese and non-Chinese sinologists felt compelled to accept when faced with supposedly illegible Chinese characters. One scholar, Charles Stone, claims that "it took [him] no more than five minutes of leafing through an unabridged four-corner index of Chinese characters to turn up two real characters (Morohashi numbers 3062 and 7061)," in "Xu Bing and the Printed Word," *Public Culture* 6 (1994): 407–10; 407. Corrections follow in the same issue, by Tamara Hamlish, "Prestidigitations: A Reply to Charles Stone," 419–21.

39 In lieu of Mount Rushmore, the Chinese often see the mythological beauty, Ashima, in beautiful mountains. In Xu Xiaoyu, "Art without Chinese characteristics."

40 The same is true of Cai Jin, who has been painting banana plants (in Chinese, literally "beautiful people plant"—*meirenjiao*) since 1990. Her works, red and green, but mainly flesh red, are in fact abstract paintings of matter, vegetal as well as animal (human). I am sorry she only pops up in a footnote; her work is so idiosyncratic—she even discusses it in terms of the smell of the pigments she uses—that a separate chapter would be needed to discuss her work.

41 "At Beijing's Central Academy of Fine Arts in 1994, 370 out of 400 new

students opted to study oils rather than Chinese painting." Alice Cairns, "Striking oils," in *Sunday Morning Post Magazine*, April 21, 1996, 13.

42 Zhang Dali is one of the "dreamers" in Wu Wenguang's documentaries. He is seen in action, "doing" Bologna's old walls at night. Near Wu's home in Beijing, the same ciphers are visible.

43 Foster, *Recodings*, 48.

44 I have translated this sentence from the Chinese written in the work, and so it may not be Madonna's exact formulation. The reduplicated superlative immediately turns the quotation into a pastiche of Maospeak, itself always "very, very, very" 'zui zui zui.'

45 Xu Tan, in Ai Weiwei et al., [*Heipi shu*] (*Black-Cover Book*) (Hong Kong: Dadi, 1994), 118. Like the *White-Cover Book*, this, too, is untitled and referred to by the color of the cover.

46 Gu Xiong, quoted by Peggy Gale, "Jiangnan narrows the Pacific Rim," *Canadian Art* (summer 1998): 59.

47 Foster, *Recodings*, 183.

48 Foster, *Recodings*, 23.

49 Xu Lei, *The Mystery of Absence* (Hong Kong: Alisan Fine Arts, 1995).

50 These two comments were made to me by Xu during a meeting on May 4, 1996.

51 Foster, *Recodings*, 29.

52 Berger, *Ways of Seeing*, 138.

53 Foster, *Recodings*, 140.

54 For an example of his works while he was living in China, see Joan Lebold Cohen, *The New Chinese Painting: 1949–1986* (New York: Harry N. Abrams, 1987), 77.

55 Foster, *Recodings*, 213, note 21.

6 Rock Music from Mao to Nirvana

1 Zhang Guangtian, in an interview by Xu Xiaoyu in 1995, *Yiren keneng jiushi gechang (Maybe an Artist Is One Who Sings)*. Xu Xiaoyu, "Tanhua jishi daolu" (Talking one's way through), unpublished manuscript, no page numbers.

2 Liang Heping, interviewed in the video by Greg Lanning, *China Rocks: The Long March of Cui Jian*, a Penumbra Co-Production with the BBC, 1991.

3 Arnold Shaw, *Dictionary of American Pop/Rock* (New York: Schirmer Books, 1982), 316–17.

4 During a panel on popular music at the Asia Pop Culture conference, held at the University of British Columbia, April 16–18, 1998.

5 John Street, *Rebel Rock: The Politics of Popular Music* (Oxford: Basil

Blackwell, 1986); Simon Frith, *Sound Effects: Youth, Leisure and the Politics of Rock* (London: Constable, 1983).

6 Simon Frith, "The cultural study of popular music," in *Cultural Studies,* ed. Lawrence Grossberg et al. (New York: Routledge, 1992), 175.

7 Street, *Rebel Rock,* 153.

8 Andrew Jones, *Like a Knife: Ideology and Genre in Contemporary Chinese Popular Music* (Ithaca: Cornell University Press, 1992); Rey Chow, "Listening otherwise, music miniaturized," in *Diaspora: Tactics of Intervention in Contemporary Cultural Studies* (Bloomington: Indiana University Press, 1993), 144–64; Gregory B. Lee, "Chinese trumpeters, French troubadours: Nationalist ideology and the culture of popular music," in *Troubadours, Trumpeters, Troubled Makers: Lyricism, Nationalism, and Hybridity in China and Its Others* (Durham: Duke University Press, 1996), 149–78.

9 Zhao Shimin, " 'Dongfanghong' de lailong qumai" (The tortuous origins of 'The east is red'), *Xiju dianying zhoubao (Theater and Television Weekly)* [Beijing] December 18, 1993.

10 An excellent book on Mao's rewriting of proverbs is by Chen Qi et al., eds., *Mao Zedong de yuyan yishu (Mao Zedong's Linguistic Art)* (Shenyang: Liaoning renmin, 1993).

11 As seen in Jiang Yue's 1995 documentary, *The Other Bank.*

12 The schoolteacher who used the rock version in his class wrote: "The rhythm was somewhat faster, and they added a bass guitar. Although it lacks solemnity somewhat, and they [Tang Dynasty] added much noise, yet it is still suitable for [teaching to] high school pupils." Zi Yun, "Guojige" yu "zhuixingzu" (The "Internationale" and the "Star Seekers"), *Beijing wanbao (Beijing Evening News)* January 5, 1993, 14.

13 Frith, *Sound Effects,* 272.

14 Street, *Rebel Rock,* 2.

15 Cui Jian, *Yiwu suoyou/Xin changzheng lushang de yaogun (I Have Nothing/Rock 'n' roll on the New Long March),* Zhongguo luyou shengxiang, 1989.

16 Cui Jian, "Yikuai hongbu" (A piece of red cloth), *Solution,* cassette tape, Zhongguo beiguang shengxiang, 1991.

17 Ray Pratt, *Rhythm and Resistance: Explorations in the Political Uses of Popular Music,* Media and Society Series (New York: Praeger, 1990), 207. Pratt, of course, does not mention Cui Jian.

18 Pratt, *Rhythm and Resistance,* 207.

19 Cui Jian, interviewed in the television special *Rock in Berlin: The Chinese Avant-Garde,* Haus de Welt, 1993.

20 He Li, "Yaogun 'Gu'er' " (Rock "Orphans"), *Jinri xianfeng (Today's Avant-Garde)* 5 (1997): 68.

21 Lee, *Troubadours, Trumpeters,* 164–65.

22 Leon Rosselson, quoted in Pratt, *Rhythm and Resistance,* 214, note 14.

23 Zhang Guangtian, "Yilu zou yilu chang" (Singing along the way), *A Collection of Modern Songs by Zhang Guangtian,* cassette tape, Zhongguo yinyue yinxiang, 1993.

24 *Far Eastern Economic Review,* September 30, 1993, 54. Another example could be given here, Zhang Chu's case, which was also covered by the *Far Eastern Economic Review,* November 19, 1992, 34–37. The caption under a photograph of Zhang states that he "sees himself as spokesman for a new generation of rock musicians." Zhang Chu poses as the figure of the sensitive, lonely guy in the big city.

25 Zhang Guangtian, "Mao Zedong," *A Collection of Modern Songs by Zhang Guangtian.*

26 Gao Xiaosong, "Tongzhuo de ni" (You who shared my schooldesk), *Xiaoyuan minyao 1: 1983–1993 (Campus Folksongs 1: 1983–1993),* tape cassette, Dadi, 1994.

27 In *Nanfang zhoumo (Southern Weekender),* March 22, 1996.

28 Rey Chow has this lovely expression: "the symphonic effects of official culture," in "Listening otherwise, music miniaturized," 150.

29 Frith, "The cultural study of popular music," 185.

30 As of 1994. He, "Yaogun 'Guer,' " 92.

31 He, "Yaogun 'Guer,' " 69. He is referring to those born in the seventies, the "second rock generation."

32 Kurt Cobain, in the documentary video *Nirvana "Live! Tonight! Sold Out!!,"* Geffen Home Video, 1994.

33 Lyrics of many of the No band songs are to be found in Sun Mengjin, *Yaogun: Jinian ban/Rock: Souvenir Album* [Beijing], limited circulation publication, 1995.

34 I thank Frank Muyard, who gave me a copy of his recording of the live performance of No at the Hanlinyuan, Beijing, October 11, 1996.

35 Cui Jian, "Jiejue" (Solution), *Solution.*

36 Zu Zhou, quoted by He Li, in "Jizhe yaogun" (Reporting on rock), *Xiju dianying zhou bao (Theater and Film Weekly),* April 1996, 5.

37 He, "Yaogun 'Guer,' " 89.

38 Sun Mengjin, "Bei yiqi de huoyan — No yuedui" (A cast-off flame — the No band) in *Yaogun/Rock,* 42.

39 This underground publication can be considered the music counterpart of the books on art published in 1994–95 with white and black covers because it also aims at diffusing cultural phenomena that are invisible in China's media.

40 In a meeting (May 5, 1996) at his home, Sun played for me bits of his show. The quotations are from those tapes.

41 Kevin Salveson, "Radioman: DJ Youdai rocks China," *Beijing Scene,* August 10–23, 1995, 4.

42 Sun, *Yaogun/Rock,* 33–35.

43 He, "Yizhe yaogun," 4.

44 Heibao, "Ai de zhenxin" (Love maxims), *Gaobie de yaogun (Farewell Rocks)/A Tribute to Teresa Teng,* cassette tape, Hubei yinxiang yishu, 1996.

45 Heibao, "Wudi zirong" (Looking for a hole to crawl into), *Zhongguo huo (China Fire),* cassette tape, Magic Stone Culture, 1992.

46 Heibao, "Lianpu" (Masks), *Yaogun Beijing (Beijing Rock),* cassette tape, Xianggang yongsheng yinyue, 1993.

47 Tangchao/Tang Dynasty, *Menghui Tangchao (A Dream Return to the Tang Dynasty),* cassette tape, Magic Stone Culture, 1992.

48 Xue Li, ed., *Yaogun mengxun: Zhongguo yaogunyue shilu (Dream-Searching for Rock: Accounts of Chinese Rock Music)* (Beijing: Zhongguo dianying chubanshe, 1993), 20.

49 In January 1997, a female bus conductor, Li Shuli, was praised by the authorities as a model worker. During a performance He Yong spurted out that she was "cute." Rumors said this landed him in jail.

50 Xue, *Yaogun mengxun,* 154–55.

51 He Yong, "Zhonggu lou" (The bell and drum towers), *Lajichang (Garbage Dump),* video cassette tape, Magic Stone Culture, 1994.

52 He, *Lajichang.*

53 Quoted by Xue, *Yaogun mengxuan,* 154.

54 He Yong, "Guniang piaoliang" (Pretty girl), *Lajichang.*

55 Dou Wei, "Zhu" (Lord), *Zhongguo huo 2 (China Fire 2),* compact disk, Magic Stone Culture, 1996. "Gaoji dongwu" (High-class animals) is from Dou Wei's first album entitled *Hei Meng (Black Dream),* compact disk, Magic Stone Culture, 1994.

56 Cui Jian, "Feile" (Gone), *Hongqi xia de dan (Balls under the Red Flag),* cassette tape, Beijing Dongxi yishu, 1994.

57 Cui Jian, "Bi'an" (The other bank), *Balls under the Red Flag.*

58 For a discussion of the male domination of rock music, see Frith, "The cultural study of popular music."

59 Ai Jing, *Wode 1997 (My 1997),* cassette tape, Dadi, 1993. This latter part of the translation (with slight modifications) is from Zha Jianying, *China Pop* (New York: New Press, 1995), 165. Zha explains very well the importance of the Hong Kong music enterprises in Beijing in her chapter 7.

60 Ai Jing, *Yanfenjie de gushi/Once Upon a Time in Yanfen Street,* cassette tape, Dadi, 1995.

61 Cobra, "Ziji de tiantang" (My own paradise), *Beijing Rock,* LP record, Xianggang yongsheng yinyue, 1993.

62 See Ajay Singh and Steven Schwankert, "Strains of their success: China's

all-women rock band finally hits it big," *Asiaweek,* November 1, 1996, 44–45.

63 Luo Qi, "Kuaile jiqi" (Pleasure machine), *Kuaile jiqi (Pleasure Machine),* cassette tape, Beijing xingdie wenhua fazhan, 1995.

64 Wei Hua, "Visa," Xiandaihua/Modernization, Zhongguo guoji wenhua jiaoliu yinxiang, 1995.

65 The Shanghai Performance Dolls, *Rap: qingchun huoli (Rap: Youthful Zest),* cassette tape, Zhongguo changpian, 1995.

66 Zang Tianshuo, "Shuo shuo" (Just say it), *Wo zhe shinian (My Last Ten Years),* cassette tape, Shanghai yinxiang gongsi, 1995.

67 Quoted in He "Yaogun 'Guer,' " 85.

Conclusion

1 Perry Link, *Evening Chats in Beijing: Probing China's Predicament* (New York: W. W. Norton, 1992).

2 Link, *Evening Chats,* 18.

3 The source is triply anonymous. It was translated from a magazine left in a Shenyang train station, says the English translation I was given (anonymously) as a photocopy.

4 Link, *Evening Chats,* 18.

5 Quoted by Geremie Barmé, "Filial impieties in China," *Far Eastern Economic Review,* January 17, 1991, 35.

6 Wang Guangming, "You suo zuowei de shidai" (An era when we can do something), *Wenlunbao (Discussion),* January 15, 1994.

7 This example comes from Pan Qingyun, ed., *Zhonghua yinyu daquan (Comprehensive Dictionary of Unofficial Chinese Language)* (Shanghai: Xuelin, 1995), 595.

8 Chao Feng, ed., *Wenhua da geming cidian (Great Cultural Revolution Dictionary)* (Hong Kong: Ganglong, 1993), 125.

9 Quoted and translated by Link, *Evening Chats,* 88–89.

10 From Wang Shuo's *Qianwan bie ba wo dang ren (Don't You Dare View Me as a Human),* quoted and translated in Link, *Evening Chats,* 184–85.

11 The examples, unless otherwise noted, can be found in all of the following works: Annie Au-Yeung, "Les nouveaux mots de la langue chinoise" (The new words of the Chinese language), *Perspectives chinoises* 33 (January–February 1996): 61–67; Pan Qingyun, ed., *Zhonghua yinyu daquan;* James J. Wang, *Outrageous Chinese: A Guide to Chinese Street Language* (San Francisco: China Books, 1994); Zhao Jianxiong, *Dangdai liuxing yu (Contemporary Popular Language)* (Shanghai: Shanghai renmin, 1994); Zheng Yefu, *Liyu, zhouyu, guanqiang, heiyu (Slang, Curses,*

Official Speech, Black [Market] Expressions) (Beijing: Guangming ribao, 1993); Zhou Yimin, *Beijing xiandai liuxing yu (Beijing's Contemporary Popular Language)* (Beijing: Beijing yanshan, 1992).

12 These last examples are to be found solely in Pan, *Zhonghua yinyu daquan,* 615, 591.

13 Gregory B. Lee, "Poetic zones, autonomous moments" in *Troubadours, Trumpeters, Troubled Makers: Lyricism, Nationalism, and Hybridity in China and Its Others* (Durham: Duke University Press, 1966), 265.

14 Pan, *Zhonghua yinyu daquan,* 816.

15 Zhou Guoping, "Hebi 'wenxin'?" (Why must it be "warm and fragrant"?), *Nanfang zhoumo (Southern Weekender)* [Guangdong], September 10, 1993.

16 Gallup 1997 Survey, *The People's Republic of China: Consumer Attitudes and Lifestyle Trends,* http://www.gallup.com/poll/special/china/chinarep.html, October 27, 1997. Topping all brandnames is Coca-Cola, which is superseded in China by only one domestic name, the Bank of China.

17 See "Chinese Dictionary finally published," *China Media Newsletter* [Beijing] 4, no. 6 (July 1996).

18 For a concise historical of China's official attitude toward AIDS, see Zhao Bian "State secrets" concerning AIDS," *China Focus* [Princeton] 4, no. 10 (October 1, 1996), 1, 4.

19 A book entitled *Beijing tongzhi gushi (Stories of Beijing Comrades)* by Zhou Huashan, a Cantonese (Hong Kong: Xianggang tongzhi yanjiushe, 1996) seems to suggest that "comrade" is already used for "gay" in mainland China. I thank Sébastien Bage for telling me about this book and lending it to me.

20 All reference books mentioned above deal with this vocabulary. However, they don't all agree on which denomination is denoted by which term.

21 Teenagers' idioms are only to be found in Pan, *Zhonghua yinyu daquan,* 606, 598–99.

22 This last group, those who have a steady, permanent job, is discussed by Zhao, 201–2.

23 Taken from a 1993 lecture given in Xiangshan (Beijing) by Chen Xiaoming and entitled "Yiwai de hemo: Jingying yu dazhong de chongdie yingxiang" (Unexpected complicity: The superimposed influences of high culture and mass culture), unpublished paper, given to me by the author.

24 Wang, *Outrageous Chinese,* 166. Wang has a very useful appendix of computer and Internet terms (155–66).

25 Yu Jian, "Zongpi shouji—shige jingshen de chongjian" (Brown-cover manuscript—the reconstruction of a poetic spirit), in *Zongpi shouji*

(Brown-Cover Manuscript) (Shanghai: Dongfang chuban zhongxin, 1997), 227–34. The statements that follow also come from this essay.

26 Yu Jian, "Wo weishenme bu gechang meigui" (Why I don't celebrate roses), in *Brown-Cover manuscript*, 65–69.

27 Zhao, *Dangdai liuxing yu*, 248.

28 I was first told in 1995 by a member of the Chinese Academy of Sciences that his then eight-year-old child's schoolmates did not know who Mao Zedong was. Skeptical, I have since asked around to be told the same. The following articles, in English, mention this, as well as the ignorance of other very recent major historical events: "What do they know? *China Focus* 5 [Princeton], June 1, 1997, 5; Ron Gluckman, "The Americanization of China," *Asiaweek* July 4, 1997, 39; John Gittings, *Real China: From Cannibalism to Karaoke* (London: Pocket Books, 1997), 168.

Index

Claire Huot is Associate Professor of

Comparative Literature and East Asian Studies,

Université de Montréal.

Library of Congress Cataloging-in-Publication Data

Huot, Marie Claire, 1954–
China's new cultural scene : a handbook of changes /
Claire Huot.
p.   cm.
Includes index.
ISBN 0-8223-2409-1 (alk. paper) — ISBN 0-8223-2445-8
(paper : alk. paper)
1. Popular culture—China.   I. Title.
HM101 .H86   2000
306′.0951—dc21   00-026442